EU Law for the Construction Industry

EU Law for the Construction Industry

Joseph Dalby
LLB(Hons), lic.sp.dr. eur,
Barrister

**Blackwell
Science**

© 1998 by
Blackwell Science Ltd
Editorial Offices:
Osney Mead, Oxford OX2 0EL
25 John Street, London WC1N 2BL
23 Ainslie Place, Edinburgh EH3 6AJ
350 Main Street, Malden
    MA 02148 5018, USA
54 University Street, Carlton
    Victoria 3053, Australia
10, rue Casimir Delavigne
    75006 Paris, France

Other Editorial Offices:

Blackwell Wissenschafts-Verlag GmbH
Kurfürstendamm 57
10707 Berlin, Germany

Blackwell Science KK
MG Kodenmacho Building
7–10 Kodenmacho Nihombashi
Chuo-ku, Tokyo 104, Japan

First edition published 1998

Set in 10/12 Palatino
by DP Photosetting, Aylesbury, Bucks
Printed and bound in Great Britain by
MPG Books Ltd, Bodmin, Cornwall

The Blackwell Science logo is a
trade mark of Blackwell Science Ltd,
registered at the United Kingdom
Trade Marks Registry

DISTRIBUTORS

Marston Book Services Ltd
PO Box 269
Abingdon
Oxon OX14 4YN
(*Orders:* Tel: 01235 465500
          Fax: 01235 465555)

USA
Blackwell Science, Inc.
Commerce Place
350 Main Street
Malden, MA 02148 5018
(*Orders:* Tel: 800 759 6102
                781 388 8250
          Fax: 781 388 8255)

Canada
Copp Clark Professional
200 Adelaide Street West, 3rd Floor
Toronto, Ontario M5H 1W7
(*Orders:* Tel: 416 597-1616
                800 815 9417
          Fax: 416 597 1617)

Australia
Blackwell Science Pty Ltd
54 University Street
Carlton, Victoria 3053
(*Orders:* Tel: 03 9347 0300
          Fax: 03 9347 5001)

A catalogue record for this title
is available from the British Library

ISBN 0-632-04067-X

Library of Congress
Cataloging-in-Publication Data
Dalby, Joseph.
    EU law for the construction industry/Joseph
Dalby.
        p. cm.
    Includes index.
    ISBN 0-632-04067-X (pbk.)
    1. Construction industry—Law and
legislation—European Union countries.
I. Title.
KJE6786.D35 1998
341.7′5–dc21   97-39127
                                            CIP

To
Niamh

Contents

Preface

The origins of this book lie in the offices of the European Commission, where I had the good fortune to spend seven months in the Construction Unit of the Internal Market Directorate-General, during 1992 and 1993, just as the Single Market was coming into being.

Working within the institutions of the European Union, and then in private practice in Brussels, offered a whole new cultural, economic and legal environment for a barrister who qualified a few years before 1992 – when European law really began to enter into the average practitioner's life – and who, for the first three years of practice, learned his craft within a national context. I had to 'Europeanise' my working practices by identifying the advantages of the Single Market; understanding the principles of primacy and direct effect; questioning the validity of national legislation; absorbing the EU approach which concentrates on interpreting the aims and intentions of a law, not the letter; and deferring to the fundamental principles of the Treaty of European Union.

From here it was only natural to look at the construction industry and construction law in the same light. A need for specialist, sector-based publications within the discipline of European law has now arisen, and accordingly this book is intended as a construction professional's reference book on European law; equally, it is the European professional's reference book on construction law relating to the EU.

Separate chapters are devoted to the four main areas of construction activity which are affected by European law: competition, procurement, trade and liability. These are preceded by a general introduction to European law and EC institutions, with an overview of the European construction industry which makes detailed reference to the European Commission's report into the sector.

European law is regulated by what the Treaty of European Union permits the institutions – including legislators – to do. So rather than concentrating on standard form contracts and liability under national laws, this book concentrates on the effects of the EU in harmonising these laws. If one acknowledges that European law serves to regulate a single market which covers the combined territories of its member states, then several questions arise:

- How does one integrate the national markets and free them up to open competition?
- By what commercial rules will contractors operate within this single market?

- How does one regulate competition between contractors for public contracts?
- What assurance does an operator have that his investment in expanding his market opportunities will not be undermined by discrimination based on his place of incorporation or nationality?
- Finally, if there is to be a single market, then what technical rules will regulate the placing of goods on the market, and safeguard workers and consumers, as well as the environment?

The answers to these questions, and others like them, will hopefully be found within the pages that follow.

I would like to acknowledge my appreciation and thanks to my former colleagues within the European Commission, to Ulrich Paetzold for his comments on the manuscript, to friends and acquaintances who encouraged me to begin to write for a number of outlets which in their way led to the completion of this book, to Julia Burden and Janet Prescott of Blackwell Science for keeping me to my word on delivery and to Tamsin Bacchus for grasping a specialist subject so expertly during editing.

Joseph Dalby
Winchester
November 1997
dalby@zetnet.co.uk

List of Abbreviations

CDM	Construction Design and Management
CEN	European Committee on Standardisation
Cenelec	European Committee for Electrotechnical Standardisation
CPD	Construction Products Directive
DSB	Dispute Settlement Body
DSU	Dispute Settlement Understanding
ECJ	European Court of Justice
ECU	European Currency Unit
EIA	Environmental Impact Assessment
EN	European Standards
EOTA	European Organisation for Technical Approval
EP	European Parliament
ER	Essential requirement
ETA	European Technical Approval
GAIPEC	Groupe des Associations Interprofessionelles Européenes de la Construction
GATT	General Agreement on Tariffs and Trade
GPA	Government Procurement Agreement
GRIM	Groupe Réflexion, Information, Management
ID	Interpretative document
IP	Intellectual property
PHARE	Poland and Hungary – Assistance for Restructuring the Economy
PPE	Personal Protective Equipment
PQQ	Pre-qualification questionnaire
R&D	Research & development
SPO	Vereniging van Samenwerkende Prijsregelende Organisaties in de Bouwnijverheid
Tacis	Technical assistance for the commonwealth of independent states
TEN	TransEuropean Network
TEU	Treaty of European Union
UPR	Uniform Price Regulation
WTO	World Trade Organisation

Chapter 1
The European Union and the Construction Industry

Overview of the European Union

The origins of the European Union

The European Union is a trading block with unparalleled legal, social and political dimensions. These elements make it much more than a free-trade zone or customs union. With its own law-making powers, and both international and domestic legal capacity, it is the biggest influence on the constitutional and legal fabric of its member states at present. One theory puts it that European law now accounts for one-third of all legislation in member states today, although even higher figures have been mentioned.

Its origins are well documented and its objectives feature prominently in the aspirations of politicians going back as far as the nineteenth century. Its present history is founded in a speech on 9 May 1950 (now Europe Day) by French Foreign Minister Robert Schuman, who was himself inspired by one Jean Monnet, later to become the first (and only) Honorary European Citizen. The Europe that had been shattered just five years earlier by the 1939–45 war was now beginning to revive and economic activity was growing. Nowhere was this more true than in Germany, which thanks to massive investment (largely originating from the United States of America under the aegis of the Marshall Plan) was once again becoming a major economic force. The earnest desire of a post-Nazi Germany to be politically accepted in Europe, and the parallel need of France to harness Germany's economic strength, led to a singular trade-off between the two – a trade-off which still persists today in the form of the so-called Franco-German Axis, metaphorically described as the engine that motors Europe.

The first manifestation of this co-operation was the European Coal and Steel Community (ECSC). A Treaty was signed in Paris in 1951 between six member states: France, Germany, Italy, the Netherlands, Luxembourg and Belgium ('the Six'). The last four of these had quickly warmed to the theme propounded by Robert Schuman and added to its momentum by asking to be involved. Other nations, principally led by the UK, participated in discussions but declined all involvement, preferring an association that was strictly limited to free trade rather than the transfer of sovereignty which the Community idea entailed. For this reason this group went its own way and drew together seven other states into the European Free Trade Association (EFTA).

Meanwhile, building on the success of ECSC, the founding fathers of the Union turned to other areas in which to bring about ever closer European ties. Treaties on political and military co-operation were promulgated but rejected, most decisively by France. However, it was in the areas of economic and nuclear energy that most consensus could be found. At a conference in Messina, Italy, the Six sat down to draw up treaties which would establish communities in both these fields. These treaties were subsequently signed in Rome in 1957 and so it happened that the European Economic Community and the European Atomic Community came into being on 1 January 1958.

Milestones through the years

Jean Monnet remarked that Europe moved in crises. That aside, the evolution of the European Union can largely be marked by enlargement or institutional and constitutional change. The first enlargement was in 1973 (the UK, Ireland and Denmark), the second in 1979 (Greece), the third in 1986 (Spain and Portugal), and the most recent in 1994 (Finland, Sweden and Austria), with a further enlargement expected early in the next century of up to five new members. Each stage has brought a widening of the coverage, ideas, attitudes and initiatives of the Community, and, as the EU grew with confidence, a deepening of its integrationalist and unionist resolve.

On the institutional side, changes have materialised in relation to the relative balance of power between the Council of European Union (as it is now known), the European Parliament, and the European Commission. The years since the European Parliament became directly elected by universal suffrage in 1979 have in particular witnessed:

- increased recourse to majority voting in the adoption of legislation by the member states in Council;
- greater power to amend, block and, more recently, jointly adopt legislation by the European Parliament; and
- more areas of competence for the Union as a whole in respect of which the power of initiative lies with the Commission.

The Treaty of Maastricht in 1992 brought about significant changes in these three principal areas of operation, with further changes when the Treaty of Amsterdam recently came into force on ratification by all member states in accordance with their constitutional requirements (i.e. by referendum or parliamentary vote). The member states have agreed to extend the power of the European Parliament to jointly adopt legislation, particularly in relation to employment and, social policy (equal opportunities and treatment). The Parliament will also be able to influence the adoption of laws on police and judicial cooperation, although this is limited to consultation only.

Constitutional change has come about in a way that was largely unexpected – from within. The extensive impact and inviolability of European law is due almost entirely to the jurisprudence of the Court of Justice. The central pillars of supremacy and the direct effect of European law to achieve a European legal system were conceived by the Court, and have been fostered and considerably extended in the many cases it has been called upon to preside over. Such progress has been achieved by this judicial reasoning that member states can now be held liable in damages for breaches of European law, just as individual persons are liable for tortious acts. It is almost impossible to imagine the same rate of development had it been left to the member states rather than a politically independent and impartial organ.

Finally, one must not ignore the political change that has both initiated and resulted in the foregoing. In one respect there has been none. Both the concept of the common market and the determination to lay the foundation of an ever closer union have always been integral to the existence of the Union since the founding Treaty. What has changed is political awareness by the citizens of Europe and a reckoning of what closer union entails. Membership of the Union is now a political football in most if not all countries both inside and outside the EU. 'Brussels' is seen as a source of disruption and disunion and not a means of escaping both. Economic and monetary union, above all, is having a divisive effect between proponents and opponents. We are entering a new era.

The situation today

The term today is 'the European Union' by which the amalgam of treaties, communities, institutions, laws and politics that have arisen out of the three original, individual communities is known. Technically, however, the three remain separate. It was only when the Treaty of European Union, or Treaty of Maastricht, was signed in 1992 that they were brought under a single 'umbrella'. In this regard it should be noted that whilst each of the three communities (Coal and Steel, Economic and Atomic) have legal personality, and can make binding laws, the European Union itself does not. The EU, at present, has no institutional or legal force and truly is an association of nation states. There is some confusion in the interchangeability of the terms 'European Community' (formerly 'European Economic Community') and 'European Union'. In common parlance one can use EU abstractly, but this does not reconcile with the fact that the law itself is 'EC' made. This book will, in accordance with current convention always use the term European Union unless it is necessary to refer to the Community or to Community law to avoid confusion.

The state of the Union in business terms

The geographical area

Geographically (and politically), the Union comprises fifteen states, with Finland, Sweden and Austria being the last to join. The next phase of enlargement will open up the Union into Central and Eastern Europe. Hungary, Poland, Slovenia, Slovakia and the Czech Republic are all to commence negotiations for entry early in the twenty-first century. The territories of these nations combined represent the territory of the EU. Exception is made with regard to some territories within certain member states. Technically, places such as Greenland or the Channel Islands do not form part of the Union although they do benefit from special treatment.

If one considers the territory in which rights which originate in the founding Treaties may be relied upon then one will discover that this is larger than the fifteen states. The principal instrument to engineer this is the concept of the European Economic Area (EEA). This was established by a separate agreement between the member states of the EU and those of EFTA and was principally designed to bring applicants from the latter up to speed on legislation prior to accession. It contains, amongst other things, single market, competition, state aid, and free movement provisions similar to those found in the Treaty establishing the European Economic Community. Thus in business terms, the catchment area of the single market because of the EEA, should really be regarded as embracing eighteen states – that is 'the Fifteen' plus Iceland, Norway (which has twice applied for and then rejected membership of the EU) and Liechtenstein.

By another route one should also consider the 'corridors' of access that trade agreements with specific 'third' countries offer. Switzerland and, more recently, Turkey both have trade agreements with the EU. In addition, countries that were formerly dependent colonies of one of the EU member states also have a special trading relationship. Whilst there are fewer benefits to operators in the EU, the Lome Convention gives these African, Caribbean, and Pacific states (known as 'ACP' countries) preferential access into the EU market.

Finally, although they are of limited economic significance, one should not forget the variety of association and co-operation agreements between the EU and certain third countries. Co-operation agreements are little more than a diplomatic 'handshake' between friendly nations. They generally consist of a statement of economic aspirations and respect for human rights and a commitment to work together in the future. One of the more recent co-operation agreements was concluded with South Africa. Association agreements on the other hand are of slightly more economic significance since they reflect continuing trade ties between the parties. There are agreements existing with Jordan, Israel, Morocco, and, closer to home, Poland, Hungary, the Czech Republic, Slovakia (collectively, the 'Visegrad group') and Slovenia. They are of some economic significance since they cover general trade arrangements and, from the point of view of Slovenia and the Visegrad group, are regarded as a first step towards eventual full membership of the Union. Indeed a growing number of these states have made formal applications to join the European Union.

The economic dimension

The Treaty of European Union is first and foremost an instrument for economic prosperity. That means putting together the best conditions to enable business, and not least the construction industry, to operate.

The economic element is vital because the only rights and duties the Treaty bestows or imposes are those which are exercisable in an economic context. This is borne out by the list of activities found in the Treaty of European Union (Articles 2 and 3). These comprise a common market and economic and monetary union, sustainable and non-inflationary growth, and high levels of employment, social protection and standards of living. This translates into some twenty different but interrelated policy areas of which a number are featured in this book. Those which are not but which do have some pertinence to the construction industry include a common commercial policy (regarding relations with the rest of the world), transport, industry, research and technological development, consumer protection, and energy.

The institutions (including the Court) are bound to act within the powers conferred by the Treaty and the scope of such powers is characterised by the activities listed in the Treaty. It is better to say 'characterised' rather than 'limited' or 'restricted' since the approach of the Court (and also the Commission) is to interpret the Treaty and its provisions in a large sense and to treat exceptions restrictively. In this way, whilst it is obvious that the fundamental freedoms and the competition rules are clearly economic in character, so too, because of the Treaty, are employment laws, health and safety, environmental measures, technological development and consumer policy.

In contrast, the one area which one can say is outside the scope of the Union is that of fundamental and human rights, such as those enshrined in the European Convention on Human rights and those which are common to the member states. As the Court of Justice held in its recent opinion on whether the European Union could sign up to the European Convention, the Treaty has not yet conferred such powers (Opinion 2/94, March 1996). More recently it refused to give a preliminary ruling on whether a national appellate court should quash a conviction for a breach of legislation (originating in an EU directive) because certain procedural rights were not respected, since EU law was not actually in issue (C-144/95 *Mauri*).

This brings to the fore two other important factor relating to the economic dimension of European law. Firstly, it is sometimes only when an individual has *de facto* exercised a right under the Treaty that the protection the Treaty confers can be invoked. This is especially so in cases when the doctrine of reverse discrimination applies. This doctrine, developed by the Court of

Justice, states that in situations which are purely internal to a member state Union law will not apply. Thus an architect who has never lived, worked or studied abroad will not be able to enforce his rights under the Architects Directives (see Chapter 11). Conversely, doing any of these things confers on him the status of migrant worker and a beneficiary of the treaty. Companies likewise will be affected by this principle but for them it might be easier to exercise their rights by attempting to sell their services abroad.

Secondly, the Court of Justice has shown itself far from shy in overturning national procedural laws in order to give full effect to rights in Union law. A good example is to be found in the UK's former immunity of the Crown to both injunctions and liability for damages. In both cases the Court has held that a national court should set aside a national law which reduces the effectiveness or impact of a right in Union law, even if this leads to the result of overturning a constitutional rule (*Simmenthal* (106/77), *Francovich* (C-6 & 9/90), *Factortame* (C-231/89).

The economic element of the EU has been and is being achieved in stages. The first stage was represented by the common market which went a long way to remove barriers to cross-border trade in goods and services and in the free movement of workers and the self-employed, as well establishing the conditions for fair competition. Thereafter there came the single market. This emerged in the early 1980s from a judgment of Court of Justice (*Cassis de Dijon* (120/78 [1979] ECR 649, see later), was crystallised in a Commission White Paper in 1985 and formally put in place at the beginning of 1993. It is characterised by the harmonisation or mutual recognition of technical standards for the manufacture and marketing of goods and the free move-ment of services. The single market was a milestone in itself, albeit a legis-lative one which has more appeal than substance in some areas. The concept of the common market still exists but the single market initiative was designed to reinforce and re-approach the business objectives of the Union. The construction industry was one of the major components of the single market and the Construction Products Directive was one of the first so-called 'new approach' directives on harmonising standards across the Union.

The final stage – economic and monetary union – is in the process of completion. Clearly re-focusing on the macro-economic element of the Union, this has led to a slowing down of the harmonisation approach with greater reliance on the fundamental principles set down by the Court of Justice and market-led harmonisation of trading rules. Once economic and monetary union is actually achieved this will become much more important as the need to compete on cost will touch every economic entity in the EU.

The European construction industry

In *Strategies for the European Construction Sector: A Programme for Change* (European Communities, 1994) ('the SECTEUR Report') construction is described as an industry in which Europe can beat the rest of the world. That may or may not be so. It is in any event a reflection of the strength, size and depth of the industry – what Brussels might regard as an industry worth regulating, not to contain it, but to enable it to grow and develop.

That, in essence, is what the *Strategies* publication is all about. The report, fully researched, analysed, prepared and written by W.S. Atkins International is the culmination of a major study into the state of the European construction sector undertaken on behalf of the Commission in order to stimulate debate about the future of the industry. The report looks into the structure of the industry, its processes, markets, costs and prices, and competitiveness, and then examines four strategic areas of action:

- quality,
- technology and innovation,
- human resources and training, and
- the environment.

It concludes with a set of proposals for action and an indication, by the consultant authors, of the priorities for each of the main groups involved in the sector.

The issues raised by the SECTEUR Report run parallel to the objectives set by this book. To a large extent, the author could not have a better point of reference. What follows, then, is a commentary on the report in order to complete the introductory chapter of this book. The author cannot claim any credit for the comprehensive nature of what follows but he accepts the errors in emphasis and observation as his own in what is a subjective view on the European industry as depicted by the report. For a more detailed examination, the reader is referred to the original report.

Characteristics of the industry

As far as this report is definitive (and with updating material from the annual report of the European Construction Industry Federation (FIEC) it has been calculated that construction output accounts for between 10 and 12% of gross domestic product (GDP) (1995: 11.6%). Output is directed in almost equal measure between residential construction, non-residential construction, and civil engineering, with renovation and maintenance accounting for the largest portion at a third of all output. Added to this is the fact that construction is the biggest industrial employer in Europe, accounting for up to 20% of all civilian jobs in the EU spread across 1.8 million enterprises (including one person firms) (1995: one in eight). Of the number of firms, more than 90% are small and medium-sized enterprises with fewer than 20 employees. It is calculated that one person in the construction sector creates two further jobs in other sectors (SECTEUR study). Unfortunately, however, the industry is in relative crisis and decline. Participants at a national level will be readily appraised of the economic outlook for the national industry, and, with an industry which is more or less homogenous across the Union, these national outlooks are reflected at a higher level. *Strategies* reports a decline in the construction output relative to GDP of 2% and a gradual decline since the mid-1970s, but for a rallying peak in 1991.

The report seems to indicate that this is in part the industry's own doing and that it is down to the industry itself to decide its future. In the authors' view the choice is between on the one hand an industry which is high in public esteem, applying the best technology to improve Europe's landscape, providing good affordable housing, and being a vital component in building society and on the other an industry which is increasingly seen as a source of low-skilled, low-wage employment, a fragmented and non-essential industry. Predictably the solutions proposed in *Strategies* are geared towards achieving the first scenario.

The construction sector is fragmented by a variety of factors. Distinct, rarely replaced technologies range from traditional, labour-intensive, site-based crafts to sophisticated industrialised technologies supplied by a long line of specialists and both require extensive co-ordination to transform the raw materials into the completed article. Customers range from the small client wanting repair and maintenance or the one-off client wanting a quick, budgeted job to the typical developer in the public or private sector for which the construction of large projects is an on-going exercise. This range results in a huge mix of geographically spread, individual projects for an equally wide range of end-user purposes.

In consequence contractors in each of these sub-markets are differently interested in and affected by changes in the structure of the sector as a whole. The sector is dominated by small and medium-sized industries with, according to Commission figures, over 92% of all firms (including general and specialist contractors but excluding self-employed persons) having fewer than ten employees, a statistic which fluctuates with economic cycles in correlation to the number of insolvencies. There are fewer than 1% with more than 100 staff. Moreover whilst there are five to ten large firms, there are no true European or multi-national firms, although some are developing as such through the acquisition of medium-sized specialists. The removal of technical barriers through single market legislation mainly benefits large firms, whereas the main problems of small firms relate to training, information availability, management time and ability, payment problems, delays and financing costs. For these small firms EC legislation is seen as bringing new administrative burdens and no advantage from the integration of markets.

Of course construction activity cannot but attract regulations – whether at a national or European level. The size of projects and the responsibility the sector bears for the health, safety, lives and livelihoods of those involved in the design and construction of buildings contribute to a need to regulate the construction industry, which governments tackle in various ways. However, this in turn necessitates harmonisation, since only through this process can professionals and products move freely. Both are beginning to benefit from this process with a substantial trade in products of a relatively high quality which it is hoped will lead to more prefabrication of sub-systems, structural components and even whole buildings.

The prospect of technical advancement highlights the changing construction process. In procurement, there is a general desire for greater choice between main contractor, separate trades or construction management forms and a trend towards design-and-build. These developments are prompted in part by the increase in size and complexity of projects coupled with a multiplicity of duties, issues and concerns which overburden the traditional role of the architect or engineer. A solution is to distinguish between initial conceptual design leading up to the construction permit and the subsequent detailed design and execution stage. Increased standardisation, more mechanisation and labour-saving innovations, and more off-site manufacture and prefabrication will also ease the situation. Accordingly the procurement process demands changes in the construction process, which in turn involves an increased reliance on specialist sub-contractors. This is proving to be both efficient and cost-effective.

This trend has revealed significant differences in the legal and tax provisions applicable to sub-contractors and certainly in respect of contractual matters there is some justification for the call for greater information and eventually simplification of arrangements. What applies to sub-contractors applies also to the array of consultants who as a group aim to serve every possible, conceivable need of the client and contractor. In European terms, the proliferation and emergence of specialist professions raise issues of education and training and their contractual and strategic role for the purposes of mutual recognition of qualifications and cross-border movement (see Chapter 11).

The long-term objective – high growth and high productivity

The last ten years have demonstrated that the construction industry is a barometer for the market economy. Accordingly it suffers from and rejoices in the normal business cycle. Since it is essentially private investment based, the cyclical starvation and surplus in funds cause havoc with output and render the future uncertain. However, amid this uncertainty some predictable influences can be detected.

The three major markets of the world, the EU, the US and Japan, have similar levels of construction output, but the level of intensity (output per head) is the least in the EU. In other words the US and Japan achieve higher standards of living through greater investment in construction regardless of the population density, indicating that the establishment and renewal of social infrastructure is essential. In the European construction sector, the potential for investment in infrastructure is vast, especially in terms of transportation, telecommunications and utilities. The EU is presently undergoing an ambitious infrastructure investment programme with the establishment of Trans-European Networks (TENs) to assist in market integration and the liberalisation of the utilities and telecommunications sectors. This is being administered in conjunction with EU structural and cohesion funds and, coupled with the PHARE and Tacis programmes which facilitate investment and assistance in Eastern European states, indicates rapid construction industry growth despite (or alternatively by virtue of) its concentration in less developed areas of the current and possibly future territory of the EU and Europe.

On the other hand, these new areas of investment (both geographical and sectoral) are essential to compensate for the decline in steel, shipbuilding and coal mining. Moreover, pressures will come to bear in the form of environmental protection, socio-economic factors (including the level of migration), changes in fiscal priorities and a reduction in economic disparities – each in their own way placing constraints on demand.

In this context the Secteur Report predicts that the future of the industry will follow one of three scenarios: high growth/high productivity improvement, historic growth/moderate productivity improvement, or low growth/no productivity improvement. Of the three, the middle course is considered the most likely, but only if the share of construction in the GDP rises to meet the increased needs of society and the market. Aiming high, the Report sets the first course as its objective, with a number of proposed strategies to enable the industry to achieve around 14% GDP, productivity at 2% per year, increased export trade (outside the EU), and a stronger, healthier and more competitive industry all round. To achieve this, construction must grow faster than GDP, and a shopping list containing alterations to market regulation are proposed to facilitate that growth:

- speedier deregulation of utilities;
- greater use of BOOT (Build Own/Operate Turnkey) processes;
- privitisation of public buildings and facilities;
- removal of state aid;
- liberalisation of rent controls;
- co-ordinated R&D of technology;
- high-tech low cost housing;
- energy-saving awareness campaigns;
- reduction in land costs and construction permit procedures;
- longer term land-use planning; and
- judicious use of public procurement and private infrastructure concessions.

To some extent the list is a viable one and in part is already subject to the on-going process of achieving the single market. It is submitted that it depends less on the willingness of the EU but more on the readiness of the member states to model themselves and their policies along these lines. Building on these proposals the report examines five key areas, competitiveness, quality, innovation, skills, and the environment.

Competitiveness and industrial performance

Project cost differentials across the EU are wide and are on average the same as Japan but up to a third more than those in the US. Product prices also reveal a very wide range, even in respect of those products which are almost homogenous across the Union like cement and steel, but on the other hand this does not appear to have a significant overall effect on relative construction costs between states. Labour costs are invariably set according to national wage agreements and are affected by different state benefits and employment conditions. Finally, unethical business practices are impossible to predict and hard to account for everywhere.

Given that there is therefore little harmonisation in costs, it follows that each national market is self-contained. A lack of world-beating construction firms in the EU reinforces the lack of integration and is potentially a major weakness which could result in loss of market shared to non-EU competitors. In this regard, the report detects modest inroads made by US and Japanese contractors, especially in utilities and factories. However these appear to have come on the back of inward investment (Japan) or by virtue of a significant defence-related presence (USA), and are therefore limited if not in decline. Nevertheless, both the US and Japan have a significant grip on the systems and manufactured components market. The main threat to the EU contractors is said to come from eastern Europe and the former Soviet republics, and is at present unquantifiable. Whilst in the short term these countries are concentrating on and even require assistance in their own rebuilding and rejuvenation programmes, they also boast massive construction industries with, for the time being, low wages and with the physical capacity if not the financial capacity to supply demand well beyond their own borders. They also have the ability to provide heavy construction equipment (again at cheaper cost) as their defence oriented manufacturing stock adapts to the reduction in East–West tension.

It would appear therefore that the EU industry has the opportunity to counter the threat from Eastern Europe by concentrating on developing heavy equipment and production and construction materials and the ability to undertake mega-projects throughout the world, but especially in its own 'back-yard'. On the design side, however, the report considers that the EU is in the happy state of producing world-class architecture which is aesthetically advanced and also acts as a catalyst for innovation in the manufacture of materials and components, especially in the development of environmental technologies – a foundation, it would appear, for the EU industry to build upon.

Quality in construction

Quality concerns every person connected to the construction process and needs to be evident in both products and services. Manufacturers of components and materials need to meet the requirements of the designer (on behalf of the customer) and, indirectly, the expectations of the public. The designer should only use those components and materials to the extent and for the purposes intended, and give proper instruction and specifications to the contractor for that. Finally, the contractor must follow those instructions accurately and report back to the designer faults and unforeseen problems in incorporating the components and materials. Each participant is geared towards satisfying the needs of customers and the public alike. Customers want value for money, the public demands buildings which are comfortable and safe. The industry is anxious to meet both requirements and so the issue here is to what extent they do so.

Quality is closely linked to price, and in a market characterised by intense price competition quality is liable to suffer. Generally it is perceived that quality in the construction industry is a basic problem (for a range of reasons from over-specification to defective design) but one which has lessened over the last ten years because of improvements in materials and products. Equally there is general support for improvement in all departments and moves are afoot, to a greater or lesser extent, to develop five tools to control quality.

- Firstly, common product standards (presently on-going in the form of the Construction Products Directive (CPD) will iron out differences between states providing minimum standards in the form of essential requirements (see Chapter 10).
- Secondly, technical control is somewhat linked to the CPD but revolves around adequate inspection at a local level according to local conditions and customs.
- Thirdly, liability and guarantees bind the contractor to the client and in single market terms are subject to long on-going discussion (see Chapter 12).
- Fourthly, there is much support for more registration and qualification of contractors and consultants based on their capabilities. These exist in some states and therefore become subject to the rules on mutual recognition (see Chapter 11).
- Fifthly, there is a trend towards developing quality management and assurance as an essential element in the construction process. In one way there is now a legislative basis for quality assurance in the form of the Temporary or Mobile Construction Sites Directive (see Chapter 14), although this is confined to health and safety.

Technology and innovation

The long-term future of any industry will significantly depend upon the making and incorporating of technological advances further to stimulate and maintain demand for its goods and services. Since the inception of European Union (but not on account of it) higher performance materials, more extensive use of machinery, the development of prefabrication systems, the application of computer aided design (CAD), and new structural solutions have all contributed to a major change in the construction process. In the future the Secteur Report forecasts extensive use of CAD and computer integrated manufacturing, use of composite materials, more off-site construction, building for recycling and even the gradual introduction of robotics, all of which reflect the shift of emphasis from the labour intensive, site-based process to a more industrialised one.

The inducement for change originates in the user sectors of the industry, including housing, commercial and industrial and civil engineering clients, each of which has changing needs. However this is often in the face of resistance from those who fear the reduction in traditional design and construction skills – in certain respects with some justification since change has sometimes resulted in a poorer quality product. In the final analysis it will be the market place which will dictate the pace of change and its demand for improvements in productivity and value for money mean that the whole supply chain from raw materials to site erection is constantly in the process of development.

In any event there will be no change without dissemination of technology, and therefore the pace of change depends upon how quickly ideas (which will often only turn out small improvements) pass from research and development (R&D) to exploitation and use. In this regard the speed of innovation is hampered by a lack of knowledge, skills or choice by the decision makers, and a not inconsiderable amount of risk and difficulty in disseminating large volumes of technical information to the multitude of small firms. This places the construction sector below other industries in terms of the level of R&D, although certain sub-sectors and certain member states do have their strengths (for instance nuclear power construction in France, offshore construction in Scotland, etc.). Nevertheless this issue prompts the call in the Secteur Report for a new strategy.

The new strategy has three policy priorities.

Improvements in dissemination and adoption of existing technology

Various suggestions are put forward:

- improvement in the training and education systems;
- the use of construction parks (analogous to industrial parks) where construction services are concentrated;
- better marketing and publicity by all firms and trade organisations;
- a duty on behalf of public bodies to promote innovation in public procurement of buildings and civil engineering;
- greater use of registration and qualification systems; and
- the raising of environmental and construction standards and planning controls.

More co-ordination between states and operators

A number of factors are to blame for difficulty in disseminating technology across borders including the traditional fragmentation of markets, but also uncertainty in demand and complex liability legislation. Quite apart from the cross-border difficulties, the structural make-up of the industry, particularly in separating design from construction activities, and the uncertain role of the manufacturer present problems which are equally handicapping. Each can be overcome by more co-operation between the different sides of the industry as well as between the different national industries so that information and innovation can become widespread.

An increase in the volume of R&D in construction

There are important gaps in the industry's R&D which can be filled by increasing the present level of expenditure, now 2 to 3% of construction industry turnover. EU and government money or compulsory contributory systems plus other incentives are required to achieve this, but it is envisaged that the single market should instil greater confidence in the prospect of a reasonable return. The priority areas are:

- research into the performance of buildings in terms of running costs and maintenance;
- environmentally friendly technologies;
- extending the working life of existing materials;
- the development of standard components and systems to reduce costs;
- intelligent buildings; and
- *in situ* diagnostic and repair technologies and the application of IT to construction.

Skills, training and labour market issues

Notwithstanding the shift towards mechanisation and prefabrication, the construction industry still depends upon a huge and variably-skilled workforce, which, if these characteristics are to be optimised, requires improved working conditions and job satisfaction. These are regarded as the most important long-term aims of the sector and well they might since the Secteur Report predicts a crisis if the industry does not change its approach to the recruitment and training of the right people for site work from a dwindling labour market. The report suggests a strategy to avoid this crisis.

In part the solution is a cultural one; the construction industry needs to be presented as an exciting and well-paid career not as the dirty, dangerous and insecure job it is presently perceived to be. On a more practical level the crisis will only be averted by improving employment conditions, improving education and training and the much heralded use of registration and mutual recognition of operators.

The prerequisite to improving training is to improve health and safety conditions, pay and contractual conditions, and career prospects in the industry. As well as improving employment conditions these three objectives would assist in eliminating improper competition where health and safety is compromised in order to cut costs and would decrease worker migration from states where pay is low. They would also limit the extent of temporary work and self-employment presently aimed at minimising tax and social security payments. On the training side, it is submitted that the number of complaints and the pace of technological change mean that a priority must be given to improving site skills. All firms need to adopt this but there is a strong disincentive to fund training since the labour force is mobile and largely temporary. Once again the greater good is undermined by undercutting on cost. However, once a solution to this pervasive problem is found, particular attention should be applied to the training of first-line supervisors because of the key role they play in determining the performance of the industry.

   In this regard, the Union needs a common terminology to discuss skill and training and a common system of craft and skill definition with their essential training requirements. This is presently under way in the professional sector, where the process of harmonisation should advance to creating individuals with a 'holistic' outlook by establishing training which creates deep specialisms on a very broad base of multi-discipline initial training. This implies a set of core elements covering the social responsibility of construction, architecture and town planning, environmental principles, project management, law, economics, finance and accounts, as well as construction technologies and engineering principles. Finally, harmonised training and employment conditions must lead to greater use of pre-qualification systems, although to a certain extent this should be market led.

Environment

The construction industry affects the environment both positively by its construction of the built environment and negatively by its consumption of resources and generation of waste. Thus it is essential that it is seen as a promoter of sustainable development. This can be achieved by focusing on a number of issues.

Energy consumption

About half of EU energy resources involve buildings. They are thus a principal target for conservation. New technology for building automation and climate control will help make building services more efficient, although commercial pressures can work against efforts to reduce energy consumption through the introduction of passive thermal techniques. The greatest scope for savings is thought to come from refurbishment of existing building stock. Demand for this will be greatest in eastern European states, and this should motivate manufacturers of energy-intensive materials.

Resource use, waste and recycling

The construction industry is a major producer of waste. Only improved site management and more constructive design will reduce pressures on the decreasing availability of resources caused by increasing conflicts in land use. With waste comes the third environmental factor, pollution and hazardous substances. Non-degradable materials such as plastic and solvents result in toxic gases and other by-products. Construction sites need to be operated according to 'best practice' in order to reduce the contamination of land.

Environmental improvement

More research on factors such air quality, sick building syndrome and emissions from land and building materials will improve the internal environment; good public relations will assist in pointing out the way construction can improve the external environment.

Conclusions – a programme for change

The purpose of the programme of action put forward by the Secteur Report is threefold:

- to contribute to social and economic objectives for the natural and built environment;
- to improve quality of construction; and
- to increase competitiveness and value for money.

In achieving these objectives the report assigns priorities for each of the participants connected to and involved in the construction process.

The EU needs to carry out comparative studies on the training arrangements for construction crafts and professions. The Union should support measures and studies leading to increased mobility and mutual recognition and commonality of training and competence, and increase the support given by its various training programmes. The work being done on standardisation needs to be speeded up and made appropriate to the construction sector. Similarly, more needs to be done to develop compatible insurance and liability regimes, as well as ensuring that existing legislation on health and safety, environment, working conditions and procurement is enforced. Finally, there needs to be more support for and co-ordination of R&D in construction. National governments meanwhile are set the task of implementing measures to create an open and competitive European construction market and provide stability in doing so. The introduction of measures to promote private construction demand and to free construction from public expenditure constraints would greatly assist in this regard. They also should promote training and research activities.

Moving onto the construction sector itself, clients and users need to establish stronger representative bodies to promote their interests. In consequence they will be able to promote good procurement procedures and labelling schemes. On the other side, the main objective for contractors' and consultants' associations is the need to improve the standard and quality of self-regulation, and to be more flexible and media friendly. The use of flexible guarantees, prequalification, codes of practice, better training and quality assurance will all assist in achieving these objectives. Contractors themselves need to implement a range of measures to ensure that the general initiatives at the institutional level find a sympathetic and motivated audience. In addition they need to build supportive relationships between main contractors and small firms. 'Upstream' construction products producers' associations whose work is closer to the actual raw materials should play their part in accelerating standard-making and technical approvals whilst disseminating their research on environmental control and process improvements more readily. The producers themselves should collaborate in research ventures with main contractors and invest in technologies which save process energy. As for designers, they are central in improving multi-discipline working and therefore have to be attentive to changes going on all around them.

The impact of European law on the construction industry

The Secteur Report sets the lofty but not impossible ambition of high growth and high productivity from a technologically advanced, environmentally friendly, aesthetically superior, mobile, flexible, multi-disciplinary and operationally safe industry. At present, however, it is fragmented, short-sighted and largely under-trained. The industry therefore requires constructive government and institutional support, but with a firm regulatory base to ensure high standards of quality, health and safety, in a wider, homogenous yet liberalised market. In consequence it is easy to suggest that the single market, defined as an area without internal frontiers in which the free movement of goods, services and workers is assured, will move substantially towards establishing the right commercial framework in which to achieve this objective.

The essential methodology of the single market is to establish harmonised standards, mutual recognition of qualifications and the elimination of all technical and other barriers to trade and movement. The Union legal system is therefore essentially an enabler for greater prosperity. By the same token it is regulatory, consisting of a defined body of rules which limit the powers of national authorities and states whilst implementing and enforcing minimum requirements to be met by operators.

This double dimension is routinely reflected in the chapters that follow. Integrating the markets involves freeing up cross-border restrictions to allow goods and materials to be used in sites all over Europe so that the single market and not the national market dictates their price and quality (see Chapter 10). Contractors and professionals alike need to be able to rely on their qualifications and experience being recognised as equivalent to those which are required in the host state. Moreover they want to be able to bring in their staff and machinery without having to establish themselves on a permanent basis (see Chapter 11). All contractors and professionals need to operate under the same competition rules (see Chapter 5), not only with regard to access to trade associations but also in protecting the investment in R&D which alone will enable standards to be pushed up. They also need common rules for incurring liability for defects (see Chapter 12). This is especially so in the case of contracts awarded by governments and national authorities (see Chapter 7).

However achieving this greater prosperity must not be at the expense of various interest groups with varying degrees of influence. The client wants better value for money, the consumer and end-user want safer buildings, the worker wants a safer environment in which to work, whilst the environment itself must be protected. Accordingly, whilst barriers are broken, such matters should not be brought down to the lowest possible common denominator. There needs to be a constant effort towards improving quality through technological innovation. A more prosperous market will raise standards, but there must be safeguards to ensure that minimum standards are observed in respect of the materials used in construction and civil engineering and that they are safe and reliable (see Chapter 10). No-one should be able to compete unfairly by risking the health and safety of site staff (see Chapter 14) or exploiting scarce resources and damaging the environment (see Chapter 13).

Chapter 2
General Principles of European Law and Procedure

European law has only recently become a compulsory topic for study at some universities and colleges. Moreover, whilst European legislation takes up increasing space in the statute books, the lawyer's craft is still based on national traditions and laws. The space available in this book cannot do justice to the depth and breadth of the subject but it may be helpful to provide an introduction here.

The institutions

The Council of European Union

The Council comprises representatives from the governments of the member states and is the Union's legislator. This makes it the most powerful, and hence, the most politically motivated body, although it is (as with all the institutions) bound to act within the confines of the Treaty. This is slightly academic since the member states can agree, outside the immediate confines of the Council (that is to say inter-governmentally) to increase or reduce its powers as they are collectively, ultimately and categorically the origin of sovereign power. In this respect, it is perhaps only political persuasion and the higher ranking rules of fundamental rights that can act as a check on its authority.

The Council is presided over by all member states by rotation, each state holding the presidency for six months in turn. The Presidency who is the Minister for Foreign/European Affairs of the state concerned, will represent the Union in all its international dealings, in co-operation with the President of the Commission if need be. Each Presidency will set its own priorities for its term of office in addition to continuing the longer-term initiatives which are in progress. Virtually all of the most important decisions are taken at Council level and all but a few legislative acts are adopted by it. Increasingly it is being required to share the power to adopt legislation with the European Parliament but it is still the institution whose assessment of proposals put to it by the Commission is the most important.

Decisions are taken by vote. A vote will either require unanimity or simple majority (very rare), in which case each state has one vote, or a weighted or qualified majority, in which case each state is assigned a number of votes, according, in effect, to its political and economic status. Many decisions, including the internal market directives (such as the Construction Products Directive) are taken on a qualified majority, but a few still require unanimity (e.g the environment). The level of support required for each area of law is provided for in the Treaty.

Individuals and businesses will rarely have contact with the Council as an institution. This said, if the construction industry or a section within it is extremely desirous of seeing certain policies or laws adopted, then a combined lobbying effort, targeting directly and individually the member states, would be in order since they are always a body of influence on the Council and therefore on the EU. In these and other cases contact should be made with either the government minister responsible for the portfolio or the member state's representative on the Committee of Permanent Representatives, known by its French acronym as COREPER. This body undertakes the day to day work of the Council, chiefly by examining issues, policies and legislative proposals as they arise and separating those which can be agreed by the Council without further discussion from those which require debate at the higher political level the Council offers.

The European Commission

The Commission functions as the initiator of Union action, a watchdog on the application of Union law, and as the executive body. Accordingly, this gives it an unusually high profile for an institution which carries the bulk of the Union civil service.

The nucleus of power in the Commission is concentrated in the college of Commissioners appointed by common accord between the members states. In one way these Commissioners act as government ministers since their remit to initiate and manipulate policy is extensive. However, that remit is in the main limited to the power of proposal. Hence, Commissioners tend to operate on the basis of consensus and consultation (often wide and public) so that they concentrate on only those proposals which stand a realistic chance of materialising as law or official policy.

There are presently twenty Commissioners, of whom one is appointed as President by the member states, and the rest appointed in consultation with the President. Since 1992 appointment of the college of Commissioners has required the approval of the European Parliament. Each Commissioner is given a number of portfolios which he or she must promote and defend in public, before the relevant industry or sector concerned and before the national and European Parliaments. Each Commissioner will be assisted by his or her own *Cabinet* and, in relation to each portfolio, a Directorate General made up of administrators who give effect to policy decisions and initiatives reached by the Commissioner. Table 2.1 lists the Directorates General.

The construction industry will feature in several different portfolios and will thus be administered by different Directorates General. Competition

Table 2.1 European Commission Directorates General.

DGI	External economic relations (including common commercial policy, relations with World Trade Organisation)
DGIA	External political relations (including association and cooperation agreements with Central and Eastern European states)
DGII	Economic and financial affairs (including economic and monetary union)
DGIII	Industry (including construction and associated sectors and standards)
DGIII	Competition (including merger control and state aids)
DGIV	Employment, industrial relations and social affairs (including health and safety)
DGVI	Agriculture
DGVII	Transport (including trans-European networks and infrastructure)
DGVIII	Development (including overseas aid and investment)
DGIX	Personnel and administration
DGX	Audio-visual media, information, communication and culture
DGXI	Environment (including pollution, waste, and conservation)
DGXII	Science, research and development (including production and materials technology and environmental research)
DGXIII	Telecommunications, information industries and innovation
DGXIV	Fisheries
DGXV	Internal market, financial institutions and company law (including technical harmonisation and procurement)
DGXVI	Regional policy (including structural funds)
DGXVII	Energy
DCXVIII	Credit and investments
DGXIX	Budgets
DGXX	Financial control
DGXXI	Customs and indirect taxation (including common customs tariff and VAT)
DGXXII	Co-ordination of structural policy
DGXXIII	Enterprise policy, distributive trades, tourism and co-operatives including SME co-operation and market access)
DGXXIV	Consumer policy

aspects are always administered by DGIV and industrial policy comes under the industrial affairs portfolio (DGIII). However harmonisation directives, such as the CPD as well as the procurement directives, will also come under the responsibility of a separate internal market porfolio (DGXV). Employment, industrial relations and social affairs (including health and safety) are assigned to DGV, the environment to DGXI, and consumer policy to DGXXIV. This nomenclature is subject to change but it can be helpful when one is in direct contact with the Commission to have an idea about how it is organised internally. In fact since the Commission is the largest institution it is the one which individuals are most likely to come into contact with (at least until the European Parliament becomes more central).

Anyone is free to contact the Commission if they feel the institution can be of help. For instance a direct request for information can often be dealt with easily, depending on the issue. Alternatively, a business may wish to make a complaint about the commercial activities of a competitor, difficulties in obtaining product approval or access to the market of another member state, or about the way in which a member state has interpreted Union law or preferred one activity or firm to another in the aid it gives. The Commission is under a duty to monitor and enforce Union law, and in this respect most of its information comes from individuals and businesses. In order to carry out its enforcement role the Commission has extensive powers, particularly with regard to competition matters. Thus the Commission can exert a real influence on behalf of those complaints who feel they are suffering under an imbalance of power.

Finally, contact may come via one of the many committees, consultative bodies and other sources of information and venues for dialogue that the Commission either presides over, supports, commissions or has an informal liaison with. The Commission will often given credence to even an informal body or organisation if it feels it has integrity, a democratic, professional or representative role, and is able to make a valuable contribution to current debate. Accordingly, the construction industry, as a highly organised, varied and communicative area of life, makes a substantial contribution via many groups, bodies and organisations, some of which are referred to later in this chapter.

The European Parliament

The Parliament is made up of 626 members elected by direct universal suffrage for a term of five years of whom one will be President. Its monthly plenary sessions are presently held in Strasbourg although mini-sessions and much of its committee work is done (and some sessions held) in Brussels. There is a continuing controversy over which of these two cities should be the permanent home for the EP with considerable building activity taking place in each in order to provide appropriate facilities. It will inevitably be one or the other. The European Parliament does not have a legislative role unlike its national counterparts. It does take part in the legislative process but it is only recently that its contribution could be described as decisive. In nearly all matters it has a right to be consulted and to debate proposals of the Commission. It can also debate and adopt recommendations on any matter on its own initiative. However, it is only in respect of certain areas that it can either block or jointly adopt legislation.

As a body the EP can offer influence over the legislative process, and over recent years the Parliament has been under serious consideration as a source and a means of more direct power. In addition to its legislative participation the European Parliament can also:

- conduct Committees of Inquiry into alleged contravention or maladministration in the implementation of Union law;

- handle petitions from individuals on any matter which comes within the Community's field of activity and which affects that person directly; and finally
- appoint an Ombudsman to conduct inquiries into instances of malad-ministration of the Union's institutions or bodies on the basis of individual complaints.

Whilst the second and third of these offer rights of substance for individuals, all three are really only a check on the internal workings of the Union. Nevertheless, as the Union becomes increasingly important in the daily lives of European citizens these rights of recourse should not be considered too lightly.

The Court of Justice

The Court of Justice is made up of fifteen judges appointed by common accord by the member states. Whilst it is not required that each member state nominate or appoint a judge, that in practice is what happens. The Court's jurisdiction is as extensive as the European Community, but not so as extensive as the Union. In practical terms, the economic rights and duties that feature in this book are all within the remit of the Court. In many respects the Court is the highest authority available since all other institutions are accountable to it. The only check on its activities will be the member states themselves acting as the founding sovereign powers, and they can only limit or change the jurisprudence of the court by way of amendment of the founding Treaties. Naturally that would require unanimous agreement.

Subject therefore to fundamental change by the member states, the Court has exclusive competence to interpret the Treaty and interpret and determine the validity of all acts of the institutions. The Court may do either when called to hear actions brought before it and references made to it from national courts, which are themselves required to co-operate in the application and interpretation of Union law.

Since 1989 and the creation of the Court of First Instance, the Court of Justice has been a tribunal of appeal over all matters within the jurisdiction of the inferior court. The Court of First Instance was created to reduce the workload of the Court of Justice. It only deals with direct actions of which the most relevant are competition and state aid cases.

Other institutions and bodies

The European Council is an institution formed to give the heads of state and government of the member states a platform to give routine guidance, direction and motivation to the Union. It meets twice a year, each time in the member state holding the Presidency of the Council of European Union. The purpose of the six-monthly summits is to demonstrate the unity of object and action between the member states and to take certain political decisions. Its decisions are non-binding in the legal sense but in political terms cannot be ignored. For instance the removal of a number of legislative proposals, including one for a directive to harmonise the liability of service providers, was a direct result of the Edinburgh Summit in 1993, at which the then twelve member states made effective use of the principle of subsidiarity.

The Economic and Social Committee (Ecosoc) is a body on which the construction industry will be represented in one form or another. Ecosoc brings together representatives of employers and employees, professional groups and public services. It is purely a debating chamber which may be consulted by the Commission when putting forward its proposals for legislation. Its opinions are non-binding.

The Committee of the Regions is an institution created in 1993 which brings together representatives of municipal authorities. In crude, national terms it could be regarded as the second democratic chamber shadowing the European Parliament, save that it is neither directly elective (members and alternates are nominated from elected councillors and the like from local authorities) nor does it have an effective role in the legislative process.

The adoption of legislation

The Treaty has divided the power to make laws between the four primary institutions:

- the Commission will typically propose a measure;
- the European Parliament will debate that measure or be consulted on it;
- the Council of European Union, if necessary jointly with the European Parliament, will adopt it; and
- the Court of Justice will review its validity and give interpretation as and when it is called on.

To this one can also add the duty of member states to give effect to Union law.

Forms of legislation

The Treaty itself is the primary form of legislation. However it is the product of an inter-governmental process and not of the procedure described briefly above and in more detail below. Accordingly amendments to the Treaty are only possible through international agreement concluded between the members of the European Union and ratified by each state in accordance with its own constitutional requirements. Thus any major changes in the competences of the Union and the powers of the institutions can only come about through the unanimous agreement of all participating member states. This gives each a state a direct and effective say over the direction the Union is taking and the substance of its powers, and the absolute right to disagree. Ordinarily, it is in the spirit of international relations to reach a compromise on all contentious issues and to abandon any initiatives which cannot muster an agreement. Exceptionally the Union will press on regardless of the objections of one member state. This famously occurred with regard to the Social Chapter. The UK was the sole member state to object to the inclusion of new provisions in the Treaty to extend Union competence over employment conditions. The rest were in favour and thus decided to reach an agreement on those provisions by way of a protocol appended to the Treaty. The UK has since agreed to the incorporation of the Social Chapter into the main body of the Treaty, when the 1997 Treaty of Amsterdam came into force (after ratification).

Within the Treaty the institutions with the power to adopt 'secondary' legislation may exercise that power by making *regulations*, issuing *directives*, taking *decisions*, making *recommendations* or delivering *opinions* (Article 189 TEU). There are differences in use and implementation between these measures.

Regulations

A regulation is binding in its entirety and is directly applicable in all member states. The principle of direct applicability is explained below but for now a regulation can regarded as standing as a law in itself which does not require specific implementation by national authorities. Once a regulation is adopted it is of general application and binding on individuals and national authorities alike. Measures will be adopted in regulation form if the Union has exclusive competence to regulate certain activities (such as agriculture, competition and international commercial policy) and whenever it is inappropriate to leave member states a discretion in the form and manner of implementation.

Directives

These are binding on the member states to which they are addressed insofar as certain prescribed results must be achieved. However directives leave to the national authorities the choice of form and method of implementation. In this regard implementation is a vital element in the legislative process since, unless a member state takes measures to give effect to a directive, it cannot in principle become enforceable. As will become apparent, the Court of Justice has stepped in to prevent the useful effect of directives being denied through the inactivity of national authorities in implementing them. Directives are frequently used in the adoption of Union law since they are the ideal means to 'harmonise' different national laws to regulate certain activities. For instance they were almost universally used to establish the single market. However by their nature they can only achieve approximation of national laws. Therefore in principle some differences will persist which can only be ironed out with certainty by firstly having regard to the provisions of the directive itself and perhaps secondly seeking the definitive guidance of the Court of Justice.

Decisions

Decisions are, like regulations, binding in their entirety, but only upon those to whom they are addressed. They are something of an administrative and legislative hybrid in that they comprise the means through which an institution can take specific measures pursuant to a more general power.

Recommendations and opinions

These are two methods by which the institutions can encourage a course of action or take a standpoint without the ability or need for compulsion. The Council, Commission and Parliament will often make recommendations on their own initiative to attempt to achieve ends for which there is no legal power or political will to adopt legislation, and any institution which has a right to be consulted will communicate its observations in the form of an opinion.

The Commission has added to the range of policy instruments by issuing *Notices* and *Communications* to give interpretation on existing law and *Green and White Papers* to outline policy and proposed legislation. None of these are binding although Recommendations (and Notices) can occasionally have legal effect insofar as they contain guidance on the implementation and enforcement of legal powers.

The Commission's power of initiative

Save in certain minor cases – but in respect of all the subjects covered in this book – the Commission has an exclusive power to initiate legislation, and so it is to this institution that one looks for detailed statements of policy. Occasionally the Council will call upon the Commission to act or propose certain measures, but this is not a precondition to the Commission putting forward a proposal. Such is the power of initiataive that save in certain cases the Council cannot adopt a piece of legislation unless it has been proposed by the Commission, and moreover it can only modify a proposal of the Commission by unanimous vote. Further, for so long as the Council has not acted on a proposal the Commission can modify its text.

The Commission therefore has a very wide discretion to mould and dictate the shape of Union law. It is also open to influence and, prior to issuing any proposal, it will invariably seek out the opinions of those who are likely to be affected by the measure in order both to 'fine tune' the text and to give it some democratic legitimacy. In this regard a well organised sector can both encourage and discourage the proposal of measures. This is something that is acknowledged and taken advantage of already by the European construction industry. For example, elements of the industry were very successful in postponing and effectively preventing plans for a proposed directive on liability and warranties in the construction sector (see Chapter 12).

It should not be forgotten that the Commission can in certain instances adopt measures itself without the intervention of the Parliament or the involvement of the Council. However the Commission can only do so when the legislative power has been specifically delegated to it. The area where this power is exercised most frequently is probably in competition matters, but it is also used in adapting certain legislation to technological innovation, and in the approval of technical standards drawn up by member states.

The role of the European Parliament

Over the years the European Parliament has, through Treaty amendment or inter-institutional agreement, considerably raised its profile and status, and increased its influence over the adoption of legislation. It is no longer a mere unelected Assembly that had to be consulted but could be ignored; it is now a democratically elected chamber with the power to veto certain proposed acts.

On almost all matters within the scope of this book it is required that the EP at the very least be consulted by the Council. A failure to consult is a substantial procedural violation which can lead to the annulment of the measure concerned (*Maizena* v. *Council* (139/79)). In certain matters, including social policy (that is employment legislation) and professional/ vocational education, the Council is required to co-operate with the EP so that Commission proposals are adopted after the latter has given its approval (*avis conforme*) or has submitted amendments which are incorpo- rated into the text. However, this procedure cannot preclude the Council from adopting a proposal unanimously in the face of opposition from the EP.

In a large range of matters, including single market legislation, free movement of workers and services, health, consumer policy and the envir- onment, measures are required to be adopted by both the Council and European Parliament jointly. The EP can therefore effectively block legisla- tion it does not approve of. Very briefly the procedure is as follows. The Council reaches a common position (that is political agreement) on a Commission proposal, which is assessed and then accepted or rejected by the Parliament. If rejected, the measure is debated in a Conciliation Com- mittee convened between Council and Parliament, following which both institutions will then adopt, respectively, a further common position and *avis conforme* which will finally lead to the adoption of the measure in its mod- ified form. If no agreement is reached the proposal is abandoned.

In the legislative process, the European Parliament potentially offers a considerable but nevertheless uncertain means of influence. One cannot be assured that its influence will count since the EP is not central to the adoption of legislation. Party allegiance is less decisive, although with, for example, the Socialist party in the ascendancy, support from this group for or against a common position of the Council can determine the fate of a Commission proposal. Nevertheless, interest groups with limited access to the Commission may find the European Parliament more accessible via their local MEP or via an MEP who takes a special interest in their affairs. There are, for instance, a few groups within the EP seeking liaison with the construction industry. For example the Crane Group currently brings together a broad range of construction interests including environmental concerns. It is sponsored by two MEPs, Slanislaw Tillich, an engineer from Germany, and Roberto Mezzaroma from Italy, who had previously tried to create something similar called the Built Environment Group. The forum is open to everyone connected with or interested in the construction sector, including contractors, suppliers, service providers, investors, developers and machine manufacturers, as well as environmentalists and consultants.

Accounting for national interests

As previously stated it is the Council which adopts legislation, either independently or jointly with the European Parliament. In any event the position the Council takes is vital to the fate of a Commission proposal.

The Council is the place where national interests meet head on with each other and with the European Union interest. The member states tend not to form groups as one would find in a parliament, although the Franco-German axis (known as 'the engine that motors Europe') is an almost permanent fixture. Instead, states are more likely to team up with anyone who gives support and one can never be quite certain what deals and compromises have been reached aside from the Council table. Moreover, Ministers meeting in Council are as likely to be concerned with the domestic repercussions of a proposed measure as with reaching a compromise between nations. If the necessary majorities cannot be mustered the outcome is deadlock, and this is often the destiny of measures proposed by the Commission but which cannot be agreed upon by the member states in Council.

On the question of voting, much has been made of the facility of qualified majority voting. Each member state is given a weighted vote according to its size and economic power. When the Council votes a qualified majority (of 62 out of 87) must be achieved. This enables either the small states or a combination of large and small states comprising more than 25 votes to block a measure. In certain situations where a particularly important or sensitive interest of one state is at stake, then the Council will seek to achieve a compromise which will assuage or minimise the prejudice any directive or regulation might possibly cause.

Application and interpretation of European Union law

To understand the way European law impacts on national law requires a familiarity with certain fundamental principles, either of the Union's own making or development, or borrowed from the constitutional traditions of the member states. Of chief concern here are the twin pillars of direct applicability/direct effect and of supremacy; and several general principles, which primarily guide the Commission and the Court in ensuring the enforcement and uniform application of Union law.

Direct applicability and direct effect

It was in 1963 that the Court of Justice observed that:

> 'The Union constitutes a new legal order of international law for the benefit of which states have limited their sovereign rights, albeit within limited fields, and the subjects of which comprise not only the member states but also their nationals. Independently of the legislation of member states, Community law therefore not only imposes legislation on individuals but is also intended to confer upon them rights which become part of their legal heritage.' (*Van Gend end Loos* (26/62) [1963] ECR 1; [1963] CMLR 105).

So it was thus that the Court of Justice declared that certain provisions in the Treaty and instruments adopted by the Union institutions applied directly to individuals without the intervention of the member states to 'implement' those provisions into national law. That is to say they stood as laws in their own right. Accordingly for a member state to attempt to transpose them through 're-enactment' into national law would itself be a breach of Community law since it would be failing to give appropriate effect to those provisions. In this the Court has, through the years, warmed to its theme, culminating in its landmark decision which held that member states could be held liable in damages to private individuals for the non-implementation of European law (*Francovich* v. *Italy* (C-6 & 9/90), [1991] ECR I-5357).

The key to both understanding and applying European law is in recognising whether a particular provision,

(1) requires implementation by the national authorities into national law (direct applicability), and
(2) gives rise to rights which are enforceable by individuals before national courts (direct effect).

In so doing one has to avoid the confusion over these terms. A provision is directly applicable law if, once adopted by the Union (i.e. the Council and, if necessary, the EP), it does not need to be and should not be purposefully implemented by a national authority in the form of legislation or administrative regulation. A member state is not precluded from adjusting its existing legislative and administrative provisions to give effect to a specific provision, and it is required to remove all provisions of national law which conflict with that Union measure. Clearly then the need to act will depend upon the circumstances in question. In any event, however, a directly applicable instrument or provision provides an immediate source of rights and obligations.

The principle of direct effect, on the other hand, is a case law rule of interpretation which is used to denote that a provision of Union law is enforceable before a national court whether or not it requires implementation by the national legislature or national authorities to give it full effect. A provision will indeed be directly effective if its terms (i.e. the rights or obligations it imposes) are clear, concise and unconditional. At this juncture one should note that a directly applicable measure will (if it is clear, concise and unconditional) automatically be directly effective. However a provision which is not directly applicable may nevertheless be directly effective. A brief examination of each kind of legislative instrument will demonstrate this apparent dichotomy.

Treaty provisions are a directly applicable source of rights and obligations and should be treated as primary rules in the same way as national legislation. They can also confer rights which are enforceable before national courts against national authorities and individuals. To date all the important provisions of the Treaty (as illustrated by this book) have been recognised as being clear, concise and unconditional. As mentioned earlier, regulations are declared to be directly applicable (Article 189(2) EC); thus they do not require implementation and should be treated as if they were primary legislation. As a result they can, like Treaty articles, regulate dealings between individuals and confer rights which are enforceable in national courts.

Directives on the other hand are expressly addressed to member states leaving them the discretion as to the choice of form and method of implementation. They are therefore not directly applicable. However, as the Court observed:

> 'Where the Community authorities have, by directive, imposed on member states the obligation to pursue a particular course of conduct, the useful effect of such an act would be weakened if individuals were prevented from relying on it before their national courts and if the latter were prevented from taking it into consideration as an element of Community law.' (*Van Duyn* v. *Home Office* [1974] ECR 1337; [1975] 1 CMLR 1.)

Accordingly, a directive is enforceable (i.e. is directly effective) against the state and all agencies of the state because it is addressed to the state. Furthermore, a state/agency cannot rely on its own failure to implement or comply with a directive. However, an individual cannot rely on the terms of an unimplemented directive as against another individual (i.e. it is not horizontally directly effective (*Marshall* v. *Southampton and SW Hampshire AHA* (152/84) [1986] ECR 723; [1986] 1 CMLR 688). This is because to extend the principle of direct effect in relation to directives to the sphere of relations between individuals would be to recognise in the Union a power to enact obligations for individuals with immediate effect, whereas it has competence to do so only where it is empowered to adopt regulations or decisions

(*Faccini Dori* (C-91/92) [1994] ECR I-3325). Nevertheless, if there is national legislation in existence which is designed to achieve the same or similar objectives as the directive but actually fails to do so then national courts are required to give effect to the non-implemented directive so that national law accords with it (*Von Colson* v. *Land Nordrhein-Westfallen* (14/83) [1984] ECR 1891; *Marleasing* v. *Commercial Internacional de Alimentacion* (C-106/89) [1990] ECR I-4135).

Supremacy of European law

The principle of supremacy or primacy of Union law is a fundamental pillar of the Union legal order, and like the principle of direct effect, has been recognised since the early 1960s. In one such case the Court held:

'The law stemming from the Treaty, an independent source of law, could not, because of its special and original nature, be overridden by domestic legal provisions however framed ... The transfer by the states from their domestic legal systems to the Community legal system of the rights and obligations arising under the Treaty carries with it a permanent limitation of their sovereign rights, against which a subsequent unilateral act incompatible with the concept of the Community cannot prevail.' (*Costa* v. *ENEL* [1964] ECR 585; [1964] CMLR 425).

In consequence the principle of primacy impacts on all agencies and manifestations of the state including the courts. This is reinforced by Article 5 of the Treaty which requires member states to take all appropriate measures whether general or particular to ensure fulfilment of the obligations arising out the Treaty or resulting from action taken by an institution, and further requiring them to abstain from any measure which could jeopardise the attainment of these obligations. This has led the Court to rule that a national court should set aside any national rule conflicting with Union law, including procedural rules which make it virtually impossible or unreasonably difficult to exercise rights conferred by Union law (*Simmenthal* (106/77) [1978] ECR 3595; *R.* v. *SS for Transport, ex parte Factortame (No. 2)* [1990] ECR I-2433).

Other general principles

The principles of direct effect and of supremacy are fundamental to the application and implementation of Union law. To these one must add several other general principles which are of the Union's own making or derive from the constitutional traditions of the member states. Dealing briefly with the latter source, the constitutional traditions of the member states can be best illustrated by the European Convention on Human Rights. Whilst the Union itself is unable to ratify the Convention because it does not meet the specific objectives of the Treaty – which as has been explained are economic in nature – it is nevertheless a privileged source of law which the Court of Justice has declared itself sworn to uphold and over which some of the supreme and constitutional courts of the member states have likewise refused to reduce their jurisdiction.

As regards the principles of the Union's own making, to a certain extent they also derive from the constitutional traditions of the member states. They have become the Union's own through adoption and adaptation.

Firstly, with regard to rights set out in the Treaty (and covered in this book), each right will be interpreted and applied within the general scheme of the Treaty. This general scheme is evident in the preliminary articles of the Treaty stating the objectives and tasks of the Union. The general scheme is essentially economic and integrationalist in nature, although it does have certain social dimensions. It is characterised by the single market which seeks to achieve open competition, freedom of movement and a prohibition against discrimination with a view to creating ever greater prosperity. Accordingly any legal provision (whether Union or national), concept, principle or other matter which does not have an inherently economic purpose is neither affected by Union law nor subject to it. In commercial terms, however, this does not amount to a great deal and certainly there would be very few incidences within the context of the construction industry where Union law did not apply for the want of an economic element.

Equally, the primary rights in the Treaty will always be extensively applied. Thus where rights are conferred on an undertaking or a worker then the definitions of 'undertaking' and 'worker' will be broadly construed so as to be applied inclusively and not restrictively. At the same time any exceptions to the primary rights will be narrowly construed. Exceptions are provided allowing a member state to impose measures which hinder trade, restrict freedom of movement, or are contrary to the spirit of the Treaty. The burden in this case is on the national authority to demonstrate that a specific exception both can and should be employed to limit or prevent the enforcement of the primary right. In this regard, it is necessary for the authority to give reasons which are objectively justified and not arbitrary.

The Union's institutions, including the Commission and the Court of Justice, are extremely sympathetic to the fundamental interests of a member state with regard to public policy, security, language and cultural differences, and also its finances. They will therefore uphold the use of restrictions where they serve one or other of these requirements, unless they can be protected in other ways. In this regard, however, there is a further principle of Union law which requires all measures imposed by a state to be proportional i.e. the measure chosen must be the least restrictive method of achieving the desired objective. The principle of proportionality also applies to the Union institutions is enshrined and in Article 3b TEU directing the Union not to act beyond what is necessary to achieve the objectives of the Treaty.

It will be clearly seen from this that member states do have a residual power to protect their interests as opposed to their markets. They only lose that power when the Union has adopted legislation which either subsumes those interests or eliminates them on the grounds that they are no longer relevant. When the Union does so act it is said to 'occupy a field' which was previously the preserve of the member states. In other words, it has acquired exclusive competence with respect to that field. For instance, when the Union harmonises the rules which regulate certain activity then, unless its method of harmonisation has been minimal, it removes all discretion on the part of the member states to act, other than to implement fully and properly the common European rules.

This begs the question as to when the Union should act to occupy a field. This is governed by the principle of subsidiarity which is also set out in Article 3b. This provides that in areas which do not fall within the exclusive competence of the Union, action shall only be taken if and in so far as the objectives of the proposed action cannot be sufficiently achieved by the member states and can be better achieved by the Union. The principle creates the assumption that all power rests with the member states unless it is more appropriate for the Union institutions to exercise their powers. However, in so far as it is more appropriate for certain activities to be regulated by the member states, then they are bound to respect the primary rights in the Treaty and the general principles of European law. These include the requirements that the national authorities act with certainty, without discrimination, with appropriate transparency and respecting the legitimate expectations of individuals.

Practical reliance on Union law

There is a natural tendency to view European rights and obligations as relevant to certain instances where, for instance, a cross-border element exists in contractual or tortious relationships. Whilst this element is a key and prevalent factor to the application of Union law it is not always a condition precedent. In certain circumstances a company or individual, never having exercised the right to freedom of movement, might be barred from exercising other rights derived from European law in an entirely domestic situation in the home state (the so-called doctrine of reverse discrimination), but in others a cross-border element is superfluous (e.g. sex discrimination).

This confusion is exacerbated by the fact that different Union laws are enforceable in different ways. Hence, whilst articles in the Treaty of European Union and regulations are binding on member states and individuals alike without further enactment, the same is not so for the large body of rules adopted in the form of directives, which generally require enactment. This can lead to the situation in which national law requires one thing whilst Union law requires another.

Faced with this dilemma a company or individual may well conclude observance of the national law is the more compelling solution since the risk of sanction will be greater. But, depending on the situation, it is suggested that the following policy be adopted. In private contractual or tortious relationships where one party seeks to enforce rights or obligations which are at variance with a Treaty Article or regulation but required under national law then the other party may rely on Union law and ask the Court to set aside the national provision. In contrast, in private contractual or tortious relationships where the European rule at issue is found in a directive (which the member state concerned has failed to implement properly into national law) then there would be some justification for the claimant relying on national law. However, it is only if the national court is completely unable to interpret national law in accordance with the relevant Union directive that this claim would stand any chance of success. For the defendant in these circumstances this would be a claim which would be hard to resist since individuals cannot rely on directives as between themselves. The only solution would be to seek indemnity from the national authority, either by way of third party proceedings or as a new cause of action.

However, in any situation where there is a direct risk of penal sanction at the hands of the national authorities, by way of prosecution for instance, then the doctrine of direct effect in relation to directives will enable the defendant individual or company to rely on either the directive or the national law according to preference. This is because an individual can rely on a directive against a state, whereas the state cannot rely upon it against an individual where it has itself failed to implement the directive or done so wrongly.

A good example of this is provided by a recent case before the Court of Justice on a reference from a court in Belgium, concerning the alleged non-compliance with technical standards by a manufacturer – a situation which could easily happen in the construction sector. The plaintiff was suing two competitors for libel after they had voiced their opinion that its product did not meet Belgian technical standards. Technically this was true, since the plaintiff was without authorisation to sell the product, but two important facts arose – firstly, Belgium had not notified its standards to the Commission pursuant to an EU directive, and secondly, the product had in fact been imported after manufacture to French specifications which, it so happened, had been duly notified and accepted. The Court held that litigants have a right to expect national courts to refuse to enforce national technical regulations which have not been notified as required, and so the plaintiff was able to argue that its failure to obtain authorisation for its product was of no consequence (*CIA Security SA* v. *Signalson SA* (C-194/94), not yet reported). There are important ramifications of this decision in the context of the construction products directive (see Chapter 10).

Chapter 3
Remedies for Breaches of European Law

The European Union constitutes a new, comprehensive legal order, albeit within a limited framework set by the objectives in the founding treaty and subsequently amended. It is therefore not surprising that it should offer its own remedies as well. In fact the Court of Justice has long justified the availability of remedies in the EC legal system. It was back in 1962 that the Court acknowledged that the Community constitutes a new legal order of international law (*van Gend en Loos* (26/62), [1963] ECR 1. In a slightly later case it added that by creating a Community of unlimited duration, having its own institutions, its own personality and capacity of representation on the international plane and, more particularly, real powers stemming from a limitation of sovereignty or a transfer of powers from the states to the Community, the member states have thus created a body of law which binds their nationals and themselves (*Costa* v. *ENEL* (6/64) [1964] ECR 585).

Traditionally, a litigant in search of a remedy will want either

- to force a defendant to act in a certain way (i.e. to honour a duty or obligation), or
- to stop a defendant from acting in a certain way (preventing a breach of such a duty), or
- to seek compensation from another for acts or omissions in the past which have caused him loss.

Within an EU context these remedies need to be examined in several ways.

- Firstly, those which are available at the Union level to regulate and review the actions of the institutions.
- Secondly, those which already exist at a national level to regulate and review the actions of national authorities and private individuals but which need to be seen within a Community context. In this respect one also has to consider those remedies which the Court of Justice has said must be made available within a national context even if they do not already exist.
- Finally, a minor but still very significant category, there are those remedies which have become available at the Union to regulate the actions of national authorities.

The common purpose of all these remedies is that they are designed to protect and/or enforce rights of individuals which are conferred by

European law by sanctioning, or in places compensating for, breaches of the same by institutions, national authorities and other individuals and thereby ensure effective and uniform application across the Union.

Remedies before the Union institutions

The Union institutions are wholly products of the Treaty of European Union and so it is to the Treaty that one must look for remedies to regulate and review their activities.

The Union institutions, in practice the Council of European Union and the European Commission, are able to regulate the actions of individuals through legally binding decisions. The Treaty therefore provides for three causes of action by which the Union courts may, on application made by a company or individual, review the legality or validity of these acts:

- the action for annulment,
- the action for failure to act, and
- the action for damages.

These are causes of action in the classical sense. To this one can add two administrative remedies consisting of

- petitions to the European Parliament and
- complaints to the European Parliamentary Ombudsman.

In the context of the construction industry these five causes of action will be of infrequent but not irrelevant use. An individual or company will only be in a position to contemplate having recourse to them if it is involved in a course of dealings with an EU institution.

Proceedings before the Court of Justice and the Court of First Instance are subject to their own rules of procedure which it is not intended to go into here. These will not be too unlike national rules of procedure (characterised by limitation procedures, form and incidence of pleadings, and powers of the court to hear and collect evidence) although the procedure is largely written. Parties must appear by lawyer admitted to the Bar or Law Society of a member state. One aspect of proceedings which will not be familiar in common law countries is the involvement – before the Court of Justice – of the Advocate General. After the close of hearings he gives an impartial, reasoned opinion on all legal aspects of the case. The Court is not bound to follow his conclusions but very often does so.

Action for annulment

By an action for annulment a party will seek to have the Court of First Instance overturn a decision taken by an institution which affects its interests.

An action for annulment under Article 173 of the Treaty may be brought against any act of any of the institutions which, whatever its nature or form, is able to produce legal effects. An act will produce legal effects if it substantially affects the interests of those concerned, for instance by exposing them to grave financial risk (*Cimenteries CBR* (8 & 11/66) Rec 93 116). The complainant should therefore distinguish definitive, binding acts taken following a special distinct procedure from those which are more preparatory and which do not in themselves bring about the same effects (for example a decision to launch an investigation is different (and non-reviewable) from the ultimate decision reached by that institution (*IBM* v. *Commission* (60/81) [1981] ECR 2639; [1981] 3 CMLR 635).

Member states and, generally, the institutions have unrestricted recourse to Article 173, however a natural or legal person may only institute proceedings in relation to a decision which is of direct and individual concern to that person. These criteria will be met if a decision is addressed to a person, for example in competition proceedings. However, given that it is possible for someone to be affected by a decision addressed to another, then it is open for that person to challenge the decision. Moreover, given also that it is not only by a specific 'decision' that the institutions can affect the activities of individuals but by regulations (which are ordinarily general and not specific), Article 173 actions may also be invoked in respect of these regulations.

In any event the key element to establish is that the act of the institution is of direct concern to the applicant. Such an act will be of direct concern if the effects of the decision on the applicant's interests do not depend on the discretion of another person or institution. In fairly simple terms this could be regarded as a test of remoteness where the act of an intervening third party 'neutralises' the acts of the institution (*Bock AG* v. *Commission* (62/70) [1971] ECR 897; [1972] CMLR 160). A decision will be of individual concern if the measure affects the applicant on account of certain attributes which are peculiar to that applicant, that is to say by reason of circumstances differentiating the applicant from all other persons and by virtue of which the applicant is distinguished individually, i.e. just as if the decision was in fact addressed to the applicant (*Plaumann* v. *Commission* (25/62) [1963] ECR 95). Decisions taken in the context of competition, anti-dumping and state aid can often place an applicant in the position of direct and individual concern. Whereas, a decision taken in the context of product specifications or import and export regulation which is not addressed to the applicant will tend to fall outside these conditions.

An action has to be brought within two months of the decision – this being either the date of publication, the date of notification or the date of awareness of the act being challenged. The Court of First Instance is empowered to overturn such an act on one of four grounds.

- Firstly, lack of competence by the institution concerned, in that the institution acted without legislative or Treaty authority.
- Secondly, infringement of an essential procedural requirement in, for

example, failing to consult or hear arguments and submissions in respect of a central issue.

- Thirdly, infringement of the Treaty or any rule of law relating to its application; this embraces Articles of the Treaty and general principles in its application, as well as fundamental principles of law including those set out in the European Convention on Human Rights.
- Finally, one can argue a misuse of powers.

In the case of all these, applicants should have regard to all elements of procedure and substance which gave rise to the decision in question, including matters which were not considered but should have been.

If the Court of First Instance finds that the application is well founded it can declare the act concerned to be void *erga omnes*. However, in the case of regulations (as opposed to decisions) the Court has a discretion to state which parts of the regulation are to be considered as definitive and continuing to apply. Meanwhile, the institution which took the now annulled decision is required to take the necessary measures to comply with the Court's judgment. This obligation is without prejudice to any claim to damages the applicant might have against the institution.

Action for failure to act

Since the EU institutions are organs of official authority and therefore are required to act in accordance with the instruments to which they owe their existence and powers, it follows that there should be and in fact is a cause of action for a failure so to act. These actions are brought before the Court of First Instance.

Article 175 provides that an action will lie against an institution if, after having been called upon to act, it has not 'defined its position'. One might describe the preliminary stage as a letter before action, but it is compulsory not discretionary. The applicant must have made an explicit request to the institution to act in a specific way, leaving no doubt that in the event of default an action for failure to act would follow. The applicant should give the institution two months to act, failing which there are a further two months to institute proceedings before the Court of First Instance. Again member states and institutions have an unrestricted right to bring these proceedings, whereas individuals are confined to any act other than a recommendation or opinion. Since regulations are of general application and directives can only be addressed to member states, the only act which an individual could force an institution to take is a decision. This, naturally, would be of direct and individual concern to the applicant so if the applicant disagrees with the position adopted, it may bring an action for annulment instead. Indeed, whenever the institution does define its position the right of action under Article 175 lapses.

Action for damages

The Treaty does not confer a general right to damages for breaches of European law – although it is now arguably available through the jurisprudence of the Court of Justice (see later in this chapter) – but it does confer a right to compensation in cases of non-contractual liability for damage caused by the institutions' or by the Union's servants in the performance of their duties (Article 215(2)). Under Article 178, the Court of Justice is granted jurisdiction in respect of this provision.

In order to establish an admissible claim it is necessary to show an unlawful act or omission on the part of a Union institution which causes pecuniary loss to the claimant. The action is autonomous in that it is not subject to the procedural rules nor to the requirements as to *locus standi* which are applicable in actions for annulment. Moreover, actions are admissible even when the administrative act in question was taken by a national authority, so long as the measure at the heart of the dispute was one adopted by a Community institution, and the national authority was bound to act on the institution's (normally the Commission's) instructions without any discretion. In this regard, a claimant cannot be denied damages on the basis that the remedies against the state have not been exhausted; nor on the ground that any award would be tantamount to nullifying the legal effects of the individual decision that has passed (*Krohn Import-Export* v. *Commission* (175/84) [1986] ECR 753). The limitation period is five years running from the date of damage.

Proof of fault, it will be observed, has not been mentioned, but it should not be concluded that liability will arise strictly or in the absence of fault. The Court is required to judge liability in accordance with the general principles common to the laws of the member states. Whilst the position is by no means clear, in general one can say that proof of fault will be required, but the standard of that proof will differ from case to case. Again, generally, some kind of wrongdoing must be shown, but the Court has not always awarded damages simply on the basis of a mistake. For instance the 'mere' incorrect interpretation of a regulation may not suffice, whereas disclosing confidential information will. Equally, bad administration, negligent acts by servants when performing their duties, and the adoption of illegal or invalid acts can all qualify.

Liability on proof of fault becomes more controversial when loss and damage arise out of legislative acts on the part of an institution. The Court recognises that the legislator must have certain prerogatives and accordingly has decided that, in the case of acts involving choices on economic policy, the Union will not incur non-contractual liability unless the claimant can demonstrate a 'sufficiently flagrant violation of a superior rule of law for the protection of the individual' ('The Schoppenstedt formula') (*Aktien-Zuckerfabrik Schoppenstedt* v. *Council* (5/71) [1971] ECR 975). A 'superior rule of law' consists of Treaty provisions, certain regulations which provide a vital and substantial framework for part of the Union's activities, general principles of Union law (including the principles of proportionality, legal certainty, and legitimate expectation), and fundamental principles of law such as those contained in the European Convention on Human Rights. Liability will arise if the institution has manifestly and gravely disregarded the limits on the exercise of its powers.

In all cases, damages are available for all forms of loss including economic loss, but there is a duty to mitigate loss (including taking action to protect interests or assets) and the Court will reduce damages on account of contributory negligence.

Petitions and 'actions' for maladminstration

As well as conventional causes of action in the form of judicial review and actions for damages involving the Court of Justice, a certain amount of control over the actions and omissions of the institutions is available through the workings of the European Parliament. The Treaty confers the right on all individuals to submit petitions to the EP itself and to make complaints to the EP Ombudsman in respect of maladministration on the part of an institution.

A petition may be addressed to the EP from any natural or legal person residing or having its registered office in a member state, individually or in association with others, on a matter which comes within the Union's fields of activity which affects him, her or it directly (Article 138d). A petition is arguably admissible in respect of all acts and omissions of the Union, including non-binding acts of policy of a general or specific nature. However, in the case of binding acts or omissions for which judicial review or damages are available then, given on the one hand the availability of causes of action before the Court of Justice and on the other, the relatively weak powers of enforcement on the part of the EP, a petition will only be appropriate as a last resort.

In such cases, the EP will entertain a petition on any matter which at the very least comes within one of the Union's tasks and objectives (set out in Articles 2 and 3 of the Treaty).

However, the most that the EP can do is to investigate and report on the petition and, if appropriate, seek to influence the institution responsible for the actions or omissions which aggrieve the petitioner. Whilst the EP is often a willing party to enforcing the rights and expectations of EU citizens, its unwillingness to interfere with any matter which should be resolved at a national level considerably reduces the effectiveness of this remedy.

The office of Ombudsman was created in 1992. The incumbent is appointed by the European Parliament to receive complaints from any national or legal person residing or having its registered office in a member state concerning instances of maladministration in the activities of the Community institutions, with the exception of the Court of Justice and the Court of First Instance acting in their judicial role.

On receipt of an admissible complaint the Ombudsman may conduct inquiries, and, on finding to his satisfaction instances of maladminstration, is required to refer the matter to the institution concerned. This institution will have three months in which to make submissions following which the Ombudsman will draw up a report to the European Parliament, the institution concerned and the complainant. The Treaty does not provide for any further procedure or means of enforcement after this point, but it is assumed that the transparency of the process including any finding of wrongdoing will be sufficient to 'force' the institution to remedy the situation.

Remedies before national courts

National remedies in a Union context

It is not the purpose of this book to explain in any depth the remedies which are typically available within the English legal system. However, it is appropriate to look at them in a Union context, pointing out not only what Union law expects of national remedies in order to give effect to Union rights, but also how indeed English law has adapted itself to accommodate rights arising from the founding Treaties and jurisprudence from the Court of Justice.

The starting point is the general principle of primacy, by which if national law and Union law conflict then the latter must prevail. In the context of remedies, Section 2(1) of the European Communities Act 1972 – through which the principle of primacy is given effect in English law – provides that all such remedies and procedures from time to time provided by or under the Treaties are (without further enactment) to be given legal effect or used in the United Kingdom. As is now observed, the 1972 Act makes it clear that it is the duty of a national court, when delivering final judgment, to override any rule of national law found to be in conflict with any directly enforceable rule of Union law (*Factortame (2)* [1991] 1 AC 603).

It follows, therefore, that if national courts are to give effect and protect rights in Union law then breaches of the same ought to be actionable before those courts. What, though, is the nature of the cause of action? Before the English courts it was held in 1984 that breach of a duty imposed by the Treaty should be treated as a breach of statutory duty; so the Court held in *Garden Cottage Foods* ([1984] 1 AC 130 at 141) in relation to Article 86 of the Treaty which, it observed, was for the benefit of private individuals to whom loss or damage is caused by a breach of that duty. Breach of statutory duty is all but officially established as the acknowledged remedy for all infringements of Union law. However, the very existence of this form of action is due more to landmark rulings of the Court of Justice (see later in this chapter) than to a serious development of the doctrine at a national level. Historically, the *Garden Cottage Foods* approach could be described as an exception to the main rule that infringements of Union law can only be dealt with through the common law remedy of misfeasance in public office; so the Court of Appeal concluded in *Bourgoin SA v. MAFF* ([1986] 1 QB 716) in relation to a breach of Article 30. However, it is widely considered that this authority has been overtaken by events at the Union level.

Having determined the cause of action, what remedies may be attached to it? The European Communities Act and indeed Union jurisprudence dictate that all remedies are to be available. In this regard the English courts have followed suit. *Garden Cottage Foods* acknowledges the proposition that the rights created in favour of individuals are ones which national courts must protect by the normal remedy of damages (see also *Plessey Co.* v. *General Electric* [1990] ECC 384). Likewise, injunctions and other forms of interim relief ought also to be available when a Treaty Article contains a prohibition – and most of the important ones do so. In this regard, it is worth pointing out that the Court of Justice states that the availability of injunctive relief at a national level ought to be the same irrespective of whether the applicant is contesting the compatibility of national provisions with Union law or the validity of secondary Union legislation (*Zuckerfabrik* v. *HZA Paderborn* (C-92/89) [1991] ECR 1145.

In respect of restitution, again the House of Lords has acknowledged that where a party has been unjustly enriched as a result of a breach of directly effective Union rights, the victim should in principle be entitled to bring a restitutionary claim in order to protect his Union rights. Finally, judicial review may be employed for the purpose of challenging the incompatibility of national law with Union law (*R* v. *Secretary of State for Employment, ex parte Equal Opportunities Commission* [1994] 1 WLR 409). One significant action upon which there has been no pronouncement is the representative action. Such actions, by single issue or general interest groups and associations, are limited in English law but work is afoot to enable such groups to bring cases in respect of Union law. Indeed a case has been referred to the Court of Justice from the English Courts as to whether one such interest group, the National Consumer Association, ought to be able to bring a representative action in respect of the government's implementation of the Unfair Contract Terms Directive.

Union law requirements on national remedies

The previous section set out the national remedies in a Union context, but of course Union law does have a number of basic requirements for those remedies.

The general principle is found in Article 5 of the Treaty by which member states must take all appropriate measures to ensure the fulfilment of the obligations arising out of the Treaty. This duty has been extended to cover the courts. Every national court must, in a case within its jurisdiction, apply Community law in its entirety and protect rights which that law confers on individuals. It must accordingly set aside any provision of national law which may conflict with Community law, whether prior or subsequent to the Community rule (*Simmenthal* (106/77)). Applying the principle of co-operation laid down in Article 5 of the Treaty, it is the national courts which are entrusted with the legal protection citizens derive from the direct effect of the provisions of Community law (*Rewe-Zentralfinanz* v. *Land-*

wirtschaftskammer für das Saarland (33/76) [1976] ECR 1989)). In this regard, the system of legal protection established by the Treaty, as set out in Article 177 in particular, implies that it must be possible for every type of action provided for by national law to be available for the purpose of ensuring observance of Community provisions having direct effect (*Rewe-Handelsgesellschaft Nord* v. *Hamptzollamt Kiel* (158/80) [1981] ECR 1805).

Building on the general principle, the Union courts have directed their attentions to different aspects of the national legal systems for protecting rights. It is a fundamental tenet of the Court of Justice that, in the absence of Community rules on a matter, it is for the domestic legal system of each member state to designate the courts having jurisdiction and to determine the procedural conditions governing actions at law intended to ensure the protection of the rights which citizens have from the direct effect of Community law (*Rewe-Zentralfinanz* v. *Landwirtschaftskammer für das Saarland* (33/76) [1976] ECR 1989). However, this comes with a proviso that these conditions are not less favourable than those relating to similar actions of a domestic nature nor framed so as to render virtually impossible the exercise of rights conferred by Community law (*Emmott* v. *Minister of Social Welfare* (C-208/90) [1991] ECR 1-4209).

What Union law has, generally, not insisted on is an obligation on the part of the member states to create new remedies to give effect to Union law. Although the Treaty has made it possible in a number of instances for private persons to bring a direct action, where appropriate, before the Court of Justice, it was not intended to create new remedies in the national courts to ensure observance of Union law requirements other than those already laid down by national law (*Rewe-Handelsgesellschaft Nord* (158/80) [1981] ECR 1805).

However, this has not prevented the Court from, in some cases, bringing about substantial changes in the scope and availability of existing remedies. For instance it is not sufficient for damages to be available; they must be adequate. The Court has held that, where financial compensation is the measure adopted to achieve an objective, it must be adequate in that it must enable the loss and damage actually sustained as a result of the wrongdoing to be made good in full, in accordance with the applicable national rules (*Marshall II* (C-271/91)). Likewise in relation to limitation periods, a time bar resulting from the expiry of the time limit for bringing proceedings cannot prevail over the need to protect rights conferred on individuals by the direct effect of provisions of a directive while the defaulting member state responsible for those decisions has not properly transposed the provisions into national law (*Steenhorst-Neerings* (C-338/91) [1993] ECR 1-5475). In addition, the full effectiveness of Union law would be impaired if a rule of national law could prevent a court seized of a dispute governed by Union law from ensuring full effectiveness of the judgment to be given on the existence of the rights claimed in Union law. It follows that if a court in those circumstances would grant interim relief, if it were not for a rule of national law, it is obliged to set aside that rule. (*R* v. *Secretary of State for Transport* ex parte *Factortame Ltd* (C-231/89) [1990] ECR 1-2433).

Article 177

The Court of Justice's justification for interference is based on the 'partner-ship' that it perceives existing between itself and national courts. The point of interaction and indeed the symbol of that partnership is Article 177 of the Treaty.

Article 177 enables the Court of Justice, in any and all proceedings before a national court or tribunal, to give preliminary rulings concerning the inter-pretation of the Treaty and the validity and interpretation of secondary acts. Note that it is presumed that Treaty articles are inviolable whereas the validity of acts of the institutions may be open to question. All courts or tribunals which are empowered by law to give decisions of a judicial nature *may* request the Court of Justice to give a ruling on any question of Union law if the court considers that guidance is necessary to enable it to give judgment. However, where any such question is raised in a case pending before a court or tribunal of a member state, against whose decision there is no judicial remedy under national law, then that court or tribunal *must* bring the matter before the Court of Justice. Exceptions are provided for in both cases where the interpretation is clear, or where the Court of Justice has already given adequate guidance in an earlier case. However, in both cases it is said that there is something of an obligation to refer since national courts may not interpret or judge the validity of Union law. The obligation to refer a matter to the Court of Justice is based on co-operation, established with a view to ensuring the proper application and uniform interpretation of Community law in all member states (*CILFIT* v. *Ministry of Health* (283/81) [1982] ECR 3415).When a preliminary ruling is given then all courts are bound by its authority; however this does nor prevent fresh questions being raised on the same point of interpretation or validity.

Actions against national authorities

In the hierarchical structure of the European legal system, member states stand as the point of contact between the individual and the Union institution. It is the sovereign nation which signs up, ratifies and enters the EU, and it is the sovereign nation to which one looks to give full effect to European Union law. Article 5 is so general in its terms that it can be relied upon, ultimately, in any situation in which an individual seeks to enforce rights against a member state.

What though is a 'member state'? This becomes of vital importance because of the ability of individuals to sue national authorities for damages for breaches of Union law. The Treaty of European Union does not define the scope of the term, although the Court of Justice has been on hand to assist.

The Court has held that the liability of a member state under Article 169 (infringement proceedings brought by the Commission) arises whatever the agency of the state whose action or inaction is the cause of the failure to fulfil its obligations, even in the case of a constitutionally independent institution (*Commission* v. *Belgium* (77/69) [1970] ECR 237 [1974] 1 CMLR 203). Moreover, in relation to giving effect to directives, all organs of the administration (including decentralised authorities such as municipalities) were obliged to apply the provisions (*Costanzo* v. *Commune di Milano*) (103/88) [1989] ECR 1839). However, the definitive test is whether the organisation or body is subject to the authority or control of the state and/or has special powers beyond those which result from the normal rules applicable to relations between individuals (*Foster* v. *British Gas* (C-188/89) [1990] ECR I-3313). In the Court of Justice's opinion, it followed from this that a body, whatever its legal form, which has been made responsible, pursuant to a measure adopted by the state, for providing a public service under the control of the state and has for that purpose special powers beyond those which result from the normal rules applicable in relations between individuals, is included in any event among the bodies against whom the provisions of a directive capable of having direct effect may be relied upon. Thus, a professional body exercising official authority is bound, like the state itself, to obey the directive (*Auer* v. *Ministère Publique* (271/82) [1983] ECR 2727).

The Court reinforced this in one case in relation to the ability of a professional tribunal to refer matters to the Court of Justice. If a tribunal may take advantage of Article 177 then it follows that it is bound to give effect to Union law. In the Court's opinion this means that if, under the legal system of a member state, the task of implementing provisions adopted by the Union institutions is assigned to a professional body acting under a degree of government supervision, and if that body, in conjunction with the public authorities concerned, creates internal disciplinary and appeal procedures which may affect the exercise of rights granted by Union law, it is imperative that the Court should have an opportunity to rule on issues of interpretation and validity arising out of such proceedings. In other words, in the absence of the possibility of appeal to a national court from a body which, after an adversarial procedure, delivers decisions which are in fact recognised as final, this body must, in a matter involving the application of Union law, be considered as a court or tribunal which can refer issues requiring a preliminary ruling to the Court of Justice (*Broekmeulen* v. *Huisarts Régistratie Commissie* (246/80) [1981] ECR 2311; [1982] 1 CMLR 90).

Now this line of authority and its conclusion is significant across the deregulated and private sectors and not just the construction sector. It means that an organisation such as the Royal Institution of Chartered Surveyors could be regarded as an agent of the state and therefore under a direct duty to give effect to Union law where it can. The reason is that it regulates the surveyors' profession by Royal Charter, which is an act of delegation by the state which it executes exclusively. Accordingly, it is able to:

- control entry into the profession;
- maintain the standards required to hold a licence; and
- discipline individuals who breach rules of conduct, for which the ultimate sanction is expulsion.

In this position it is able to impose, or bring about compliance with, certain rules of practice such as the terms upon which a surveyor offers his services to the public. The natural consequence of this state of affairs is that the RICS is bound, from the date a directive comes into force, by those of its provisions which are clear, unconditional and sufficiently precise. As a consequence individuals invested with rights arising out of such a directive may directly rely on such provisions against the RICS in a court of law (as they can against the state or agent thereof), even in the absence of complete and proper transposition of the directive by the state itself. Moreover, in the event of incorrect or non-implementation by the RICS it could be liable in damages for loss suffered by individuals.

On the question of damages, the general principle is that that state will be liable for loss and damage caused to individuals as a result of breaches of Union law for which that state can be held responsible. This is said to be inherent in the system of the Treaty. Individuals who have suffered damage have a right to reparation where three conditions are met. These conditions are:

- the rule of law infringed must have been intended to confer rights on individuals;
- the breach must be sufficiently serious; and
- there must be a direct causal link between the breach of the obligation resting on the State and the damage sustained by the injuries.

A failure to take any measure to transpose a directive in order to achieve the result it prescribes within the period laid down for that purpose constitutes *per se* a serious breach of Community law and consequently gives rise to a right of reparation subject to the two other conditions (*Dillenkofer* (C-178/94, not yet reported)).

The concept of state liability is still an emerging one, and so only formative conclusions can be made about its scope and definition. It seems relatively clear that a claim could be made when there is a failure to implement or a breach of directly effective provisions in what are essentially conditions which are similar to non-contractual liability of the Community under Article 215(2) (see above). In this regard any breach must be 'sufficiently serious', although this is not the hard and fast standard for liability it might appear to be since proof will depend upon how much discretion was left to the national authority taking into account a number of factors (clarity, intention, excusability, good faith, uncertainty of EC law, involvement of institutions, existence of precedents, etc.). The Court declares that all this is to be decided upon by the national court, but that, where there is narrow or no discretion, then there will in all likelihood be an automatic breach – especially for failure to transpose a directive.

The demarcation lines for state liability are probably most blurred when one compares liability for incorrect transposition (by parliament or a local authority) with liability for incorrect implementation (by a national authority or one of its agents in a non-legislative capacity). The first situation, the Court has held (*BT* (C-392/93)), involves the use of a wide discretion and is possibly excusable if it is not sufficiently serious; whereas the latter case will be governed by principles of direct effect, in relation to which there is effectively no discretion.

The measure for damages must be commensurate with the loss or damage sustained so as to ensure the effective protection of rights, and it is worth noting that national rules which totally exclude loss of profit as a head of damages cannot be accepted. However, recovery of any and all loss is subject to a duty on the loser to mitigate his loss. The injured person must exercise reasonable diligence in order to avoid the loss or damage or limit its extent. This may mean availing himself in time of all the legal remedies available to him.

Actions between individuals

It must be recalled that the primary purpose of the Treaty is to regulate institutions and member states, therefore one does not look to the Treaty for private remedies. Accordingly, recourse to domestic proceedings remains the only option for an individual who seeks to enforce his rights under Union law against another. Neither the Treaty nor the rules of procedure allow for direct actions to be brought by one individual against another before the Union courts, but private actions do regularly come before the Court of Justice on a preliminary reference from a national court during the course of pending proceedings in which a point of European law has arisen in respect of which the national judge requires guidance.

Nevertheless, Union law not only imposes obligations on individuals but it is also intended to confer on them rights which become a part of their legal heritage (*van Gend en Loos* (26/62)). However, these rights are only enforceable if they are founded in Treaty Articles or in Regulations. It will be recalled that both are directly applicable and therefore do not and should not require implementation. In such cases, the individual at fault would be in breach of a statutory duty, just as the state would be.

However, this option is unavailable in relation to directives. According to Article 189 of the Treaty, the binding nature of a directive exists only in relation to 'each member state to which it is addressed'. It follows that a directive may not itself impose obligations on an individual and that a provision of a directive may not be relied upon as such against a person (*Marshall I* v. *Southampton and SW Hampshire AHA (Teaching)* (152/84) [1986] ECR 723). The Court of Justice has refused to countenance any method of making directives directly applicable against individuals because, as it observes, the effect of extending this doctrine to the sphere of relations between individuals would be to recognise a power in the Community to enact obligations for individuals with immediate effect, whereas it has competence to do so only where it is empowered to adopt regulations or decisions (*Faccini Dori* v. (C-91/92) [1994] ECR1-5325). Most recently it held that there is no method of procedure in Community law allowing the national court to eliminate national provisions contrary to a provision of a directive which has not been transposed where that provision may not be relied upon before a national court (*Arcaro* (C-168/95)).

The effect of this line of authority is to prevent absolutely one individual from relying upon the provisions of a directive against another individual.

On the other hand, there are one or two chinks of light in this otherwise robust statement of the law. It is of the Court's own making. Often it will be the case that a national court will be asked to apply a national law in accordance with a directive even though the former did not specifically implement the latter. In these cases, so long as both national and Union measures seek to achieve the same objective, then, whether the national provision in question was adopted before or after the directive, the national court called upon to interpret it is required to do so, as far as possible, in the light of the wording and the purpose of the directive in order to achieve the result pursued by the directive (*Marleasing* (C-106/89)). In such cases then, the specific failure to implement is overcome because of pre- or post-existing national law which must be interpreted in line with the directive.

The second, it is suggested, can be developed by making use of national procedural law and the facility to join parties. Rather than putting the plaintiff to the expense of suing the state in addition to establishing factual liability on the part of the other party to the contract or the tortfeasor, then the plaintiff could either join the state as a defendant in the action against the contract breaker or tortfeasor.

Precedents in English law indicate that the joinder facility is appropriate when the different defendants are jointly or alternatively liable to the plaintiff in respect of the same subject matter. It is submitted that this is quite different from the interdependence of liability that would exist in an action which joined the private party as a defendant on the facts along with the member state as having legal liability. In this way, the actions of the defendant of fact only give rise to a finding of liability on the basis of which the plaintiff can derive compensation from the member state if the member state is at fault for failing to give effect to a directive. Conversely, the member state's failure to give effect to a directive will only give rise to a finding of liability – again one from which the plaintiff would receive compensation – if the actions of the defendant of fact come within the scope of that directive.

Nevertheless, one can see that this interdependence of liability is commensurate and compatible with the tests for establishing liability on an individual basis. For the defendant of fact this will be either the tests in contract or tort. For the member state, then this will be the three-pronged conditions established in the *Francovich* line of cases (see Chapter 2).

Enforcement of European law through complaints to the Commission

It is an emerging but unfortunate fact that the proper functioning of the European Community legal order depends, to a considerable extent, on the

willingness of the member states to behave in conformity with their Community obligations. For example, the implementation of many Community measures, including the vast array of directives to implement the internal market programme, requires the respective governments of the member states to transpose these measures into national legislation, while at the same time retaining the principles and spirit of the original Community measure (see *Litster* v. *Forth Dry Dock and Engineering Co. Ltd* 1989 SLT 540 (HL); [1989] IRLR 161; [1989] 1 All ER 1134). In fact, even though Community law more often than not confers directly enforceable rights on private individuals, the failure by member states to transpose Community legislation can effectively deprive individuals of such rights.

A private individual who finds that the UK government, or the government of another member state for that matter, has failed to live up to its obligations will quickly discover that the EC Treaty contains no express remedies allowing recourse to the European Court against the responsible authorities to remedy any injury caused by such an act or omission. Direct proceedings against member states before the Court of Justice are the reserved prerogative of member states and Community institutions.

It is true that the decision of the European Court, under the preliminary ruling procedure established by Article 177 of the EC Treaty, in *Francovich & Others* v. *Italian Republic* ([1992] IRLR 84) did establish the precedent that individuals have a right to compensation for injury attributable to the unlawful acts of member states, but this remedy must be pursued in the national courts. Further, the court has still to clarify the scope of this right and it is clear that litigation to enforce such rights will be both complex and costly to the individual concerned.

As an alternative to such court proceedings, a procedure exists whereby the European Commission may pursue an action in the European Court on the basis of a complaint made by a private individual alleging a violation of a Community obligation by a member state. This avoids the need to revert to national courts and tribunals which may be reluctant to apply the rule in *Francovich* despite the decision of the European Court.

This procedure, it must be conceded, is hardly a completely satisfactory alternative to a direct action in the European Court, but it has the virtue of offering private individuals a possible cost-efficient remedy. A solicitor representing a client in such a position must weigh up the pros and cons of such an approach in light of the needs of the client, taking into consideration the role of the Commission in the enforcement of Community law, the procedure for making complaints and the steps the Commission would adopt in enforcement proceedings in order to determine the advantages and disadvantages of proceeding via the European Commission as opposed to litigation.

The Commission's role in enforcing Community law

Under Article 5 of the EC Treaty member states are charged with the duty to take all appropriate measures to ensure the fulfilment of the obligations contained in the Treaty. This provision is often repeated in individual pieces of legislation. In an ideal world the process of implementation of Community law by member states should prove routine; after all, with a few notable exceptions, Community law is generally the product of inter-governmental negotiation and compromise wherein the common resolve is to agree legislation which is domestically digestible.

In reality, member states are occasionally out of step with their Community obligations and hence the European Commission is instructed in the EC Treaty to supervise the enforcement of Community law (EC Treaty, Article 155). In this capacity, the Commission acts as the executive branch of the Community in policing the actions of member states and Community agencies to ensure no infractions of Community law.

The most common violations of Community law involve national laws or regulations that are incompatible with the terms of the Community treaties. For example, if the French authorities refuse to certify as safe a product manufactured in the UK and marketed in France, even though the product in question complies with the relevant EC safety standards, the Commission is authorised to bring France before the European Court for failing to comply with Community obligations.

Equally, proceedings are frequently instituted by the Commission on the ground that a member state has failed properly to transpose Community directives into national law, either because the state has failed to enact national measures within the correct time period or because the national law when enacted does not correctly reflect the contents of the directive.

It is in the context of the completion of the internal market programme that proceedings on this basis are most often instituted. In the future commercial environment envisaged, clients will want to maximise or maintain their advantages in the Community marketplace. The horror for traders will be the scenario whereby, say, the UK government or its appropriate department has implemented or interpreted Community legislation incorrectly and in a way that creates a comparative disadvantage to British competitors. This could easily occur, for instance at the technical level, since, in accordance with the new approach of the Council, many directives adopted as part of the internal market programme are relatively succinct and leave the exact details and mechanics for facilitating the free movement of goods, persons, services and capital to the individual national authorities of each member state.

At this point it should be noted that complaints alleging anti-competitive practices by businesses are not considered violations of Community law for present purposes since the persons involved in such infringements are generally private parties and not agencies or organs of any member state. The state bears no liability for the actions of private individuals, even if nationals, at the Community level.

In pursuing compliance the European Commission, through the individual sectoral units (known as 'Directions') of the various Directorates-General, periodically reviews the activities of member states. In the event that it believes enforcement action is necessary, it can commence proceedings in the European Court against the member state in question (EC Treaty, Article 169).

But by far the greatest source of intelligence on possible infringement comes from private individuals. The Commission often receives complaints alleging that particular actions or measures taken by a member state are incompatible with Community law. In fact, without a healthy stream of private complaints it is difficult to see how the Commission could effectively execute its surveillance role. Private individuals, companies, firms and, in fact, all natural and legal persons are entitled to make a complaint if they believe that their Community rights are being infringed. Frequently these complaints are drafted by lawyers acting on behalf of aggrieved individuals.

However, in this respect, lawyers in the UK often seem reluctant to bring complaints to the attention of the Commission on behalf of their clients. This stands in sharp contrast to their continental counterparts. There is nothing unusual about a French or German company employing lawyers to draft complaints to the European Commission claiming violations of Community law by their own state or, more frequently, other member states.

Within the English legal profession, there is reticence about such an approach. Is the reason for this a lack of expertise, or are we deterred by geographical circumstances – an 'island mentality' factor? Although readers will have to satisfy themselves on the second count, the first reason, with all due respect to our colleagues in Brussels, should be treated as a mere lack of confidence.

Private complaints to the Commission

The procedure for commencing a Commission investigation into an alleged violation of Community law by a member state is not set out in any provision of the EC Treaty nor in any general measure of Community law. The general rule is simply that an investigation may be commenced once a complaint has been received from an interested private party.

In contrast to the position under Article 173(2) of the EC Treaty (actions to annul acts of the institutions), the status of a complainer is not a key prerequisite affecting the admissibility of a complaint, although the Commission is likely to be suspicious of any complainer appearing to act simply for altruistic reasons. In any event, it can be assumed that there are few individuals who would initiate a complaint unless they stand to benefit from requiring a member state to honour its Community obligations.

The first stage in representing a client in lodging a complaint is research: collating the relevant national and Community legislation. Once an infringement has been identified, it is necessary to determine which department of the Commission has responsibility for the subject-matter of the complaint. This can be done by contacting the Commission itself in Brussels, Edinburgh, Cardiff, Belfast or London, through the UK Civil Service, or a trade association. Direct verbal communications with the Directorate-General responsible for the matter prior to submitting the complaint can often be of considerable assistance in drafting the final correspondence.

For the sake of convenience, rather than procedure, the Commission has devised a form by which private individuals may submit their complaints and these are available from all Commission offices. Otherwise, and it is suggested in any event, the complaint should be fully set out in that ubiquitous tool of communication, the letter. For litigation lawyers used to form and precedent, issuing proceedings by letter may come as a novelty compared to the stylised language of pleadings. In fact, faced with such rare simplicity the lawyer could find himself lost for words! This can be overcome by following the somewhat schoolmasterly advice of keeping the letter succinct and coherent, bearing in mind that your addressees' first language may not be English.

The complaint should be supported with evidence substantiating the allegations made on behalf of the client. For example, if the subject of the complaint relates to inconsistent national legislation, a copy of the relevant statute or regulation should be included as an appendix. Similarly, if a client has been denied approval for marketing a particular product or service in a member state, copies of the relevant correspondence between the client and the national authorities should be included with the complaint.

The complaint itself should be addressed to the Secretariat-General, which maintains a register of all complaints received by the Commission. It should be noted that this register is quite separate from the register of complaints alleging breach of the competition rules maintained by DGIV. The complaint will be allocated a number and passed on to the relevant department. Because of the Leviathan proportions of the Commission it is also worthwhile sending a copy of the complaint to the department which will eventually be seized of it. Once the department has received the complaint from the Secretariat-General it is required to send an acknowledgement.

At this point it is worth noting that, although the Commission is not strictly obliged to communicate with the complainant, it has adopted internal rules on this matter. These are a feature of open administration and are intended to protect the interests of all interested parties to the investigation. Thus, in addition to an acknowledgement, the complainer should subsequently receive a letter explaining the representations made to the authorities, and one informing the complainer that proceedings have been initiated or that the case has been closed. Over and above this the complainer may receive letters requesting further information.

Depending upon the client's needs, the strength and sensitivity of the case, any soundings received from the Commission, and the degree of co-operation on the part of the member state concerned, one must judge how much contact to have with the Commission. This judgment is largely subjective, and will be assisted by good interpersonal skills and a moderate degree of faith in the Commission representative. Lobbying can range from a simple periodical telephone call to visiting the Commission personally, and all possibilities should be considered.

In short, the procedure is relatively straightforward and flexible and is compatible with a lawyer's usual manner of practice.

Commission enforcement proceedings against member states

Contrary to popular belief, the conduct of investigations into private complaints by the Commission is a relatively expeditious way to proceed on behalf of a client. In fact, the Commission has imposed upon itself a one-year time limit within which the case must either be closed or made the subject of formal infringement proceedings.

Provided that the complaint sets forth a compelling legal case for action and is supported by sufficient evidence of unlawful behaviour, the Commission can quickly collate the information required to justify bringing the matter to the attention of the member state concerned. Article 169 of the EC Treaty specifies a particular pre-litigation procedure, but in practice the following steps are taken by the Commission.

First, the Commission forwards the essential details of the complaint to the relevant national authorities for their comments and requests observations on the matter within a stated period. If the member state maintains that the measure or action is justified, the Commission reconsiders the matter in light of the observations submitted. If the Commission is dissatisfied with the justifications offered by the member state, it delivers a reasoned opinion on the matter outlining the legal principles applicable and explaining why the measure or act is incompatible with Community law. Again the member state is given a stated period in which to comply with the position as set out by the Commission.

If no settlement of the matter is reached at this point, the Commission issues a formal letter of notice containing the Commission's reasoned opinion and indicating the action that the Commission will take if the position is not rectified. This notice is drafted by the Directorate-General responsible for the matter with the assistance of the legal service of the Commission. Once again the relevant member state is offered a further opportunity to respond with corrective measures.

In the absence of a suitable reply, formal legal proceedings are initiated by the Commission before the European Court. Once this stage is reached there is little likelihood that the matter will be resolved out of court; unfortunately a period of at least one and a half years will then elapse before the court reaches a decision on the merits of the case.

Should the court rule in favour of the Commission, the member state is obliged to comply with the judgment of the court under Article 5 of the EC Treaty. Although at present there are no sanctions available to the Commission if a member state refuses to comply with the judgment of the court, it should be borne in mind that Article 171 of the EC Treaty allows the Commission to recommend fines to the court for non-compliance with decisions.

In practice, however, only a fraction of investigations initiated by the Commission on the basis of a legitimate complaint proceed to the European Court. Naturally, some member states are more willing to adhere to the views of the Commission than others and the UK and Germany have the least number of cases brought against them. But overall, according to

Commission estimates, over 50% of all investigations conducted are resolved even before a reasoned opinion is issued.

Advantages and disadvantages of complaints to the Commission

Making a complaint to the European Commission on behalf of a private individual has a number of clear advantages over litigation against government bodies in the courts of the state alleged to have been involved in the unlawful behaviour.

The first, and perhaps most significant, advantage is cost. A complainer incurs nominal legal costs in the prosecution of the case because the Commission, if it agrees to pursue the matter, assumes responsibility for the action and therefore its own legal costs. This is a significant advantage when the member state alleged to have been involved in the violation is a state other than the UK because otherwise it would be necessary to instruct foreign legal counsel to pursue a claim in the national courts of the other state.

The second advantage is that the mere weight of the Commission behind a complaint may have the effect of expediting a settlement of the problem without the need to revert to formal legal proceedings. Since the European Commission provides the member state with a statement of legal reasons why a particular course of conduct is believed to infringe Community law, there is substantial motivation for a state to change its practices.

A notable example of such an informal settlement arose in connection with a complaint to the Commission in 1989 that the French government was planning to impede imports of passenger vehicles made in the UK by a Japanese company on the grounds that the vehicles did not contain a sufficient value of Community material to satisfy the Community rules of origin. Since the merits of this argument were completely unfounded, the European Commission notified the French government that such behaviour would result in France being brought before the European Court. The threat was sufficient to compel the French government to back down.

Enforcement proceedings through the Commission may also allow the complainer to remain anonymous. Often, companies are reluctant to institute public legal proceedings against governments because they wish to remain on cordial terms for a variety of reasons, such as, for example, the procurement of public contracts. As a general rule, anonymity is better secured through Commission proceedings than in litigation.

In addition, the investigation conducted by the Commission is inquisitorial, not adversarial. There is no burden or standard of proof to discharge (although, one may need to convince the Commission that, *prima facie*, there is a case to answer); rather the Commission carries out an investigation in which the member state is obliged to co-operate and to provide the information required.

Finally, and perhaps most prosaically, it will become apparent that the Commission is only a telephone call away – a fact to take advantage of. Although the formal acts of the Commission have to be executed with suitable officialdom, the rules of procedure in making a complaint are a great deal more user friendly than in the case of formal legal procedures.

It must also be pointed out, however, that there are several drawbacks in complaining to the Commission rather than proceeding by way of litigation in national courts. The most important is the fact that the Commission retains absolute discretion as to the appropriate course of action to follow in the event of a notification of a violation. The Commission may decide that, for a variety of reasons, enforcement proceedings are not the most appropriate means of compelling a member state to comply with its Community obligations.

Even a private party alleging injury as a result of an unlawful act cannot compel the Commission to institute proceedings against the state. This somewhat unsatisfactory situation was well illustrated in *Star Fruit Co. SA* v. *EC Commission* ([1990] 1 CMLR 733). In that case the applicants complained that the Commission had failed to institute infringement proceedings against the French government which was operating import quotas on the supply of fresh fruits into its market which they considered incompatible with Article 30 of the EC Treaty. The Commission took little positive action on their behalf and so the applicants lodged a complaint with the Court of Justice claiming that the Commission had failed to act. The admissibility of the complaint was heard as a preliminary point and the Court resolutely declared that the Commission is not bound to commence proceedings, and the intention of the Commission in such proceedings cannot be pre-empted by private individuals.

A further disadvantage of a Commission complaint is that it does not give the complainer an automatic right to damages or compensation for injuries sustained. Enforcement proceedings brought by the Commission under Article 169 of the EC Treaty are, at least in theory, of a declaratory nature and do not give rise to a duty to pay compensation either to the Community institutions or to affected private individuals.

But, at the same time, the finding by the European Court that a member state is in violation of its Community obligations is conclusive evidence that the state has breached its obligations and may be relied upon in any subsequent suit in a national court by a private individual. In fact, in *Francovich*, the European Court relied upon the fact that Italy had already been held by the European Court to be in breach of its obligations in an earlier enforcement proceeding to support the liability of the state to the individual. It is not, however, clear whether such a proceeding is a prerequisite to a successful claim under the principles elaborated in *Francovich*.

In any event, if the Commission refuses to pursue a complaint on behalf of an individual, it is required to provide the complainer with a statement of reasons. But again it is stressed that this obligation is self-imposed as a matter of internal procedure and not strictly a matter of Community law.

Conclusions

It seems clear that making a complaint to the Commission is a preferred course of action where the complainer has a strong case to put forward, where no serious degree of injury has been sustained by the private party, and where the complainer wishes to minimise costs. In such circumstances, a Commission complaint may be the most effective way of proceeding on behalf of a client.

Chapter 4
EU Competition Law

Introduction

It is the task of the European Union to establish a system of competition in the internal market which ensures that such competition is not distorted. Accordingly, the competition rules of the European Union are of universal application to all traders operating within its territory, whether or not they are established there. Whilst the rules apply to all enterprises, professional or otherwise, many operators will not be directly affected by them in the routine execution of their business. In general competition law concerns medium-sized and large undertakings, but any company dealing with such an enterprise will itself be indirectly affected by the competition rules. Therefore no undertaking or professional can afford to ignore their existence and effect since, whenever a market player co-operates or integrates with other participants in a defined project, joint venture, trade association or other grouping, this is likely to affect competition in the market place.

The competition rules comprise Articles in the Treaty, supplemented by individual regulations and other instruments. They govern both public and private undertakings and confer rights on individuals which are directly enforceable before the courts and competition authorities at both a national and Union level.

The essential purpose of the competition rules is to prohibit conduct which restricts competition. This might happen if two or more undertakings agree to a certain course of conduct, or if a single undertaking, which is in a dominant position in a particular market, abuses that position. On the other hand, the courts and competition authorities are ever mindful not to stifle innovation and advancement which would actually benefit the market, and especially consumers. In practice it is a matter of maintaining a balance between the two.

By extension the competition rules also include rules governing state aid. These are mainly found in the Treaty. This is an area which should not be dismissed out of hand on account of the fact that, ultimately, aid or subsidies to one undertaking (whether public or private) will affect others in the market place. This is particularly so in the emerging trend towards privatisation, partnerships between government and industry and private finance. Again, rules on state aid also confer directly enforceable rights on individuals.

This chapter concentrates on three factors which are regarded as having an unacceptable influence on the market:

- collusion between undertakings and the application of Article 85 TEU;
- abuse of a dominant position and the application of Article 86 TEU;
- unlawful state aid and the application of Articles 92–93 TEU.

Thereafter the chapter will include with an examination of remedies which are specifically available in the context of the competition rules.

Collusion between undertakings

Agreements and undertakings covered

The primary competition rule consists of a prohibition. Article 85(1) TEU makes it unlawful to act in a way which has the object or effect of preventing, restricting or distorting competition, on the grounds that it is incompatible with the common market. The type of activities which are assumed to be anti-competitive are listed to include:

- directly or indirectly fixing prices or any other trading conditions;
- limiting or controlling production, markets, technical development, or investment;
- sharing markets or sources of supply;
- applying dissimilar conditions to equivalent transactions with other trading parties, thereby placing them at a competitive disadvantage; and
- making the conclusion of contracts subject to the acceptance by the other parties of supplementary obligations which, by their nature or according to commercial use, have no connection with the subject of such contracts.

This is a non-exhaustive list and one needs to refer to the jurisprudence of the Union courts and the decisions of the European Commission for other instances of anti-competitive conduct not readily falling into one of the foregoing categories.

The prohibition applies to agreements between undertakings, decisions of associations of undertakings, and concerted practices. An 'undertaking' is construed broadly as any combination of resources which are brought together to pursue a commercial economic objective, whether public or private, profit or non-profit making. Hence it will almost certainly include the independent architect or firm of engineers, and the main and sub-contractors, as well as any other participant in the construction process – including artists.

Special note should be made of the fact that a group of companies is treated as a single economic unit (*Centrafarm* v. *Sterling Drug Inc.* (15/74) [1974] ECR 1147) Two or more companies become a group when control of one is conferred on another either by capital acquisition or board control. In consequence, agreements between a parent and/or its subsidiaries do not infringe Article 85(1) (although they could be considered as an abuse under Article 86). Moreover, any single subsidiary within the group will be treated as having the turnover of the whole in its dealings with the world at large – relevant in respect of *de minimis* thresholds. In this regard, anyone dealing with one or more subsidiaries of the same group must ensure that they themselves do not inadvertently become party to agreements which would, by virtue only of their participation, fall foul of Article 85(1). Groups of companies which are created by or made the subject of a merger or takeover could, if of a sufficient size, fall to be considered under the Merger Control Regulation. This will, however, only concern the largest contractors. Otherwise, where a capital acquisition does not confer control but enables the 'parent' to influence the behaviour of the 'subsidiary' then Article 85 may apply.

Individual members of a professional or trade association will be treated as a single undertaking, but any *grouping* of 'undertakings' will be regarded as an 'association' – no matter what its form, whether it is a loose unincorporated entity or an incorporated body of limited liability – and will thus be subject to Article 85(1). That is to say, the association itself must conduct itself in accordance with the law just as each member must (hence the fining of Cembureau by the Commission for its part in the cement cartel case in 1995). The definition also includes associations of associations (federations). It matters not whether the rules of membership or the 'decisions' the association takes are binding or merely suggested, or whether the association is temporary or permanent. It is clear that the Commission does not need to find a high or sophisticated level of complicity in order to establish an infringement. It has stated that:

> 'To be held responsible, an association need not expressly list anti-competitive practices as one of its institutional objects. Nor is it necessary for the association or its representatives to have been entrusted formally by its members to discuss restraints of competition. The Commission considers it to be sufficient that the association or its representatives participate *de facto* in activities which infringe Article 85(1).' (see para. 150, *Competition Report*, 1994)

Accordingly, construction associations, either trade or professional, must be careful that they do not succumb to the belief that they know what is best for the industry. There is a special danger of this happening when the association becomes the recognised body for a sector or specific discipline and, on the strength of that, draws up rules of conduct, quality or procedure. Chapter 5 will make a closer examination of this.

The prohibition in Article 85(1) applies to agreements and concerted practices. Following on from the generality of the approach so far, it will come as no surprise that the term 'agreements' is also construed broadly. It connotes not only the typical contract, either express or implied, written or oral, but also atypical 'gentlemen's agreements', incidental agreements within the context of a long-term contract, understandings between companies, and standard written terms of contract which a manufacturer imposes on its dealers as part of a selective distribution network. In construction terms, with written (and standard form) contracts being such a feature of the industry, whether or not there is an agreement will not arise. However, there may still be an issue in relation to long-term co-operation agreements, bidding joint ventures, and commercial agreements not linked to a particular project.

Care should also be taken with agreements imposed, favoured, encouraged or sanctioned by the government or other public authority. The seal of approval by the state is not a defence to a breach of Article 85(1). Thus, the drive to refocus contractual relationships in the construction process in the wake of the Latham Report, *Constructing the Team*, cannot be regarded as an open invitation to suspend Article 85 even though it received governmental support. However, should a member state make certain contracts compulsory then undertakings would not be individually liable.

Finally, the prohibition covers 'concerted practices' This refers to any behaviour which cannot already be identified as an agreement or decision. They are defined as any form of co-ordination between undertakings which, without having reached the stage where an agreement properly so-called has been concluded, knowingly substitute practical co-operation between them for risks of competition (*Dyestuffs ICI* v. *Commission* (48, 49, 51-57/69) [1972] ECR 619). However, this does in itself satisfactorily contain the concept. In other cases, the Commission and Court have added that it is not necessary to have a common plan – mere parallelism of behaviour will not suffice, although it may amount to strong evidence. Any producer is free to change his prices to compete with his competitors so long as this interdependence falls short of co-operating with competitors by, for instance, determining a co-ordinated course of action relating to price increases. In the final analysis, the Commission and Court are looking for economic operators who are free to exercise their autonomy.

Agreements which are anti-competitive

To expand this heading, it should read 'activities which are anti-competitive under the EU rules as opposed to national rules'. To enlarge on the terms of the prohibition, Article 85(1) states that agreements, decisions and concerted practices will be unlawful if they affect trade between member states, and have as their object or effect the prevention, restriction or distortion of competition within the Common Market. The two criteria here are as much a test for the application of EU law *per se* as for anti-competitive behaviour. European law will always take precedence over national law, no matter what the circumstances, but only if its criteria for application are met. If not, one is then concerned with an entirely domestic matter, unless and until another 'cross-border' feature arises.

Competition law looks at the size of undertakings, the market they operate in, their relative shares in that market, their relationship to each other, any agreement between them or conduct in which they all participate, and the effect thereof on the market, before concluding whether a given agreement or course of conduct is lawful. Generally, undertakings that do not in any-way compete with each other, either directly or indirectly, actually or potentially, are unaffected by what follows. The same applies when the parties to an agreement are seller and ultimate consumer, so long as, it must be said, neither are in a dominant position in the market (see later in this chapter).

Therefore any two undertakings contemplating an agreement ought to examine their relationship to each other. They do this by looking at all the markets they operate in. They are competitors if they are concerned with or have an interest in the same product or service market, either at the same or at different stages of production, and whether directly, indirectly, actually or potentially. If so they must therefore be cautious in their dealings with each other.

Whilst in principle all undertakings (as previously defined) come under the control of Article 85(1), there is an assumption that undertakings and agreements below a certain size and value will not be detrimental to trade between member states. Likewise the Commission has indicated certain activities which it believes do not in themselves distort competition even though they amount to co-operation between competitors.

Thus once the substance of the relationship is established each party must look at its overall size and market share. In this task, European law lays down *de minimis* threshold criteria. It is significant to note that these are drawn up to facilitate co-operation between undertakings where econom-ically desirable, particularly between small and medium-sized under-takings. If the undertakings concerned find that they are below these thresholds they do not need to be concerned whether their agreement is anti-competitive.

Under European law, undertakings to an agreement will fall outside the scope of Article 85 if the parties have

- an *aggregate* annual turnover of less than ECU 300 000; and
- a *combined* market share of less that 5%.

It should be noted that turnover is exclusive of taxes achieved in the last financial year, and, where one undertaking has concluded similar agree-ments with other undertakings in the past, then the turnover of all partici-pating undertakings should be taken together. Finally, the relevant market is the one for the goods or services which are the subject of the agreement/relationship, including any which are considered as equivalent or direct alternatives in the area of the common market affected by the agreement. The relevant geographical area is the area in which the agreement produces effects, which will usually be the whole Union unless there are reasons to make it smaller.

Moreover, regardless (in principle) of the size of the undertakings, there are instances when co-operation is welcomed without the need for scrutiny or extensive control. The Commission has, through a Notice on Co-operative Agreements (*OJ* 1986 231/2), declared that certain activities do not immediately suggest anti-competitive conduct. These include:

- exchanges of opinion and experience – so long as it is not of a commercial nature;
- interaction with regard to accounting matters and debt collecting;
- research and development – so long as there is full disclosure of the results to all concerned;
- interaction about production, storage and transport facilities;
- working partnerships – i.e. collaborating to complete a specific order which one undertaking on its own could not do;
- joint selling and joint advertising; and
- co-operation on labels and standards.

The foregoing are good examples where competitors may be willing to co-operate with each other. It will be noted that they consist of overtly non-competitive activities which happily accord with the basic principle that competitors must not co-operate in a way that means that they are unable to compete. In this, whilst one of the above may form the object of an agreement, the effect of the agreement must not be forgotten. Since the Commission's Notice is indicative, not regulatory, it is not legally binding. Caution is therefore needed that the effect of the agreement does not cause it to 'spill-over' into becoming anti-competitive.

Accordingly, if there is doubt that an agreement cannot be described as *de minimis* or be regarded as concerning only non-strategic or commercial matters, then it is then necessary to examine whether the two principal criteria contained in the prohibition apply.

The first, that the agreement has an effect on trade between member states, involves an assessment of the impact the agreement has on the volume of trade. However, this does not make it an exercise in macro-economics. Rather, it is no more than an excuse for a very wide definition. This is because once it is known that an agreement affects trade between member states it comes under the competence of the Union institutions, notably the Commission which is well known for administering Union competition law.

According to the Court of Justice, an agreement will affect trade between member states if it is possible to foresee, with a sufficient degree of probability and on the basis of a set of objective factors of law or fact, that it may have an influence, direct or indirect, actual or potential, on the pattern of trade between member states such as might prejudice the aim of the single market (*Grundig* v. *Commission* (56 & 58/64) [1966] ECR 299). The breadth of the prohibition is revealed in the use of the adjectives 'directly, indirectly, actually or potentially'. In fact, the frequency should be taken as an indication of how wide the scope of European law of competition proves to be. Thus an agreement between two undertakings in the same member state which concerns anti-competitive conduct and which is expressly limited to the territory of the member state may still be anti-competitive since it may have the effect of restricting the entry of other foreign, or even domestic competitors into the market.

Whether an agreement does affect trade between member states is a question of law and fact, and each agreement of concerted practice must be looked at on its merits in order to establish whether it might have a direct or indirect, actual or potential influence. The ability of new firms to enter the market is a major factor, but specific advice can only be given according to the circumstances. In special cases, the Commission may regard an agreement as the sort which could influence trade flows if it is of the type that if it was in ready and wide use within the industry it would foreclose the market notwithstanding the fact that any two parties concerned would not affect trade themselves.

The second criterion for assessing the anti-competitiveness of any agreement is to ask whether the agreement or concerted practice has as its object or effect the prevention, restriction or distortion of competition. An agreement which has the object of distorting competition (for instance to share price information) is *de facto* a breach of Article 85(1) and it is not necessary to prove its effect. But when only proof of effect will support a claim for anti-competitive conduct then, as the Court has held, it is necessary that the consequences of the agreement prevent, restrict or distort competition to an appreciable extent (*La Technique Minière* v. *Maschinenbrau Ulm GmbH* (56/65) [1966] ECR 235). The restriction will be appreciable if a competitor could not have entered or maintained a presence on the market during the currency of the anti-competitive agreement.

The effect of the prohibition

Any agreement or concerted practice between undertakings or any decision of associations of undertakings which affects trade between member states and distorts competition is void (Article 85(2)). In consequence, any one who suffers loss or damage as a result of such an agreement, concerted practice or decision may bring an action claiming compensation for that loss. Alternatively, one can complain to the Commission which may investigate the matter. If the Commission discovers that two or more parties have agreed to collude between themselves to the detriment of competition then it has the power to impose fines of up to either 10% of their combined turnover or ECU 1 million.

Agreements which are exempted

It is generally acknowledged that the activities of any one or more operators in a market will have an effect on competition. With the spectre of fines and litigation to reinforce a robust prohibition on anti-competitive activity any market would simply stagnate. It is therefore acknowledged that new technology or market conditions might require operators to make strategic alliances or become larger through merger or takeovers. It is also recognised that the regulatory framework should allow for structural changes in the market place.

If an agreement necessarily falls foul of Article 85(1) but the parties still wish to pursue it then it may be permissible in the following circumstances:

- The agreement improves the production or distribution of goods or promotes technical or economic progress.
- Consumers are allowed a fair share of the resulting benefit.
- It only imposes restrictions which are indispensable to the attainment of these objectives
- It does not afford such undertakings the possibility of eliminating competition in respect of a substantial part of the products or services in question.

These four conditions are set out in Article 85(3) which states that the prohibition may be declared inapplicable in the case of agreements which meet all these criteria. This marks the belief that co-operation between enterprises can be beneficial and means such an agreement is perfectly valid in the form it is notified to the Commission.

Exemption is available either by the European Commission examining individual agreements on the basis of the four criteria referred to above or through the secondary legislation which offers automatic exemption to certain categories of agreements. In the former case the parties are required to notify their agreements to the Commission, in the latter case the parties deliberately draft their agreement so as to benefit from one of the block exemption regulations that have been adopted by the European Commission.

It is not necessary to obtain specific exemption when the parties reach an agreement modelled on a group exemption. Moreover, by Article 4 of Regulation 17/62 individual exemption is not necessary in three further circumstances.

(1) Where the only parties to the agreement are undertakings from one member state and the agreement does not relate to imports or exports between member states.
(2) Where not more than two undertakings are party to the agreement and it only restricts the freedom of one party in determining the terms of trade upon which goods obtained from the other party may be resold, or imposes restrictions upon the rights of an assignee or user under contract of industrial property rights.
(3) Where the agreement has as its sole object the development or uniform application of standards or types joint research and development specialisation in the manufacture of products which do not, in a substantial part of the common market, represent more than 15% of the volume of business done in identical or similar products and where annual turnover of the participating undertakings is less than 200 million ECU.

Group exemptions

Group exemption has been given to a number of categories of agreements, and a short overview of the ones most relevant to the construction sector follows.

Exclusive distribution agreements

Exemption is available to agreements between two undertakings for the exclusive supply of certain goods for resale. This is covered by Commission Regulation 1983/83 (OJ 1983 C101/2) which expires at end of 1997 but is to be replaced in either the same or similar form.

Under this regulation, the parties may agree certain restrictions which ordinarily would breach Article 85(1) but which are regarded as meeting the requirements for exemption under Article 85(3). To obtain automatic exemption the agreement should not impose any restrictions on competition other than:

(1) the obligation on the supplier not to supply the contract goods to users in the contract territory; and
(2) obligations on the distributor:

- not to manufacture or distribute goods which compete with the contract goods;
- to obtain the contract goods only from the supplier; and
- not actively to sell or market the goods outside the contract territory.

In addition the supplier is free to require the distributor to purchase complete ranges of goods or minimum quantities, to sell them under certain trade marks or to take measures to promote sales. However, the agreement may not prevent the distributor from responding to requests to supply made by users or intermediaries located outside his contract territory – i.e. there can be no contractual provision prohibiting passive selling.

It should also be noted that where a manufacturer maintains a selective distribution network, of which membership is subject to certain qualitative conditions relating to technical ability, then the network will be lawful so long as the criteria of purely qualitative tests are objective and objectively applied. Requirements as to specialist knowledge, adequacy of premises and customer service are considered as acceptable (see the Commission decision in SABA (76/159/EEC) OJ 1976 C28/19).

Exclusive purchasing agreements

Group exemption is available for agreements between two undertakings for the exclusive purchase of certain goods for resale. This is provided by Commission Regulation 1984/83 (OJ 1983 C173/7), expiring at end of 1998 but also to be replaced.

Under this regulation, the parties may agree, on the same terms as with distribution agreements, that the supplier shall not distribute the contract goods or goods which compete with the contract goods in the reseller's principal sales area and at the reseller's level of distribution. It also permits the supplier to insist that the reseller

- does not distribute competing goods;
- takes measures to promote sales by purchasing complete ranges or minimum quantities of goods;
- sells them under trade marks;
- advertises; and
- provides customer services.

However, the agreement may not be concluded to run for more than five years nor may it cover more than one type of goods where these are neither by nature nor usage connected to each other.

Specialisation agreements

Group exemption is available to agreements between more than two undertakings for the purposes of specialising on the manufacture of certain products. This is provided by Commission Regulation 417/85 (OJ 1985 C53/1).

Under this regulation, two or more undertakings may agree either to enter into reciprocal obligations not to manufacture certain products, leaving it to other party or parties to do so, or to manufacture certain products jointly. This obligation may be linked with other obligations:

(1) not to enter into specialisation agreements which compete with those which are the subject of the central agreement;
(2) only to purchase the contract goods from the other party or parties (subject to the 'purchaser' having the right to purchase the contract goods on more favourable terms elsewhere); and
(3) to grant the other party or parties exclusive distribution rights.

It is envisaged that the parties to such an agreement will be potential competitors. Exemption is, therefore only available if the aggregate market share of all parties to the agreement in respect of the contract products (plus any products which are regarded by users as equivalent) is not more than 20% of the market. By amendment to the regulation, the parties may also agree to market and sell the products jointly so long as their joint market share is less that 10%.

Joint research and development

Group exemption is available for certain agreements to carry out research and development into technical knowledge and 'know-how'. This is provided for by Commission Regulation 418/85 (OJ 1985 C53/5) which expires at the end of 1997.

Under this regulation, two or more undertakings may agree to undertake joint R&D of products or processes, joint exploitation of the results or both. This may be by means of a joint team or organisation, by entrusting the task to a third party, or by specialising on certain elements of a project. The parties may do this only on condition that the objectives and the field of work of the R&D are clearly defined, and that all parties have access to the results and the right to exploit the results independently. Where there is to be joint exploitation then the parties can only do so in relation to such decisive results that are protected by intellectual property rights or constitute know-how that substantially contributes to technical or economic progress. It does not matter whether the manufacturers are competing, although where they are then the exemption is additionally subject to an aggregate market share of not more than 20% of the common market or a substantial share thereof.

Additional conditions may also be imposed, e.g. not to carry out independent or competing R&D, to purchase R&D products only from the joint venture company (if any), or to feed back experiences in exploiting the results. Whilst generally there can be no joint sales or restriction on sales imposed on any party, in an R&D agreement one party may be given the exclusive right to distribute the contract products (on a choice of terms to counterbalance the concession) whilst another may (separately) agree not to compete in the same territory reserved for the contract products the subject of R&D for a fixed period of time (not exceeding five years). Nor can the parties agree not to compete in respect of any contract products outside the scope of the R&D programme or agree to quotas, prices, customer limits, passive sales.

Technology transfer agreements

Group exemption is available for certain categories of technology transfer agreements involving patent and or know-how licensing. This is provided by Commission Regulation 240/96. Under this regulation, no more than two parties may conclude agreements which contain one or more of the following obligations:

- a sole and exclusive licensee; licensor protection in areas within the EU not covered by the agreement;
- restraints on active and passive sales outside the exclusive territory;
- trade mark use; and
- limits on production.

Pure patent agreements and mixed patent and know-how may be concluded for as long as the entire patent system for the manufacturer's product or process is in existence although, if the exemption is for a restriction on passive sales, it is limited to five years. Pure know-how agreements may be concluded for ten years but bans on passive sales may only last for five years – although the obligation not to divulge confidential information which remains secret and substantial will remain exempted for the lifetime of the agreement. There can be no price restrictions, export restraints, customer restrictions, specified quantity restrictions, excessive territorial restraints, or (perhaps remarkably) no-competition clauses. This has no effect on the obligation of the licensee to use his best endeavours to exploit the licensed technology, the right of the licensor to terminate the agreement exclusively or to stop communicating improvements to him.

Abuse of a dominant position

At one end of the market there are small traders whose actions or inactions are unlikely to distort trade in the common market or a substantial part thereof. At the other there are companies in a position of 'unchallengeable ascendancy' over all competitors in terms of market share. Where these undertakings have the power to behave independently then anything they do can have serious implications on the market. There is nothing unlawful about being in a position of dominance; however they are placed under the duty not to abuse that position.

According to Article 86 TEU it is unlawful for one or more undertakings to abuse a dominant position within the common market or in a substantial part thereof insofar as it affects trade between member states. Again the Treaty offers a non-exhaustive list of conduct which would be an abuse. This comprises:

- directly or indirectly imposing unfair purchase or selling prices or other unfair trading conditions;
- limiting production, markets or technical development to the prejudice of consumers;
- applying dissimilar conditions to equivalent transactions with other trading parties therefore placing them at a competitive disadvantage; and
- making the conclusion of contracts subject to acceptance of supplementary obligations which by their nature or according to usage have no connection with the subject matter of such contracts.

Dominance can be established by examining an undertaking's market share and a variety of other factors, including the availability of technological knowledge, raw materials or capital. The power to behave independently translates into a power to determine prices or control production or distribution for a significant part of the products in question. This power does not necessarily have to derive from an absolute domination enabling the undertaking to eliminate all competitors. It is only necessary that the undertaking is strong enough as a whole to influence the market.

Determining the existence of an abuse of a dominant position involves considerable economic analysis in light of a few well-defined principles developed by the Court of Justice. It is first necessary to assess the relevant product market. A market is defined by determining whether a sufficient degree of interchangeability exists between all the products forming part of the same market so far as *specific use* in concerned. A readily appreciable example is provided by a case which came before the Court of Justice in 1978 as to whether the market for bananas was sufficiently distinct from the market for fresh fruits. Here it was not as much a question of 'specific use' – as might be more germane to construction products for instance – but interchangeability between products. The Court decided that the market for bananas was a distinct one. This case shows that if one narrows down the market sufficiently, one will always find an undertaking in a dominant position. In fact, this process is not unknown, even down to defining a market by reference to a 'brand', as opposed to a general product.

It is then necessary to determine the geographical market for the products in question to determine whether there is any dominance. The geographical requirement is met if the dominant position covers, at the very least, a substantial part of the EU, as assessed in terms of the pattern and volume of the production and consumption of the product market in question, how-soever defined. Thus if the market for a certain construction product is concentrated in very few but large areas across the Union, then any single such area could amount to a substantial part of the common market.

The dominance of the undertaking's position is then assessed by reference to its economic strength in the geographical market for the goods in ques-tion, and in particular the diversity of its sources of supply, the homogenous nature of its products, the organisation of its distribution and marketing network, and a number of other factors.

Finally, an undertaking in a dominant position is said to abuse that position if as a result of its conduct the degree of competition in the market is weakened or hindered. In proving this aspect, it is conclusive to show that the undertaking has exploited its position unfairly, to the detriment of actual or potential competitors. Thus for example, an abuse of a dominant position has been shown when

- the actions of the undertaking in question reduced the amount of traders on the market;
- when the undertaking systematically discriminated between purchasers; and
- when it either refused to supply, pursued a policy of predatory pricing, tied purchasers into a range of products when they only required one, charging unfair prices or imposed other unfair terms.

Where the Commission finds such an abuse it will order the undertaking concerned to terminate its infringement and, if appropriate, impose fines.

Enforcement of competition law

Enforcement of competition law merits attention on account of the range of legal and administrative remedies which are in addition to or distinguishable from the principles and procedures of general enforcement. They should, however, be seen in the context of the latter.

In many cases the aggrieved complainer will be presented with a choice as to how enforce his rights which may be welcome, given that cost is a significant factor. However if damages are a priority this narrows the available options. The principal remedies lie before the European Commission, and thence to the European Court of Justice, or alternatively before the national courts, possibly involving the Court of Justice. In addition and in due course further remedies may be available before national competition authorities.

Enforcement by the European Commission

The Commission, as guardian of the Treaties, is generally empowered to enforce Union law, and moreover in respect of Articles 85 and 86, it has considerable delegated power to enforce principles of competition law. This translates into powers to investigate, pass judgment on and, as appropriate, fine individual companies for anti-competitive conduct. It is therefore a forum to be considered by aggrieved parties.

These powers and procedures are specifically contained in the First Council Regulation on implementing Articles 85 and 86 of the Treaty, adopted under Article 87. Convention has given this the short form title 'Regulation 17'. Some provisions have been covered in the previous chapter, and reference is made to the availability of negative clearance and the notification of new and existing agreements.

The complaint

By Article 3 of Regulation 17 where the Commission, upon application by any individual company or person or upon its own initiative, finds an infringement of Article 85 or 86, it may require the undertakings concerned to bring their agreements or practices to an end. Those entitled to make an application are member states, and natural or legal persons who can demonstrate a legitimate interest. This is a matter of demonstrating a *prima facie* case of a breach of Articles 85 or 86 which is having an actual or potential detrimental effect of the complainant's business activities.

One of the great advantages of the remedy is the option conferred on the complainant to preserve its anonymity. In particularly sensitive sectors or situations a complainant may ensure that both its complaint and the information it provides remain anonymous. Accordingly the complainant is unlikely to elect to take advantage of the right to present observations at a hearing. On the other hand, publicity might be sought with a view to putting commercial and political pressure on competitors.

The Commission is under a duty to consider a complaint submitted to it under this provision, and failure to do so could be relied upon under an application under Article 173 for failure to act. If, however, it decides not to do so and shows good reasons why not then the Court of First Instance (and on appeal to the Court of Justice) will rarely interfere with the Commission's decision. (Case T-24/90 *Automec Srl* v. *Commission* [1992] ECR II-2223)

The investigation

Should the Commission decide to take up the complaint, the form of its investigation is inquisitorial. Here the complainant has the opportunity to provide a considerable amount of information and evidence since it is in its interests that the Commission has sight of everything which might assist in finding a violation.

Alternatively, the Commission has power under Regulation 17 to obtain information itself in a number of ways. It may, first of all, submit a request under Article 11 to any government, authority, undertaking or association of undertakings for all necessary information. There is no duty as such to comply, but there are penalties for failing to supply or for supplying false information, intentionally or negligently. These penalties may take the form of a small fine (Article 15(1)(b)) or daily penalties (Article 16). Moreover, it is largely up to the Commission to decide what it thinks is 'necessary'. Thus, the request may be of either a general or specific nature. Those called upon to supply information should consider obtaining legal advice before complying. Information supplied is covered by a duty of confidentiality on the part of Commission officials (Article 214 TEU).

Secondly, the Commission has power to undertake all necessary investigations into undertakings and associations of undertakings. To this end it may:

- examine and take copies of an undertaking's books and business records;
- enter any premises (land or means of transport) for the purpose of doing so; and
- ask for oral explanations on the spot (Article 14, Regulation 17).

These so-called 'dawn raids' by which Commission officials literally turn up at an undertaking's offices unannounced and with authority to enter and investigate are relatively rare, but the Commission usually has no hesitation in carrying them out.

As an institution created by international convention, the Commission must act within its powers when executing an investigation. The decision sanctioning the raid must have been taken and properly adopted by the Commission, and its officers must produce their authorisation in writing, specifying the subject matter and purpose of the investigation. If time permits the Commission is additionally required to notify and consult with appropriate national authorities.

An Article 14 decision does not have the force of compulsion that a police warrant or Anton Piller order has. However (unlike under Article 11) undertakings are obliged to submit to such investigations. Their effectiveness is, in fact, reinforced in three ways:

(1) Member states have a general duty to give effect to all manner and measure of Union law, including these decisions which will be without prejudice to the scope for judicial review by the Union Court. Thus, the Commission decision may be accompanied by an order from the Commercial Court or an official from the national competition authority may be present to give greater weight to its authority.

(2) The Commission will impose fines up to ECU 5000 per day for any obstruction during the investigation; a point blank refusal will invariably suffer such a penalty. In this regard, the officers and other key staff within an undertaking should be wary of the on-the-spot interrogation. The Court has held that the right against self-incrimination is not available in Article 14 investigations. (*Orkem* v. *Commission* (374/87) [1989] ECR 3343) However, the Court will honour the principle of legal professional privilege in respect of communications between the undertaking and independently practising lawyers (i.e. excluding in-house Counsel).

(3) The Commission may also carry out enquiries in the market or EC construction sector or delegate that task to national authorities.

The hearing

Following its investigation but before it reaches its decision the Commission is required to give the undertakings or associations of undertakings concerned the opportunity of being heard on the matters to which the Commission takes objection (Article 19). This is specifically required in any decision which clears, prohibits or exempts an agreement or practice, or imposes fines. Article 19 also permits the Commission to offer this same opportunity to anyone with a sufficient interest.

The procedures leading up to and for holding this hearing are as follows:

● The Commission issues a statement of objections containing the case against those who whom it is addressed.
● The undertakings concerned will be given two to three months to make submissions and provide arguments in their defence – a period which may be extended.
● During this time the Commission will probably give limited access to its file. Nowadays it usually appends a list of documents it has in its possession which may be inspected – including those documents which are manifestly exculpatory. Confidential documents are listed but not available for inspection.

- Thereafter the 'hearing' will be held at the Commission's offices in Brussels. Again this is inquisitorial, with the Commission acting more like a continental-style investigating magistrate than a party to proceedings before a impartial tribunal.

This inquisitorial nature is a characteristic that has attracted considerable criticism, which is why the Commission now appoints a Hearing Officer to conduct the hearing. Whilst employed in the competition directorate of the Commission, the Hearing Officer nevertheless injects an element of neutrality into the proceedings. This is further evidenced by the presence of third parties, including perhaps the original complainant, having a right to be heard and hearing such evidence which is not confidential in nature.

Deferring only to allow an Advisory Committee of national representatives to be consulted, the Commission will then reach a decision as to whether the practice complained of or simply being investigated is in breach of Article 85(1), and whether it should be fined or exempted under Article 85(3). The power to fine is not insignificant. Article 15(2) provides for fines of up to ECU 1 million or 10% of the turnover for the previous year.

Remedies before the European courts

As indicated in Chapter 3, there is no direct access for individual entities before the Court of Justice and the Court of First Instance other than provided by the Treaty, but this permits actions for annulment, for failure to act and for damages for negligence.

Thus in the context of competition matters, anyone aggrieved with a decision of the Commission following Regulation 17 proceedings would 'appeal' to the Court of Justice by applying for an annulment of the Commission's decision on one of the grounds provided for in the provision of the Treaty. This would be admissible not just against 'final' decisions but against a decision in the course of infringement proceedings which produces legal effects, affecting the interests of the applicant by bringing about a distinct change in his legal position; for example a fine or penalty, but not a decision to issue a statement of objections. (*IBM* v. *Commission* [1981] ECR 2639)

Likewise a failure to adopt a position with regard to a complaint is reviewable before the Court of First Instance under Article 175.

In any situation where an act (i.e. a decision, a breach of confidentiality or an irregularity of procedure) or omission causes economic loss, then an action can be brought under Article 215(2).

Remedies before national competition authorities

As agents of the state, national competition authorities are bound by the statutory rules which create them and thus are indirectly bound by the EU competition rules. However, there is a clear division of competence between the Commission and the national authorities given that the latter are primarily responsible for the application and enforcement of national rules whilst the former has exclusive competence for the application of Articles 85 and 86. Nevertheless, moves are afoot to increase the role of national competition authorities in co-operation with the Commission.

Remedies before national courts

Articles 85 and 86 are directly applicable without the need for further implementation and contain rights which are clear, concise and unconditional making them both horizontally and vertically directly effective. They thus enable undertakings to enforce these rights before national courts, not just against national authorities and Union institutions, but also against other undertakings (*BRT* v. *SABAM* (127/73) [1974] ECR 51).

National courts are empowered (and in fact required by virtue of Article 5 TEU) to enforce Articles 85(1) and 86. They can therefore determine whether an agreement or the conduct of certain parties infringes the basic prohibition against anti-competitive practices. They cannot, however, exempt agreements according to the criteria in Article 85(3), although they do have the facility to determine whether a specific agreement meets the criteria for automatic exemption under one of the Commission's regulations. Insofar as a court requires guidance on the application of Article 85 or 86, an economic analysis of a specific market, or advice on the extent to which an agreement affects trade between member states, then it may seek this directly from the Commission. This is in addition to the facility in Article 177 to seek a preliminary ruling from the Court of Justice on a point of law. Where the court action is running parallel to a Commission investigation then the court has a discretion as to whether or not to stay proceedings.

Actions of the state

Much of the Treaty of European Union is concerned about achieving a single market which it does by curtailing the power of the state to restrict or hinder cross-border trade. In the context of the competition rules, the focus so far has been on the conduct and activities of private undertakings. Although even in this regard the state is not forgotten. By virtue of Article 90 TEU, Articles 85 and 86 extend to the activities of public undertakings. Certain undertakings are excluded, in particular those which are entrusted with the operation of services of a general economic interest or have the character of a revenue-producing monopoly, insofar as the competition rules would obstruct the performance of those tasks. Otherwise any undertaking to which a member state grants special or exclusive rights must respect the competition rules. Therefore, public undertakings are precluded from entering into agreements which distort competition or, and this is more likely to be the case, abuse the dominant position they are in. If they do so then any interested party has a directly effective right in Article 90 which it must exercise in conjunction with another directly effective right (such as Article 85) to seek damages in a national court. With regard to the abuses of a dominant position it can be noted that in some cases the mere grant of a special or exclusive right can be a breach of Article 86 if, in consequence of the same, the public undertaking would be induced to exploit its position (*Merci Convensionali Porto di Genova SpA* v. *Siderugica Gabrielli SpA* (C-179/90)).

That aside, the instrument through which the state may most easily and widely distort competition in the common market is the application of aid. By virtue of Article 92(1) all aid granted by a member state or though state resources in any form whatsoever which distorts or threatens to distort competition is incompatible with the common market but to breach Article 92 it would have to favour certain undertakings or the production of certain goods and affect trade between member states. It can be difficult to identify aid as distinct from general measures of economic policy, but in order to remain outside Article 92 such measures should be non-sectoral or even non-regional.

Aid can take innumerable forms: for example, a golden share in even a private undertaking will constitute aid unless the undertaking could have obtained the amounts in question on the capital market (*Tubemeuse Belgium* v. *Commission* C-124/87) [1990] ECR 2321). Alternatively, aid granted through a regional authority or benefits offered to certain undertakings by a public undertaking might also be incompatible. In this regard, it is not necessary for the aid to come direct from the state so long as it comes though state resources (*Kwerkerij Gebroeders Van der Kooy BV* v. *Commission* (Cases 67, 68 & 70/85) [1988] ECR 219).

At the same time, it is acknowledged that the state must be able to provide such funds which are necessary to achieve certain objectives. In this regard, Article 92 also provides instances when aid will be deemed or may be deemed compatible with the common market (see below). The arbiter in the application of these exceptions is the Commission. The Commission is required to keep all systems of aid under review and decide on the compatibility of aid that states wish to apply. Accordingly, unless the aid has a social character and is granted to individual consumers or is to make good damage caused by natural disasters, the state must notify its intention to apply aid to the Commission. Furthermore it is prohibited from putting its proposed measures into effect until the Commission has reached a favourable decision. This requirement gives rise to a legitimate expectation on the part of private undertakings that any such aid applied in contravention of the notification procedure may be challenged and damages claimed. Moreover, the Commission will often require the state in question to recover unlawful aid unless this is absolutely impossible. In such instances, or whenever the Commission has ordered the state concerned to abolish all later aid and it has failed to do so, then the Commission may refer the matter directly to the Court of Justice.

There are five instances in which aid will be deemed compatible with the common market:

(1) aid to promote the economic development of areas where the standard of living is abnormally low or where there is serious under-employment;

(2) aid to promote the execution of an important project of European interest or to remedy a serious disturbance in the economy of a member state;

(3) aid to facilitate the development of certain economic sectors where such aid does not adversely affect trading conditions to an extent contrary to the common interest;

(4) aid to promote culture and heritage conservation where such aid does not affect trading conditions and competition in the Community to an extent that is contrary to the common interest; and

(5) other such categories specifically approved of by the Council.

State aid should be seen less as a source of funding (although clearly for the large infrastructure projects the state is still often the only or largest backer and in this regard option 2 above permits aid to projects forming part of a transnational European programme supported jointly by a number of governments) and more as potential threat to the market where the state directly or indirectly confers advantages on certain undertakings. Of the above instances of acceptable aid, option 3 could justify this purpose. This option lays down in positive terms the means to underwrite the needs of a particular industrial sector (defined in national and not just EU terms) and in negative terms the requirement that this aid does not excessively and adversely affect trade. The Commission enjoys the power of appraisal to judge both, and in particular the common interest.

Part of the process of reaching a decision involves hearing the submissions of third parties. All aid notified to the Commission will be published in the *Official Journal*. Undertakings whose interests may be affected by the grant of aid, particularly undertakings and trade associations, may submit observations which the Commission is required to consider as part of its detailed investigation into exercising one of the options above. The Commission decision is reviewable by the Court under Article 173 TEU, whichever way it goes, but its discretion will rarely be overturned by the Court unless its decisions are contradictory or it had provided insufficient justification for its findings. Alternatively the member state concerned may apply to the Council to decide that aid shall be considered as compatible with the common market. The effect of such an application suspends any on-going investigation by the Commission for three months.

Chapter 5
The Construction Industry and the Competition Rules

Chapter Four gave an overview of the EU competition and state aid rules which are of general application. This chapter will focus on how these rules apply in the context of the construction sector. This it does primarily by examining the situation in the aftermath of a single case: *Vereniging van Samenwerkende Prijsregelende Organisaties in de Bouwnijverheid and others* v. *EC Commission* (T-29/92) ('SPO'). The judgment of the Court of First Instance on 21 February 1995 was something of a landmark ruling in construction terms because in a single case it embraced many of the activities and idiosyncrasies of the sector

The Dutch construction industry competition case

In this case the Court dismissed an application from the main plaintiff and 28 other applicants to annul a Commission Decision which had found a breach of Article 85(1) TEU and had imposed fines totalling ECU 22 498 000.

The background

In 1952, the Netherlands building market reorganised itself and contractors began to group themselves into associations according to sector or region. Later, these numerous associations set up an umbrella association, called the Vereniging van Samenwerkende Prijsregelende Organisaties in de Bouwnijverheid ('the SPO'). According to Article 3 of the SPO's statutes, its object was 'to promote and administer orderly competition, to prevent improper conduct in price tendering and to promote the formation of economically justified prices'. To this end, the SPO's rules provided for the institutionalised regulation of prices and competition. Furthermore, it was empowered to impose penalties on contractors affiliated to its member organisations in the event of a breach of these obligations. At its height, there were 28 member associations of the SPO embracing over 4000 building undertakings established in the Netherlands.

The SPO drew up three sets of rules to which the Commission was later to pay particular attention. In 1980 it adopted a Code of Honour which imposed a uniform system of penalties for infringement of standard rules of association. Then in 1987 the SPO brought two sets of Uniform Price-Regulating Rules ('UPR rules') into force. These laid down a procedural framework for competition between contractors tendering for building works, whether public or private.

The UPR rules provided for several schemes but with two central features. Firstly, in the procurement process for any contract it enabled the members of a sectoral or regional association to designate an 'entitled undertaking' which would be regarded as the preferred bidder in the subsequent tender. Secondly, all members of that association intending to submit a tender for the contract would disclose and compare tender bids so that it could be agreed how to make the preferred bidder's offer the most competitive. This was achieved by increasing all tender prices (including that of the preferred bidder) by an agreed sum to a level which would enable the successful tenderer to reimburse, at the expense of the client, the combined tender calculation costs of those bidding and make a contribution to the operating costs of the trade organisation. The procedure followed differed slightly according to whether an invitation to tender was open or restricted. In principle, however, the contractor which disclosed the lowest bid became the entitled undertaking. He was then required to increase his bid by the agreed sum but could submit his tender to the client in the safe knowledge that he would not face any competing bids from other SPO members and that the SPO would protect him from competing bids from non-members. These other bidders would of course become the preferred bidder another time but in the meantime were assured the cost of putting together the tender. To complicate matters the UPR Rules were in effect condoned by the Netherlands government. It issued a Royal Decree banning certain practices in the award of procurement contracts but it provided for a number of exceptions from which the UPR Rules were able to benefit.

The Decision

The Commission had begun investigating the Dutch building industry in 1985 with requests for information. However, in July 1989, a complaint came from a city authority about certain parts of the SPO's rules and regulations. The Commission therefore decided to initiate a procedure of investigation under Regulation 17 implementing Articles 85 and 86 of the Treaty against the SPO. Shortly afterwards, and it would seem for tactical reasons, the SPO notified its constitution and the UPR rules to the Commission with a view to obtaining an exemption from the prohibition under Article 85(1).

In its subsequent Decision 92/204/EEC of 5 February 1992 the Commission found that the statutes of the SPO, the two sets of UPR rules and the Code of Honour constituted infringements of Article 85(1) of the Treaty (Article 1 of the decision). The application for an exemption under Article 85(3) of the Treaty was rejected (Article 2). Further, the Commission ordered the SPO and its member organisations to bring to an end immediately the infringements found (Article 3), and imposed fines totalling ECU 22 498 000 on the 28 associations concerned (Article 4).

The appeal

The SPO and the 28 member associations brought an action under the second paragraph of Article 173 of the Treaty seeking a declaration from the Court that the Commission's decision was non-existent or, alternatively, a declaration that it was void. An application for interim suspension of Article 3 was admitted. The applicants' principal claim concerned whether the decision actually existed in light of an administrative error. It is of no real consequence and was in fact rejected.

As regards the more substantive point that the decision was void on its merits, the applicants presented numerous arguments. Those which are most interesting from a construction perspective included an argument of rebuttal that, for the purposes of application of the general prohibition on anti-competitive agreements found in Article 85(1), the Commission:

- incorrectly defined the relevant market;
- misapprehended the scope of the rules and regulations at issue; and
- wrongly considered that they appreciably affected trade between Member States.

It will be noted that these go to the heart of the constituent elements of Article 85(1). In addition, and in light of the rejection of its tactical request for exemption, the SPO claimed that the Commission failed to take account of the particular characteristics of the building industry in the Netherlands and misunderstood the scope of the rules and regulations at issue.

The Court's ruling

The Court dismissed these and all other arguments put forward. It ruled that the Commission was right to conclude that the SPO and its various rules amounted to an infringement of Article 85(1) of the Treaty. It did so on a number of grounds which are of considerable significance to the construction industry and the application of the competition rules.

On a general point it ruled that it was right to treat the whole of the Netherlands building sector as the relevant market and that accordingly the rules were inherently liable to affect trade between member states. This was because they affected conditions of competition in the Netherlands by differentiating them artificially from those obtaining in other member states. In particular, when a group of contractors participated in a given project outside the scope of the rules, as in the case outside the Netherlands, the member undertakings enjoyed artificial advantages over non-member undertakings which carried on the bulk of their business in other member states. In short, if all member states were to follow suit then it would result in fragmentation of the common market.

On more specific points, it found that the system of uniformly increasing price tenders in order to fund the reimbursement of tender calculation expenses as well a contribution to the operating costs of the trade organisation constituted price fixing within the meaning of Article 85(1). In consequence this clearly restricted competition between contractors regarding calculation costs and moreover led to an increase of prices which, it observed, would actually be larger if a contracting authority or party wished to obtain competitive bids from a larger number of contractors. The fact that all this was to be borne by the contracting entities which were effectively unable to negotiate with other contractors participating in the meeting did not let consumers have a fair share of the benefits accruing.

At the same time, the mechanism of affording preference to the 'entitled bidder' constituted a sharing of the market to the detriment of the freedom enjoyed by consumers to choose their suppliers. The entire process, culminating in the designation of an entitled undertaking, took place in the absence of the party having a contract to award. The UPR system undermined the freedom of contractors to join or not to join a trade association since non-membership would deprive them of certain advantages afforded by the system. Essentially, a non-member, if bidding for a particular contract, would be faced with competing not with a number of contractors acting independently from each other, but with a number of contractors having common interests and information.

In conclusion the Court ruled that it is for the awarding party itself to reach a judgment, with the contractors, as to the comparability of their price tenders, so as to ensure that the information exchanged between members did not affect competition, and to ensure that the prices tendered by the various contractors were not altered in order to increase the competitive advantage of some or reduce the competitive disadvantage of others.

The Court therefore dismissed the application in its entirety and ordered the applicants to pay all costs arising. It should be noted, however, that the applicants have since lodged an appeal against the ruling of the Court of First Instance before the Court of Justice.

Implications for the construction industry

Many elements of the SPO case are relevant beyond the construction industry. For example, the ruling deals with questions of procedure concerning in particuliar the application of Regulation 17, the meaning of Article 190 TEU (on reasons for decisions), the definition of the rights of the defence and other matters which are possibly of more interest to European competition lawyers. On the other hand, the SPO case is particularly important to the construction industry in a number of respects. The ruling offers lessons to be learnt on the emerging European construction industry, the nature of co-operation between contractors, the role of the state, the procurement process, and the environment of self-regulation.

The construction 'product'

For the purposes of Articles 85(1) or 86 it does not matter if the concerted practice or abuse in question relates to a product or service even though the terms of Article 85 are more concerned with products than with services (see Article 85(1)(a) and the conditions of exemption under Article 85(3) which require that the agreement contribute to improving the production or distribution of goods). However in the SPO case the Court is saying that the construction process cannot, at least in competition terms, be regarded as a composite of services. Instead, the 'completed project' – that is to say the building or civil engineering structure – is a product itself.

This conclusion might be regarded as being at odds with the general perception of the building trade. The contractor, sub-contractors, specialist contractors, surveyors, engineers, architects, and project managers all provide a service that contributes to the building of the project being paid for by the client. The tangible element is the materials which are incorporated to bring about completion of the project. However these building materials do not form the subject matter of the transaction between the client and the builder or architect. They merely form one of the specifications which the project must meet. It is not only a question of perception: if one considers the Construction Products Directive (89/106/EEC) then one finds that the 'construction products' in question refer to materials that are to be incorporated into a construction or civil engineering project. Whilst the building must comply with the essential requirements of the CPD, this is only a reference point for individual products which must themselves comply with the relevant standards sanctioned by the mechanics of the CPD.

On the other hand, in considering competition between contractors, the materials are not really at issue so long as they meet the required specifications. What is of most significance is their contribution to the project costs which are the defining characteristic for any tender. What the Court expects is genuine competition in the procurement process.

Cross-border mobility

Probably the most difficult aspect the Court had to deal with was to apply rules designed to facilitate a more competitive environment across Europe to an industry which is not prone to cross-border movement.

The Secteur Report observes that because of the diversity of technology, customers, projects and market sectors the construction sector is very fragmented. If one were to add to this list, then 'tradition' might be the next most important factor. Whilst new technology will invariably find a sympathetic reception in any state if it makes the construction process more efficient, this will often have to be at the expense of 'tradition.', not in the inefficient sense of harking back to days gone by, but in the cultural sense which recognises that different national markets are made up of different components, different professions, different processes.

According to statistics compiled by the Fédèration Industrie Européene de la Construction 90% of all building contractors have fewer than 20 employees. Thus the industry is essentially made up of small enterprises. Considering the relative immobility of equipment, the large workforces, and the fixed and localised nature of the work, not only is it less than likely that many contractors will seek work in other member states, it is equally unlikely that any one contractor could command sufficient market share to exert an influence beyond a certain region which could be of the slightest legal interest to the Commission in the enforcement of the competition rules – taking in consideration the *de minimis* exemption. That said, a large number of small enterprises can, together, affect the market as a whole. This is of course the Commission's point, which was accepted by the Court. The SPO embraced some 4000 enterprises, a significant majority of the Dutch construction industry. Under the aegis of the UPR regime no one enterprise could act independently of the market which is, *de facto*, a breach of the competition rules.

Both Articles 85 and 86 refer to the notion of the common market as a geographical point of reference. Any agreement or concerted practice which has an adverse impact on at least a substantial part of the common market – regardless of where the protagonists are based – will in principle amount to an infringement. The Court takes a different approach to defining the relevant market according to whether Article 85 or Article 86 of the Treaty is to be applied. For the purposes of Article 86, it is first necessary to define accurately the relevant market before assessing the existence of an abuse (*SIV and Others* v. *Commission* (T-68/89) [1992] ECR II-1403. It is necessary to establish the existence of a dominant position in a given market, which presupposes that such a market has already been defined. On the other hand, for the purposes of applying Article 85, the reason for defining the relevant market is to determine whether the agreement, the decision by an association of undertakings or the concerted practice is liable to affect trade between member states.

Clearly, there is no suggestion that the Dutch building sector is not within the EU. However the question arose as to whether it was to be treated as a market in itself. The Court held that it was right for the Commission to treat the Netherlands as a geographical market in itself and noted, in fact, that in doing so the Commission was simply adopting the approach followed by the applicants in their notification of the UPR rules. The judgment, referring to a statement from the SPO's notification, offers a useful observation on this point:

> 'According to the SPO, the relevant product market from the macro-economic point of view is the construction market. Only that product market appears relevant from the point of view of competition law. It is an extensive market. Whilst it may be possible, in principle, to identify within that market innumerable market segments reflecting the nature and size of the constructions to be erected, it is nevertheless doubtful that such segments could be described as separate product markets for the purpose of European competition law. Both supply and demand are so diversified in that market that it would appear, in principle, impossible to isolate submarkets in which only certain categories of contract awarders and contractors operate. A necessarily artificial division of the construction

market into submarkets would, moreover, be unhelpful in assessing the competition rules in question, since, first, the Code of Honour applies to all building work and, secondly, the UPR rules cover all works in the categories mentioned.'

This was raised in rejection of the argument by the SPO that the Commission had wrongly defined the relevant market, and so there is perhaps little surprise that the contentions of the SPO in this regard were not upheld. Given that the Court would have examined the issue objectively in order to apply Articles 85 and 86 in a real economic context, one can draw from the judgment the point of principle that the actions or operators within national building markets can affect trade between member states.

Notwithstanding the SPO's original submission, the ruling might be regarded as slightly artificial in conveniently overlooking the essential characteristics of the construction industry. It is a point which will be examined from a different perspective later on, but it has already been observed that the construction industry is a relatively immobile economic activity. Given that routine mobility across the broad spectrum of contractors of all sizes is low, one can ask, with some logic, how the effect on trade between member states could be 'appreciable'. However, the Court agreed with a submission by the Commission that it is not possible to invoke the limited extent of trade between the member states in seeking to reject the notion of trade between member states being subject to an appreciable effect. The Court observed that only about 150 undertakings established in other member states (mainly Germany and Belgium) complied with the UPR rules but, that although it was limited, there was indeed real trade between member states. It ruled that, for restrictive arrangements to be prohibited by Article 85(1) of the Treaty, it is not necessary for them to affect trade appreciably between member states, but merely to be capable of having that effect (*Miller* v. *Commission* (19/77) [1978] ECR 131). Since a potential effect was sufficient, future development of trade should be taken into account in assessing the effect of the restrictive arrangements on trade between member states, whether or not such effect was foreseeable. Finally, as regards the appreciable nature of that effect, the Court stated that the more limited the trade the greater is the likelihood that it will be affected by the restrictive arrangements.

In the context of the SPO, the Court explained that an agreement or the rules of an association extending over the whole territory of one of the member states has the effect of reinforcing compartmentalisation of national markets, thereby holding up the economic interpenetration which the Treaty is intended to bring about (*Vereniging van Cementhandelaren* v. *Commission* (8/72) [1972] ECR 977). In the SPO the rules introduced in 1987 apply throughout the Netherlands and, even though they were sub-divided into separate sets of rules, none could be considered separately from the others since those rules were the subject of standardised penalty procedures imposed by a single association as from 1980.

In conclusion, it is easy to appreciate that a lack of cross-border activity can create difficulties for the Commission in its assessment of whether trade between member states is affected. One might wonder whether one disgruntled foreign contractor denied access to a particular award is sufficient cross-border trade upon which the Commission can then conclude that such trade has been affected to an appreciable extent. To get round this the Commission pointed to, and the Court accepted, the potential trade that might be affected if the concerted practices in question were allowed to persist indefinitely. Again, this might be regarded as too specious to be a rational legal justification. Of course one must accept the possibility that, in the distant future, technical progress might make it easier for contractors to move more freely across the continent. One must accept too that since most participants in the construction process are service providers, this enables them to be highly mobile. Nevertheless, the construction industry is marked by immovable property (the site) and often heavy materials and equipment, most economically provided locally. Thus, one might conclude that the Commission's assessment of the geographical market was not made in its economic context. Having said that, one might accept also that the SPO system could be a impediment to future mobility.

The procurement process

According to the applicants, the UPR rules had a twofold purpose:

- to combat the haggling in which contracting authorities tend to engage; and
- to correct imbalances between supply and demand resulting from a lack of openness on the supply side of the market and the high transaction costs incurred in preparing tenders.

The Court rejected both and in doing so made a number of interesting observations on how the competition rules impact on the public procurement regime.

The effect of the judgment is that any pre-contractual discussions between prospective tenderers amounts to collusion. The Court ruled that collusion between contractors regarding the manner in which they intend responding to an invitation to tender is incompatible with Article 85(1) of the Treaty, even where the invitation sets unreasonable conditions. It is for each contractor to determine independently what he regards as reasonable or unreasonable and to conduct himself accordingly.

On the other hand, whilst the Court expects genuine competition, it has conceded that firstly the procurement regime cannot itself deliver this and that secondly the procurement process should not be regarded as a vehicle for pure competition.

The Court gave judicial recognition to the point that the open procedure of public procurement provides the best opportunity for foreign contractors to penetrate the Netherlands market. The Court noted that the system of reimbursements for calculation costs was intended to encourage contract awarders to weigh the advantages and disadvantages of approaching a larger or smaller number of tenderers. Since contract awarders knew that they would have to bear the burden of tender costs, they would naturally focus their calls for tenders more narrowly and thus invite a smaller number of tenderers. As it was possible to limit the number of tenderers approached by contract awarders under the restricted procedure, it followed that the UPR system encouraged restricted rather than open procedures. Moreover, within the category of those restricted by the procedures, those which were most restricted were foreign firms.

One might conclude that routine recourse to the restricted procedure (for which no justification is required) would ultimately but adversely affect trade between member states. However, the Court did not reach that specific conclusion. Instead it decided to focus on the adverse effect the SPO's rules had on a contracting authority's discretion on choice of procedure, thus to some extent condoning the national rules but not the private agreement, even though each had the same consequence – to shut out or discourage cross-border trade.

However, according to the Court it is inappropriate to rely too heavily on the common purpose between the public procurement directives and the competition rules. It was argued by the SPO that the UPR rules applied in the main only to contracts below the threshold of ECU 5 million laid down by Public Works Directive, and that, accordingly, they could not be anti-competitive insofar as they did not apply. However, the Court ruled that the applicants could not rely on the threshold, agreeing with the Commission that the aims pursued by Article 85 of the Treaty and by the directive differ too much for the threshold laid down by the latter to serve as a point of reference for the level at which Article 85 applies. The legal basis of the directive had no connection with Article 85 of the Treaty and that provision is not mentioned in its preamble.

There is therefore a measure of conflict between the two. However, it would appear that this gives rise to a 'client's prerogative' to adopt an open or a restricted approach to procurement nothwithstanding that this in itself may ultimately be contrary to the spirit of the procurement regime – which is a remarkable observation since the whole purpose of the EU rules is to increase cross-border integration.

For this reason perhaps the Court was still prepared to apply the competition rules strictly with regard to the UPR rules. The Court found contractors exchanged information on the cost components of the contract, the characteristics of the tenders, the prices proposed by each contractor and fixed prices or parts of prices thereto. Thereafter, the entitled undertaking enjoyed protection from the other participants in the concerted practice since the latter would lose the right to negotiate their tender with the client.

In mitigation the applicants argued that the information exchanged did not relate solely to the invitation to tender and there was some evidence of that. Furthermore, there was also discussion about the suitability of technical solutions to a particular project. Technical advancement might be regarded as the life blood of the industry but it is not something which the Court considered as a high priority. The Court concluded that the Commission had sufficiently established that, at the meetings held under the UPR rules, the contractors exchanged information relating in particular to the costs of the product concerned, its specific characteristics and a breakdown of the price tenders, details which an independent operator would ordinarily keep strictly secret as confidential business information (*Hercules Chemicals* v. *Commission* (T-7/89) [1991] ECR II-1711).

Furthermore, the Court rejected the point that, in principle, proposed tender prices of each contractor could not be later altered and, that as a result competition did take place at the point of submission of prices to the chairman of one of the UPR meetings. It become evident that the delivery of blank figures did not end the competitive process because negotiations were yet to take place between the client and the entitled undertaking and between the client and undertakings which did not attend the meeting. The UPR rules did, however, bring to an end the possibility of the client accepting advantageous tenders from association members which had had been forced to withdraw from the tender process. In this regard, and in the context of the procurement process, the contractors deliberately substituted practical co-operation between them for the risks of competition.

The role of the state

In the SPO case the Netherlands government adopted legislation which gave tacit approval to the rules and regulations of the SPO. In doing so it implicated itself in the affair whilst demonstrating that state approval is no defence to undertakings embarking on activities which prove to be contrary to EU laws. This is a caution that all sectors should heed, but it is one which is particularly pertinent to the construction industry, which often looks to the state for special treatment in its activities because of its significant contribution to the gross national product.

Governmental support can come in many ways. Construction activity can act as catalyst for wider economic output. It is the biggest industrial employer in the EU and according to the Secteur report, one person working in the industry is served by two jobs in other sectors. Understandably, governments consider it to be in the interests of the state to foster a strong and vibrant construction industry and are accordingly often content to leave it to its own devices.

A case in point is the re-structuring of construction activity in the UK. The Latham Report into the UK construction industry recommends partnering as a new approach to construction relations, enabling the avoidance of excessive disputes and therefore extra costs, and thus leading to better competitiveness in servicing clients. Whilst this is not done on a formal or compulsory basis, the report actively encourages all undertakings (and clients) in the sector to take on the new approach.

It will be recalled however that the Commission and Court are prepared to reconcile any inconsistencies between one aspect of EU law and another and it is for this reason that they will not allow too great an interlinking of the procurement and competition rules. As a consequence the Court expects undertakings to accept direct responsibility for compliance with Articles 85 and 86. Accordingly, if a public authority authorises, favours or encourages an agreement which infringes Article 85, then the undertakings concerned cannot look to the state for a defence. Only if it is a legal requirement does such a defence arise.

Partnering is a concept which, like the term 'joint venture', often lacks a satisfactory definition. One approximate definition is: a long-term commitment between two or more organisations for the purpose of achieving specific business objectives by maximising the effectiveness of each participant's resources. This, it is submitted, is a statement which is loaded with elements which could distort competition. Partnering can immediately be rendered anti-competitive since it encourages the development of policy, structure and strategy to derive benefits from trading with the same business over and over again. Terms like 'agreement', 'co-operation' and 'commitment' can all be anti-competitive because they imply putting an obligation upon an undertaking which could restrict its ability to act independently on the market. The whole cultural emphasis of partnering is the same since it turns on open lines of communication, the selection of partners, identifying and ranking markets, and finally joint decision making. All these elements have heavy anti-competitive undertones, for each of these acts in themselves can distort the free will of an undertaking; but at the same time each element can also be taken to mean genuine and sincere co-operation.

It is clear that partnering will certainly fall foul of either European or English competition law if it meets the criteria for application. However when an industry is going though a cultural change which involves the positive encouragement of the government, state approval is not, on the basis of the SPO case, a defence. In that particular case, state approval was not argued forcefully as a defence, although it is evident from the judgment that the applicants felt that the state should bear some responsibility for deliberately permitting the SPO to exist by exemption. This defence would seem fully justified because neither the Commission nor the Court – nor even the member states themselves – recognise fully the responsibility of the member states to apply the full rigour of competition law. However, in the absence of such recognition the construction industry must watch its back.

The role of trade associations

Perhaps the most telling aspect of the SPO case for the construction industry is the complete rejection by both Commission and Court of the argument that the trading fraternity knows what is best for the industry and that they discover this for themselves through the use of trade associations. The interdependence of contractors, professionals and other service providers, plus the great variety of specialist sub-contractors, gives rise to a natural tendency for contractors to group together. Moreover, a successful project relies upon effective co-operation. Larger contractors tend to become the main contractor for a project whereas smaller contractors will undertake the numerous sub-contracting works that every project of significant size requires – especially for contracts awarded by public authorities. In these relationships, professional competence is a central factor. But so is cost. Haggling over price therefore is commonplace, and must, undoubtedly, involve pressure. Thus the removal of pressure, but with work guaranteed can motivate the competitiveness of contractors in a positive way. In other words, an open market does not necessarily reduce prices.

However, the treatment of the SPO federation of associations by the Commission and the Court must put into question whether any form of co-operation between contractors in the Union is in accordance with the EC competition rules. This, will be of particular concern to trade associations which are known to clients and consumers as the recognised association for the discipline concerned, such that only contractors belonging to this recognised association can compete effectively.

In the context of the SPO, one can understand the logic of the contractors' arguments. They drew attention to the beneficial effects which the rules had on competition, the consequent benefits for consumers. The object was to keep as many contractors as possible in business, not (as is often the case) to foreclose the market around a few enterprises intent on achieving market domination. Moreover, the associations enabled smaller contractors to have greater influence in the face of larger ones since any one contractor could lay claim to be the entitled bidder for any single contract. Each contractor was, in part, ensured of survival because some work at least would be guaranteed to it and, in any event, there would be no fear of collapse under the weight of expenses incurred in submitting bids since these would be reimbursed through the UPR regime.

The weakness in this argument is that a regulated market is an artificial one. By propping up inefficient enterprises the market is distorted for the purposes of Article 85(1). Furthermore, the Court pointed out that the beneficial effects of the rules described could not be taken into consideration for the purposes of Article 85(1) of the Treaty but were only relevant to the application of the criteria laid down by Article 85(3) of the Treaty.

This said, the Court did not rule out the possibility that the SPO and therefore trade associations generally could act in the interests of the consumer. In this regard the Court examined the UPR rules closely to see whether they contributed to the improvement of distribution of products or to promotion of technical or economic progress, giving a fair share of the benefits to the consumer.

Before the Court, the applicants made much of the macro-economic benefits of the schemes. They adduced evidence that demonstrated that the Netherlands building industry charged very low prices and had very narrow profit margins as a consequence of the rules, not least because the rules made it possible to prevent the formation in the Netherlands of 'underground cartels' of the kind found in other member states of the Union.

Against this, the approach of the Commission was to emphasise the micro-economic sphere and the effect of the rules on individual contracting authorities, as detailed above. Interestingly, it argued that the micro-economic approach was appropriate since it considered that underground cartels between contractors were not inevitable in the building industry.

In these situations, the Court unfortunately relies less on the need to reach a definitive and substantive solution and much more on ensuring that the complex economic assessments comply with the procedural rules, that proper reasons are given, that the facts have been accurately stated and that there has not been any manifest error of appraisal or misuse of powers (*BAT and Reynolds* v. *Commission* (142 and 156/84) [1987] ECR 4487). The Court found in essence that the applicants had not managed to prove a causal link between the SPO rules and the healthy performance of the Netherlands building industry; that performance might be attributable to numerous other factors. The Commission had weighed up the assertions of the applicants and, although it rejected them in the final analysis, had committed no manifest error of assessment.

The Court went so far as to confirm the correctness of the Commission's approach in that it was clear to the Court that, notwithstanding that the applicants had stated repeatedly that the machinery for protecting the entitled undertaking was intended to prevent prices from reaching an unjustified level, this simply was not corroborated by the evidence; as a result any benefit from reducing the incidence of 'playing-off' actually only accrued to the contractors. The party having a building contract to award could negotiate only with the entitled undertaking, whereas if the rules had not been in existence it could have negotiated both with the entitled undertaking and with the other contractors participating in the meeting.

In response the applicants argued that it would necessarily lead to ruinous competition, which would ultimately have adverse repercussions on contract awarders. The Court rejected this almost out of hand by adroitly observing that it is impossible to distinguish between normal competition and ruinous competition since 'potentially, any competition is ruinous for the least efficient undertakings'. For this reason the Court concluded that by taking action to counteract what they regard as ruinous competition the applicants had necessarily restricted competition and therefore deprived consumers of its benefits.

The Court dealt similarly with the argument that, by ensuring transaction costs were borne by the contract awarder in their entirety, the system facilitated a reduction in the transaction costs which would otherwise have to be borne by the contractors, particularly where they were not awarded a contract. The Court noted that it was true that a transfer of costs was not entirely without economic justification. However, it added that this pre-supposed that it would be the contract awarder wishing to offer this, since the effect of doing so or having to do so was to limit the number of contractors it wished to consult. Even if that limitation led to a decrease in the contract awarder's transaction costs, through examining a smaller number of tenders, the benefit was limited in comparison with the disadvantages to the contract awarder and the benefits obtained from the system by contractors.

Moreover, only those organisations which regularly award a large number of contracts covered by these rules would find that the benefit of contractors no longer incorporating the costs of unsuccessful tender calculations in their general costs would offset the disadvantage of bearing all the calculation costs. An organisation awarding contracts only rarely would find itself reimbursing calculation costs which would considerably outweigh the benefit, under this system, of the entitled bidder's lower tender.

A result of the system is that contract awarders who feel it necessary to approach a large number of contractors must necessarily reimburse calculation costs which considerably exceed the costs which they would have to bear if the system did not exist. Consequently, the system of reimbursement of calculation costs might reduce the overall transaction costs in the market, but it does not allow that reduction to be shared fairly between contractors and contract awarders.

The Court also decided that the entire process of selecting the entitled undertaking in the absence of the awarding party was not indispensable for the attainment of the SPO's intended objectives. The awarding party itself is best placed to reach a judgment on the comparability of price tenders, so ensuring that the information exchanged at private meetings does not affect competition, and that the prices tendered by the various contractors are not altered in order to increase the competitive advantage of some or reduce the competitive disadvantage of others.

From this it must be concluded unquestionably that the EC competition rules do apply to trade associations, no matter what their form (loose unincorporated entities or incorporated bodies of limited liability), the level at which they trade or the binding nature of their rules. This is evident from Article 85(1) itself. The Commission's 1994 Competition Report, gives a useful statement of principle on the application of the Article 85(1) to trade associations. It is clear from this that the Commission does not need a high or sophisticated level of complicity in order to find evidence of an infringement:

'To be held responsible, an association need not expressly list anti-competitive practices as one of its institutional objects. Nor is it necessary for the association or its representatives to have been entrusted formally by its members to discuss restraints of competition. The Commission considers it to be sufficient that the association or its representatives participate *de facto* in activities which infringe Article 85(1).' (paragraph 150)

The size of the association will be material, however, and it was especially here that the SPO regime fell foul of the competition rules. A regional association or those holding a small share of the market might not fall within Article 85(1). This seems to be the case in light of the *de minimis* notice and the apparent policy of the Commission to target only those trade associations that operate on a national level (for example, *Roofing Felt* ([1986] OJ L232/15), the Belgian roofing felt association; Meldoc ([1986] L348/50), the Dutch dairy co-operative association; COAPME Spanish estate agents; and, of course, the *SPO* case). However, it must be conceded that a regional association could fall under the cut of Article 85(1) if it met the relevant criteria, one of them being that the region concerned is a substantial part of the market. In the case of the SPO it was an association of associations of contractors which embraced 4,000 enterprises.

This said, it remains to be considered whether the UPR rules could legitimately be used in free market conditions. Had the SPO never been formed or had some of the member associations acted independently then perhaps the Commission would have been forced to take a different view. Could it, for instance, become a standard term of business for the tender expenses of all bidders to be met by the successful bidder and therefore ultimately the procuring authority? On balance, and on the basis of Article 85(1), it is difficult to see how it can.

Chapter 6
Public Procurement

Introduction

As far as the building contractor is concerned, it is in the award of public contracts that European legislation has had the most impact on the practice and procedures of the domestic industry. Before the UK's accession to the European Union, there was no transparent system for the tendering and award of contracts. At that time entry into the public procurement market was undoubtedly assisted by personal contacts and what the Secteur report describes as 'murky practices', which do not require elaboration here. More importantly there was little legal opportunity to open up those procedures, other than the limited scope for judicial review of acts of public authorities. By the time the UK joined, however, the Union institutions had already adopted a major tenet of public procurement law, the Public Works Directive ('the Works Directive').

The Works Directive was joined by common rules on the provision of supplies ('the Supplies Directive') and later a single system for the provision of services ('the Services Directive'). Most ambitious of all, a combined directive was issued in 1992 concerning works, services and supply contracts offered by entities operating in the utilities sector ('the Utilities Directive'). Until then these had been excluded from the scope of preceding general directives.

The addition of the Services and Utilities Directives to the range of legislative instruments, coupled with the increasing number of amendments to the original sector directives prompted by jurisprudential, legal, political and economic developments, gave rise to the necessity to codify and re-structure all the directives. This examination is based upon the most up-to-date codification. However, the framework regulating how contracts are to be awarded by any entity acting under or in pursuance of specific public power is very much a global one. Current legislation in the traditional sectors was amended in July 1997 to take account of the Government Purchasing Agreement (see Chapter 8) signed under the auspices of the General Agreement on Tariffs and Trade (GATT). Other than re-specifying thresholds in terms of Special Drawing Rights (the currency used by the GATT) and extending rights to non-EU companies, these amendments do not alter the intrinsic rights and procedures which are currently applicable to the EU supplier, service provider or contractor.

General schemes and principles of procurement

The objects of the procurement laws are open competition and non-discrimination. It is the certainty and transparency of the procedural framework by which these objectives are achieved, and the right to insist on both, which underpins the European public procurement regime. These characteristics manifest themselves in the advertising and tendering procedures, the selection of tenders for consideration and the award criteria. Despite the plurality of directives, these are components which are common to all.

Contracting authorities

The term 'contracting authority' comprises the state (that is to say the government), any regional or local authorities, and all bodies governed by public law, including associations formed by one or several of such authorities or bodies.

A 'body governed by public law' is further defined as one established for the specific purpose of meeting needs in the general interest, not having an industrial or commercial character. It must additionally have legal personality and be financed for the most part by state, regional or local authorities or other public bodies, or be subject to their management supervision. An association incorporated by a public body as a private entity would still meet these requirements, and in this regard comparison could be drawn with the concept of an 'agent of the state' referred to in Chapter 2.

Exceptions and exclusions

Each directive more or less clearly determines its field of application by its title, and then definitively in Article 1. At the same time each contains broadly the same exceptions and exclusions in relation to the contracts which, in principle, fall within its sphere of activity.

First and foremost the directives mutually exclude contracts which fall under one of the other directives. Contracts which are declared secret, or the execution of which must be accompanied by special security measures, can also be excluded. However, the directives do apply to contracts awarded by contracting authorities in the field of defence, except when the state seeks to invoke a general national security exception in the Treaty (Article 223(1)(b) TEU). As regards the EU in the world procurement market, the directives will not apply if the contract is awarded in pursuance of an international agreement and different procedural rules apply instead.

Tender procedures

A contract must be awarded by one of three procedures:

- the open,
- the restricted, and
- the negotiated.

Unless one of the grounds for employing the negotiated procedures can be justified objectively, then the contracting authority has a choice between the other two.

The negotiated procedure enables contracting authorities to consult contractors of their own choice and negotiate the terms of the contract with one or more of them. However, this procedure may only be used in certain circumstances:

- in the event of irregular tenders, in response to open or restricted procedures;
- in the case of contracts for pure, non-commercial research, experiment or development;
- in exceptional cases when the nature of the works or the risks attaching thereto do not permit prior overall pricing;
- in the absence of appropriate tenders in response to an open or restricted procedure;
- in cases of extreme urgency;
- for unforeseen additional works amounting to 50% of the initial project which are either inseparable from the initial project or, if separable, are strictly necessary to its later stages;
- when, for technical or artistic reasons or for reasons connected with the protection of exclusive rights, the works may only be carried out by a particular contractor;
- for new works consisting of the repetition of similar works entrusted to the same contractor as before, so long as the works conform to a basic project for which a first contract was awarded and in which mention was made of the possibility of subsequent contracts.

There does not need to be any justification to use either the open and restricted procedures and one or the other should be used unless the negotiated procedure is justifiable.

Under *the open procedure* a contract notice is issued inviting all interested contractors, suppliers and service providers to submit a tender for consideration, so long as they meet the minimum economic and technical standards required.

Under *the restricted procedure*, contractors, etc. are invited to express an interest in submitting a tender for a particular contract or series of contracts, but only those selected for inclusion on a list by the contracting authority will later be invited to submit a tender for a specific contract. A contracting authority might prefer the restricted procedure in order to save time when assessing the economic and technical criteria of tenderers, especially if it has a series of similar contracts to award, since this can be dealt with when drawing up the list of 'approved' tenderers. This initial process, however, ought to be conducted under the open procedure. In order to keep in with the spirit and meaning of the procurement regime and the objectives of the Union the authority would routinely have to monitor the composition of the list and from time to time make fresh invitations to contractors to be included on it. Provision is made to accelerate the procedure in cases where urgency renders impracticable the time limits laid down for restricted as well as negotiated procedures.

Under the restricted (and negotiated) procedures the contracting authority is required to select candidates on the basis of information which the prospective tenderers give on their financial and economic standing, technical expertise and previous experience. The authority is not precluded, in **appropriate** circumstances, from issuing pre-qualification questionnaires in order to pinpoint the exact requirements which are necessary to complete the contract.

In the case of the restricted procedure the authority may prescribe the maximum and minimum number of prospective tenderers it will list. Whilst the authority need not disclose what that range will be until the issue of the contract notice, it must be at least five and no more than 20. In any event the number of invited tenders must be sufficient to ensure genuine competition. In the case of negotiated procedures the number of candidates admitted to negotiate may not be less than three, provided that there is a sufficient number of candidates.

Advertising

Aside from certain contracts awarded under the negotiated procedure, all proposed contracts must first be fully 'advertised' by way of notice in the *Official Journal of the European Communities*. The Office for Official Publications of the EU publishes the *Supplement* (or 'S' Series) to the *Official Journal* specifically for these notices. It is published on just about a daily basis, on paper and in electronic form, in each of the Union languages and contains – or at least should contain – every proposed contract with a value exceeding the respective threshold criteria. It will be observed therefore that the requirement to advertise constitutes an essential procedural step, and failure to comply would render an award void.

These notices do not contain specifications but provide information about where, how, to whom and when enquiries or tenders (as the case may be) should be directed, including details on the availability of documentation.

The directives require notices to be provided at three points in the procurement procedure and model forms are given in each directive. The essential features for all procedures consist of:

- full contact details of the awarding authority;
- the nature and extent of the contract;
- the place of performance and manner of execution;
- time limits for execution;

- dates, addresses and languages for tenders;
- the person responsible for opening tenders;
- main financial and payment terms;
- the legal form of the contractor;
- any minimum economic and technical standards to be met; and finally
- the criteria for the award.

Notices in respect of the three types of procedure differ on two points, first the statement referring to the procedure chosen, and second, in respect of negotiated and restricted procedures, the reasons for accelerating the process.

A *prior indicative notice* should be published as soon as the decision is made giving approval to the intention to award a contract, regardless of the procedure or nature of the contract. This is simply a device to forewarn the industry of impending invitation to tender. It should therefore only contain the essential characteristics of the contract, important dates in the procedure and contract, and the estimated value.

Thereafter, a *contract notice* must be published. Its form should accord with the model requirements for the procedure being followed, namely, open, restricted or negotiated. Considerably more information must be supplied this time – sufficient for any contractor in the EU to make an informed decision on whether to make further enquiries.

Finally, following the award of the contract to the successful bidder, a *contracts award notice* must be published, giving information on how and on what basis the contract was awarded. This is an essential failsafe requirement to enable anyone who had a interest in the concluded contract to verify the number of offers received, the criteria for the award, the name of the successful contractor, the price offered, and the nature and extent of the services/supplies to be provided.

All notices should be sent to the Office of Official Publications as soon as possible after they are due to be issued and by the most appropriate channels. In the case of the accelerated procedure the notice should be sent by telex, telegram or telefax. Communicating by e–mail is not yet acceptable.

Time limits

Assuming that the contracting authority lawfully makes a decision to award a contract by way of public tender, it is incumbent on that authority to commence the procedure with all speed by means of and then to keep strictly to the time limits for each stage of the process. The authority is required to send its indicative notice as soon as possible after the planning, executive or administrative decision is taken. Other than the award notice (for obvious reasons) there is no compulsion to issue a notice or even commence the procedure. The obligation on the authority is to only award contracts coming within the directives by means of the rules and procedures provided for therein.

In the open procedure, the time limit for the receipt of tenders fixed by the authority must not be less that 52 days from the date of dispatch of the notice inviting such tenders. This may be reduced to 36 days if the authority has published a prior indicative notice (or in the case of the Services Directive has included the contract in its annual notice). Requests made in good time for the contract and supporting documents should be responded to within six days. Requests for additional information relating to the contract and supporting documents should be responded to no later than six days before the final date for receipt of tenders. Appropriate extensions of time must be given if the contract documents are too bulky to be supplied within the time limits or if tenders can only be made after a visit to the place where the contract is to be performed.

In restricted and negotiated procedures the time for receipt of requests to participate fixed by the authority must be not less than 37 days from date of dispatch of the notice. Candidates invited to submit tenders should be written to simultaneously, enclosing the contract and supporting documents. In the restricted procedure, the time limit for receipt of tenders must not be less than 40 days from the written invitation. This may be reduced to 26 days if the prior indicative (or, as appropriate, annual) notice had been issued. Additional information, if requested in good time, should be sent not later than six days prior to the date fixed for tenders. Likewise all time limits should be extended if tenderers are expected to visit the place of performance.

In cases of urgency, which render impracticable the time limits laid down for restricted and negotiated procedures, then the respective time limits fixed for receipt of requests and receipt of tenders should not be less that 15 days from notice, and 10 days from invitation to tender, with additional information supplied not later than four days before tender. Notices, requests and invitations should all be sent by the most rapid means of communication possible. This will normally be by fax or courier but could mean e-mail.

Finally, the award notice should be sent not later that 48 days after the award of the contract and the contracting authority should respond within 15 days to a request for reasons why an application or tender was refused.

Technical specifications

Given that goods, materials or services will invariably be defined by means of a specification, then the system will be open to abuse unless there is a common standard by which goods, materials and services originating in all member states may be judged. This is the practical result of the principle of non-discrimination which, if it were overlooked or little enforced, would create many anomalies in the massive and vital market of public procurement. The point is elaborated in Chapters 10 and 11 on the free movement of goods and services; reference should be made there for the full impact of the principles.

Suffice it to say here that anything lawfully manufactured and used in one member state is allowed to be so used in another member state, subject to intervention by the other on the grounds of health and safety. Likewise, any person qualified or approved to provide services in one state has the right to provide those same services under the same approval in another member state, subject to intervention by the latter on the grounds of the general good.

On a more technical level, specifications should be defined by reference to either national standards implementing European standards(EN), European technical approvals (ETAs) or common technical specifications. In this regard, technical specifications may not refer to particular patented or trade marked products.

European standards comprise those which have been drawn up by the European Committee for Standardisation (CEN), or, as appropriate, the European Committee for Electrotechnical Standardisation (Cenelec). Once standards have been drawn up it is up to national authorities to give effect to them. (For a useful demonstration of the standards these bodies draw up consider those compiled for implementing the Construction Products Directive.)

A European technical approval is defined as a favourable technical assessment of a product's fitness for use, based on the fulfilment of appropriate essential requirements by means of the inherent characteristics of the product in question and the defined conditions of application and use. (Again the use of ETAs can be demonstrated in relation to construction products.)

Finally, a common technical specification is a specification laid down in accordance with a procedure recognised by the member states to ensure uniform application in all member states and which has been published in the *Official Journal*.

The only dispensations from using European standards are when they would lead to problems of incompatibility or excessive cost or would limit innovation. National authorities are required to keep records of situations where only national standards are used.

The contract documents may allude to certain employment conditions. Ordinarily, the authority is not precluded from indicating (or may under national law be required to so indicate) where the tenderer may obtain appropriate information on obligations relating to employment protection and the working conditions which are in force in the member state, region or locality in which the contract is to be performed. Where so indicated, the tenderer will be required to take those obligations into account.

Contractor selection

Next to technical specifications, the most divisive element of the process is selection of candidates according to certain qualitative criteria. The directives provide for exclusion of tenders on the basis of financial and economic standing and on technical knowledge or ability.

Regardless of the merits of the tender, a tenderer may be excluded from participating in the contract if it:

- is bankrupt, wound up under the court's administration or has otherwise entered into an arrangement with creditors, or is subject to any such proceedings;
- has been convicted of a recognised offence concerning professional conduct or is guilty of grave professional misconduct;
- has failed to pay social security contribution or taxes as required; or
- is guilty of serious misrepresentations in supplying information to the contracting authority.

Evidence of financial standing may be furnished by way of a bank reference, audited accounts, or a statement of turnover. If all of these are genuinely unavailable then the tenderer may prove standing in any way acceptable to the authority.

Technical ability is a far more relative concept and in this regard principles already referred to for the free movement of services, and in particular the mutual recognition of diplomas, would apply. Building on these principles, the directives provide that evidence of the tenderer's ability and experience may be furnished by:

- educational and professional qualifications and/or those of the firm's managerial staff;
- a list of completed projects over the previous five years attested by certificates of satisfactory (or presumably practical) completion;
- a statement of the firm's plant and machinery, average manpower over the previous three years; and
- details of consultants and technicians whom the tender can call upon to carry out particular tasks.

It should be borne in mind that any official listing of accredited tenderers must be adapted to take account of tenderers from other member states. This could include a private trade organisation whose accreditation and membership schemes are treated as the industry standard, either formally or informally.

When the Public Works Directive (93/37/EEC) was adopted in its original form in 1989 it was noted that there was no common system between the member states for the registration and qualification of construction firms. States differed between centralised or decentralised lists, official and unofficial systems or no system at all. The Commission was therefore asked by the Council to draw up proposals for European legislation laying down the requirements for the qualification of construction firms covered by that directive.

The system of qualification is to be based on harmonisation of criteria and the promotion of mutual recognition. The system should permit the recognition that construction firms have the necessary attributes to carry out the particular types of works, and provide an assurance to contracting authorities that the enterprise is appropriate to the works being procured. The criteria are likely to include the legal status of enterprises, their financial position, the technical skills they should have at their disposal and their experience in the successful completion of similar work. CEN has been mandated to draw up European standards in relation to the classification of classes of enterprises in line with classes of construction work so that firms may qualify for the types of public contracts likely to be issued in practice. This will necessarily involve not only standardised criteria for qualification but also common application and notification procedures. However quality assurance certification is not to be included as a criterion of the system.

A draft text was due to be presented to the Commission by December 1996 for final adoption by Summer 1998 and implementation six months thereafter. However, CEN is in delay and no draft text is yet available.

Finally, the contracting authority may ask the tenderer to indicate in the tender any share of the contract it is intended to subcontract to third parties. However, this indication is to be without prejudice to the question of the principal contractor's liability. Moreover, tenders may be submitted by groups of contractors. These groups may not be required to assume a specific legal form in order to submit the tender but the group selected may be required to do so when it has been awarded the contract.

Award criteria

The directives provide that contracts shall be awarded on the basis of one of two criteria. This involves a final analysis of *the lowest price* or *the most economically advantageous* tender.

A contract will be concluded with the contractor whose tender most closely meets the criterion employed for that particular award. Before this final stage is reached, the contracting authority will have selected only those contractors who are not excluded through lack of financial, professional or technical integrity. However, this presumes a selection process which offers the contracting authority real choice. Therefore before the award is considered, selection must be made from a sufficient number of candidates to ensure genuine competition.

Under the open and restricted procedures an award may be made no matter how few or many tenders are considered suitable. Thus the authority has a discretion over the minimum number it will accept. Should it consider the number received to be insufficient then it may re-commence the award on the basis of the negotiated procedure. Here, however, the directives insist on a minimum of three, provided there are a sufficient number of candidates.

Moving on to the available award criteria, *lowest price* offers a simple yardstick, but it is essential for the contracting authority to stipulate exactly what work, supply or services the price should cover. Otherwise comparison would be impossible. Clearly, then, the lowest price criterion would be inappropriate when there are too many economic, technical and conditional factors adequately to determine the realistic value of a bid. Nevertheless, unless another award criterion is stipulated, all contracts will be awarded on this basis.

On the other hand, the *most economically advantageous* tender allows for a much broader assessment. The directives give a selection of the type of factors that can be borne in mind. These include

- price,
- time limits,
- costs and profitability, and
- technical merit

adapted, of course, to the nature and purpose of the contract. Clearly these will be intrinsically linked to the specifications the tender must meet. Thus, in order to indicate their relative significance to each other and overall, the contracting authority must set them out in the contract notice in descending order of importance. Even if this is done, the assessment is necessarily open to interpretation, which is why the directives provide that contracting authorities may take account of variants which are submitted by a tenderer but which meet the minimum specifications.

If a given tender appears to be abnormally low in relation to the contract then the contracting authority shall, before it can reject such a tender, request the tenderer to explain in more detail the substance of its bid. The onus is on the contracting authority to establish whether the abnormally low offer is objectively justified on the grounds of the economy or originality of the working methods proposed, because of some technical solution, or because of the exceptionally favourable conditions in which that tenderer operates. The requirement on the part of the contracting authority to probe further is reinforced by the duty to communicate to the Commission the rejection of tenders which it considers to be too low.

Post- and non-award issues

Naturally, the successful tenderer and the contracting authority will advance towards completion. However, the authority has continuing duties to the other candidates. For each contract awarded, the contracting authorities must draw up a written report which shall include matters such as

- the subject and value of the contract,
- the candidates or tenderers admitted and the reasons for their selection,
- the names of the candidates or tenderers rejected and the reasons for their rejection,
- the name of the successful tenderer and the reasons for its tender having been selected and,
- if known, any share of the contract the successful tenderer may intend to subcontract to a third party.

In the case of contract awarded pursuant to the negotiated procedure, the report should refer to the circumstances which justify the use of this procedure. This report, or the main features of it, shall be communicated to the Commission at its request.

Each unsuccessful tenderer is entitled to be advised in writing of the reasons why its application or tender was eliminated or refused. When responding the authority should provide the name of the successful tenderer. Moreover, if a contracting authority has decided not to award a contract in respect of which a prior call for competition was made, or to recommence the procedure, it must inform all candidates or tenderers who so request of the grounds on which it made those decisions. The authority is also required to inform the Office for Official Publications of that decision.

Enforcement

In addition to establishing common rules in the award of contracts, the Union has also felt it necessary to co-ordinate procedures for the review of procurement procedures. It has done this by way of directives (Directive 89/665/EEC [1989] OJ L395/33 as regards supplies and works and Directive 92/13/EEC [1992] OJ L76/1 for utilities) which are separate to the legislative instruments for general and utilities procurement. On the one hand these provisions are the logical corollary of the right of all tenderers to know the identity of the successful bidder and thereafter to seek a review if they consider the procedure to be unfair. On the other hand, such rules should not in principle be necessary since the Court of Justice has held that national procedural rules should be adapted (or if appropriate set aside) to enable the effective enforcement of rights in Union law. That said, these review procedures do give details of the manner in which grievances should be resolved.

In each member state national law should be in place to offer any person with an interest in obtaining a particular contract, and who has suffered or risks suffering loss, to obtain an non-discriminatory and effective review of decisions taken by a contracting authority as rapidly as possible. The only condition for seeking a review is the requirement to notify the contracting authority of this intention – although some member states may elect to dispense with this. The review options must include the availability of interlocutory, interim and compensatory relief to correct or prevent any alleged infringement or damage. This should include a range of powers suspending or setting aside the procedure, to include picking out particular specifications (whether technical, economic or financial) in the invitation to tender which are discriminatory. However, it is not necessary that the review itself has a suspensory effect on the procurement procedure. Whenever a procedure is suspended, notice must be given to the Commission with details of the alleged infringement and in due course of the outcome of the review procedure.

The review body may be judicial or administrative. If administrative, then so long as there is adequate appeal available to a court of law or independent tribunal with the ability to make references to the Court of Justice, this facility may be excluded from the review tribunal's powers. However such bodies must in any event give written reasons for their decisions. In the exercise of interlocutory powers, the directive respects the almost universal rule requiring tribunals to consider the consequences of the proposed measure (including, for instance, the effects of setting aside a contract in national law) and permits member states to forbid the order of such measures should the negative consequences exceed the benefits. In some states the ultimate remedy, damages, may only be available if the award has been set aside.

Finally, the Commission has the power to intervene prior to the award of any contract if it believes that there has been a clear and manifest infringement of the procurement rules. In doing so it will direct the contracting authority on the measures it should take to remedy the infringement or default, giving reasons or notice of suspension of the procedure. In these circumstances the Commission will invariably obtain their intelligence from parties involved or interested in the procedure.

Works

Regulating public works contracts

The first Works Directive was adopted in 1971 (Directive 71/305/EEC) in the wake of the General Programme for the abolition of restrictions on freedom to provide services. It was recognised that to achieve free movement required not only the abolition of restriction but also the co-ordination of national procedures for the award of public contracts. The General Programme stressed that co-ordination should be based on the prohibition of discriminatory technical specifications, adequate advertising of contracts, and objective participation and award criteria. It is this philosophy that has been followed through directives focusing on different sectors, as well as a major codification of the works legislation which resulted in the Public Works Directive 93/37/EEC.

A 'public works contract' is a contract for pecuniary interest concluded in writing between a contractor and a contracting authority which has as its object the execution and/or design of building or civil engineering works which, taken as a whole, are sufficient of themselves to fulfil an economic and technical function. The directive also applies to a 'public works concession'. This is a contract of the same type except for the fact that the consideration consists solely or in part of the right to exploit the construction.

The directive covers all such contracts have an estimated value, net of VAT, of not less than ECU 5 000 000. When calculating this amount, account is to be taken not only of the amount of the public works contract but also of the estimated value of any supplies needed to carry out the works which are made available to the contractor by the contracting authority. Where the works are subdivided into several lots, each one the subject of a contract, the value of each lot must be taken into account for the purpose of determining if the threshold is exceeded. Where the aggregate value of the lots is more than ECU 5 000 000, then all the lots need to be advertised. However contracting authorities have a discretion not to advertise certain lots with an estimated value, net of VAT, of less than ECU 1 000 000, so long as the total estimated value of all the lots exempted does not exceed 20% of the total estimated value of all lots. No works or contract may be split up with the intention of avoiding the application of the directive.

In its original form this was the scope of the directive. However two significant extensions are now provided for, concession contracts and public housing schemes.

Concession contracts

It has been recognised that they concession contracts are of increasing importance since they enable a contracting authority to divest itself of a considerable administrative burden and/or financial risk. Nevertheless they are subject to considerable regulation. The threshold for advertising (for which separate notices are provided) is again ECU 5 000 000. The contracting authority has a discretion to require the concessionaire to award contracts representing a minimum of 30% of the total value of the works to third parties. It must, however, leave the option for candidates to increase this percentage. This minimum percentage is to be specified in the concession contract.

Alternatively, the contracting authority may request the candidates to specify in their tenders the percentage, if any, of the total value of the works which they intend to assign to third parties. In this regard, the directive requires member states to ensure that these proposed third party contracts are advertised according to the procurement rules (except where negotiated contracts without publication of notices are justified). Furthermore, undertakings in a group formed in order to obtain the concession contract, or undertakings affiliated to them, are not to be regarded as third parties.

An 'affiliated undertaking' is one where there is the ability, exercised directly or indirectly, of one undertaking to dominate another or subject it to a dominant influence by virtue of:

- ownership,
- financial participation or
- the rules which govern it.

A dominant influence shall be presumed when, directly or indirectly, one undertaking in relation to another:

- holds the major part of its subscribed capital;
- controls the majority of the votes attaching to shares; or

- can appoint more than half of the members of its administrative, managerial or supervisory body.

The proposed concessionaire is required to disclose full details of all such affiliated undertakings, and any subsequent changes.

Finally, there is a slight qualification in the time limits for concession contracts. The time limit for the receipt of requests to participate must be not less than 37 days from the date of dispatch of the notice, and the time limit for the receipt of tenders not less than 40 days from that date or the invitation to tender.

Public housing schemes

The other addition to the scope of the directive consists of contracts relating to the design and construction of public housing schemes. It is recognised that the size, complexity and duration of such schemes require advanced planning and close collaboration with a team of experts. Accordingly a special award procedure may be adopted for selecting the contractor most suitable for integration into the team. In this regard, the contract notice should describe as accurately as possible the works to be carried out so as to enable interested contractors to 'form a valid idea of the project'. This information is intended to be additional to the personal, technical and financial conditions to be fulfilled by candidates.

Supplies

A Public Supplies Directive was originally adopted in 1977, (77/62/EEC) but had to be amended on a number of occasions. With the codification of the Works Directive and the introduction of the Services and Utilities Directives, it was recast in 1992 as Directive 93/36/EEC. This present directive on co-ordinating procedures for the award of public supply contracts is cast in the same form as the other two except for certain features.

A 'public supply contract' is a written contract for pecuniary interest between a supplier and a contracting authority involving the purchase, lease, rental or hire purchase (with or without the option to buy) of products. The delivery of such products may in addition include siting and installation operations (Article 1). The threshold for such contracts is, net of VAT, ECU 200 000 (Article 5). In the case of contracts for the lease, rental or hire purchase of products, the basis for calculating the estimated contract value is either the duration of the contract or (if this is more than 12 months) then its total value. For contracts of an indefinite period or in cases where there is doubt as to the duration, the estimate is calculated by multiplying the monthly value by 48. For all contracts which are regularly renewed, the estimated value is the actual aggregate value of similar contracts concluded over the previous fiscal year, or over the 12 months following the first delivery, or during the term of the contract where this is greater than 12 months. The directive cautions against the selection of a valuation method or the splitting up of the quantity of supplies with the intention of avoiding its application (Article 5).

Contracts above the threshold must be awarded in accordance with one of the procedures (Article 6), which first and foremost involves advertising. In addition to specific notices, where the total estimated value is more than ECU 750 000, contracting authorities must each year advertise, by means of an indicative notice, their total procurement requirements by product area for the subsequent 12 months (Article 9).

Services

Before 1992 and the adoption of the Public Services Directive 92/50/EEC [1992] OJ L209, there was no specific legislation for such activities. The delay was not entirely unplanned in that the object of the Services Directive was to open up public procurement insofar as this had not already been achieved by the earlier two versions. The planned adoption of the Services Directive was in part responsible for the codification exercise of recent years.

Scope of the directive

A 'public service contract' is one for pecuniary interest concluded in writing between a service provider and a contracting authority. In line with the general procurement scheme, the directive applies to the same contracting authorities affected by the Supplies and Works Directives (and principally excludes entities in the utilities sector) and does not apply to contracts which relate to matters coming within those directives. Should a contract comprise both products and services then it will only be covered by this directive if the value of the services exceeds that of the products (Article 2). In the case of service contracts awarded in connection with a works contract then the contracting authority will be required to comply with this directive when it subsidises the service contract by more than 50%.

Other notable exclusions are:

- contracts relating to land,
- arbitration and conciliation,
- employment contracts; and
- research and development.

However in respect of R&D the directive does apply to contracts where the benefits accrue exclusively to the contracting authority for its use in the conduct of its own affairs on condition that the service is wholly remunerated by the contracting authority.

Design contracts

Significantly, the directive covers design contests which lead to the award of a service contract covered by the directive. It is immaterial whether or not the contest includes the award of prizes, but where there are prizes then this is to be taken into account when calculating the estimated value of the contract. The rules of the contest must conform with the requirements of Article 13 of the directive. This states that admission must not to be limited by geographical origin or by fact that, in the law of a candidate's state of establishment, the contest is restricted to either natural or legal persons. Where contests are restricted to a limited number of candidates then there must be clear and non-discriminatory selection criteria. In any event there must be sufficient candidates to ensure genuine competition.

The jury is to be composed exclusively of natural persons who are independent of all candidates and, if necessary, with at least one-third having the same professional qualifications or equivalent. The jury is to be autonomous in its decision or opinion which it must reach, on the basis of projects submitted anonymously, solely on the grounds of the criteria indicated in the prior indicative notice. The notice of results must be sent to the Office for Official Publications as if it were an award notice (Article 16).

Requirements of the directive

Subject to minor adaptations, the advertising and tender procedures, as well as the award criteria previously discussed apply to service contracts in the normal way. In place of individual prior indicative notices, contracting authorities are required at the beginning of each budgetary period to advertise by way of notice the intended total procurement in each of the service categories covered by the directive which they envisage awarding during the subsequent 12 months, so long as this budget exceeds ECU 750 000. Otherwise, the estimated value for individual contracts, net of VAT, is not less than ECU 200 000 (Article 7(1)). For the purposes of calculating this value in contracts which involve design, the fee or commission payable is to be taken into account (Article 7 (4)). Where services are divided into lots, each one the subject of a contract, then the contracting authority may waive the normal threshold for any lot which has an estimated value of less than ECU 80 000, provided that the total value of such lots does not exceed 20% of the total value of all lots. For fixed term contracts of more than 48 months for which there is no total price, the value is calculated by taking the total value for the duration. For indefinite term contracts, or contracts for less than 48 months, then the value is estimated by multiplying the monthly instalment by 48. Finally, in the case of regular, renewable contracts, the value is either the actual aggregate cost of similar contracts awarded over either the previous fiscal year or, if appropriate, the year following the first service contract (or whole contractual term if more than 12 months).

In the case of contractor selection, insofar as candidates have to possess a particular authorisation or be members of a particular organisation in their home country in order to be able to perform the service concerned, the contracting authority may require them to prove that they hold such authorisation or membership. Any candidate or tenderer may be requested to prove his enrolment, as prescribed in his country of establishment, in one of the professional or trade registers or to provide an appropriate declaration or certificate (Article 30). To protect against any abuse of this and any other provision there is an express provision not to discriminate against tenderers (Article 3).

Utilities

Council Directive 93/38/EEC of 14 June 1993 ([1993] OJ L199) co-ordinating the procurement procedures of entities operating in the water, energy, transport and telecommunications sectors was, like the Services Directive, included in the Single Market White Paper. The main reason for its previous exclusion was that such entities were irregularly governed either by public or by private law. Accordingly, the entities to be covered had to be identified on a basis other than by reference to their legal status.

They are dealt with together because the procurement problems are of a similar nature – hence the directive combines the rules on the award of services, works and supply contracts. For instance, entities operating in these sectors do not generally purchase on the basis of community-wide competition because of the closed nature of the markets in which they operate. This is due to the existence of special or exclusive rights granted by national authorities concerning the supply to, and provision or operation of, networks for providing the service concerned, the exploitation of a given geographical area for a particular purpose, the provision or operation of public telecommunications networks or the provision of public tele-communications services. Another reason for the adoption of this directive is that it is Union policy to achieve liberalisation in all these markets. The principle (if not the practice) of telecommunications and electricity liberal-isation is well established, as it is for transport.

The directive does in large measure mirror the purpose and provisions of the other three. When awarding supply, works or service contracts, or organising design contests, the contracting entities shall apply one of the usual procedures (Article 4). Contracting entities must ensure that there is no discrimination between different suppliers, contractors or service providers (Article 4), although entities are required to give preference to goods and materials of Union origin.

On the other hand it also has some special features. The rules apply to 'a public undertaking' as well as to public authorities. A public undertaking is any undertaking over which the public authorities exercise, directly or indirectly, a dominant influence by virtue of their ownership of it. A dominant influence is presumed when these authorities hold or control the majority of the undertaking's subscribed capital or votes, or can otherwise appoint more than half the members of its administrative, managerial or supervisory body (Article 1(2)). In addition, whilst in principle the directive covers the sectors of water, energy, transport and telecommunications, the exact scope of the directive in relation to each of these sectors is minutely detailed in Article 2, which should be referred to. The common element for each is, however, the existence of 'relevant activities' which are undertaken on the basis of special or exclusive rights.

Finally, given the expected magnitude of projects in these areas, the directive permits the use of 'framework agreements', which comprise any agreement between one or more of the contracting entities covered by the directive and one or more suppliers, contractors or service providers (Articles 4 and 5 – see Chapter 7).

The thresholds used across the board are not entirely the same. In works contracts the minimum contractual amount is ECU 5 000 000 but services and supply contracts are split into categories. Contracts for the provision of water, the exploitation of solid fuels, and the operation of transport services require an estimated value of not less than ECU 400 000, whereas service and supply contracts in the case of telecommunications networks need to be at least ECU 600 000. The method of calculating each of these thresholds is the same as under the respective public sector directives.

Advertising rules are also slightly different, but one might offer the observation that the essential characteristics remain the same as under the individual public sector directives. The point is that the directive relies greatly on obtaining its procurement requirements through the call for competitions. Contracting entities may choose from any of the usual procedures so long as a call for competition has been made (Article 20). Furthermore, in contrast to the discretionary use of the negotiated procedure in the public sector directives, entities under this directive are given the option to use a procedure without prior call for competition on the same or similar grounds. This call for competition involves the use of notices published in the *Official Journal*. Ordinarily, the entity should use one of three possibilities:

- a contract notice; or
- in slight contrast to the service and supply directives, a periodic indicative notice; or
- a separate notice when the entity is to employ a qualification system.

The periodic indicative notice is used to invite expressions of interest ahead of a restricted or negotiated procedure without further publication of a notice of a call for competition. Contracting entities must subsequently invite all candidates to confirm their interest on the basis of detailed information on the contract concerned, before beginning the selection of tenderers or participants in negotiations. When a call for competition is made by means of a notice on the existence of a qualification system, tenderers in a restricted procedure or participants in a negotiated procedure shall be selected from the qualified candidates in accordance with such a system (Article 21). In addition to these specific notices, entities are required at least once a year to make known by means of a periodic indicative notice, their service, supply and works requirements for the ensuing year (Article 22). In the case of service and supply contracts, the notice must detail the value of all contracts where the aggregate is equal to or greater than ECU 750 000. For works contracts, then they must detail the essential characteristics of the works contracts which the contracting entities intend to award when the aggregate is more than ECU 5 000 000. These notices can be used as a means of calling for competition so long as the expressions of interest are invited within the ensuing 12 months.

Finally, in relation to the review of contract procedures, the review of directive provisions concerning utilities (92/13/EEC) follows the general directive relating to supplies and works contracts. There is, though, the additional requirement that contracting entities be given the option (by the member state) to have their contract award procedures and practices attested as being in conformity with the directive. Independent attestors are required to give an objective written opinion on the existence of any irregularities in the award procedures. There is no requirement in EU law for publication, but some inference of irregularities may be drawn if a contracting entity fails, in the long term, to publish as permitted notice of conformity in the *Official Journal*.

Moreover, the attestation is of a general nature and does not guarantee that the procurement rules have been correctly applied in individual cases.

Chapter 7
Public Procurement in Practice

Introduction

The purpose of this chapter is to focus on a few issues and scenarios which routinely or occasionally crop up in the procurement process and set them against the regulatory infrastructure covered in Chapter 6.

It is impossible in a book of this nature to cover every issue in as much detail as one would like; nevertheless, what does follow is a test of the rigidity of the regime in the form of a commentary on a few of the recent trends and potential problems in the procurement rules.

- Firstly, there is an issue as to whether a contracting authority, which is permitted in a given case to make use of an exception, is required to comply strictly with all aspects of that exception, or whether the authority may ignore the exception or make selective use of it.
- Secondly, and continuing with the analysis of partnering which was begun in Chapter 5, it is compelling to suggest that partnering would be ideal in a procurement situation, particularly for large projects where establishing an effective on-going relationship may be synonymous with choosing the most economically advantageous tender. However what scope is there for this in the directives?
- Thirdly, there is the increased use of pre-qualifications and the extent to which these come within the selection criteria of the directives.
- Fourthly, there are the problems that arise through the use of consortia and special purpose vehicles for extremely large projects. Must there be continuity in the composition and structure of these corporate entities throughout the award process?
- Finally, there is a brief look at the use of selection and award criteria.

Procurement rules in context

Given that the object of the procurement regime is to open up the market to competition across the Union, that object will be undermined if it is not enforced and respected within the meaning and scheme of the Treaty. This involves the direct application of primary rights, and this section examines how two major tenets of the Treaty, free movement of goods and open competition, are applied.

Free movement of goods

Except in the case of pure services contracts, public purchasing will invariably involve the buying-in of goods and materials, or their use in a works or utilities contract. Therefore any restriction on the use of certain materials which is not justified on one of the permitted grounds (see Chapter 9) will make it harder for the tenderer who is unable to use the materials of his choice to submit a competitive bid. In *Commission of the European Communities* v. *Ireland* (45/87) [1988] ECR 4929, ('*Dundalk*') the Court of Justice dealt with this point.

The Commission brought an action against Ireland for a breach of Union law in the way it handled a major project, the Dundalk Water Supply Augmentation Scheme. Part of the scheme was for the construction of a water main. An open invitation to tender was published, but one of the specifications in the contract documents provided that asbestos cement pressure pipes should be certified as complying with Irish standard specifications. One tender from an Irish undertaking, which turned out to be the lowest, provided for the use of pipes manufactured by a Spanish undertaking. These pipes complied with international standards, but had not been certified as complying with the Irish standard. Accordingly, the tender was excluded from further consideration or selection.

A sub-issue of this case was whether the contract was covered by the Works Directive at all, the argument being that if it was not, then Article 10 (prohibiting the use of technical specifications which mention products of a specific make or source) did not apply. The significance of this point will be returned to below but for now it can be noted that the Court concluded that the contract was not covered by the directive. However, it went on to consider the compatibility of the specification with Article 30 TEU.

Acknowledging that the District Council was a public body, the Court rejected all arguments that Article 30 could not apply to a contract that was essentially for the procurement of services. The prohibition in Article 30, it noted, was of a general character, and provisions on the freedom to supply services do not lay down any specific rule relating to particular barriers to the free movement of goods. Consequently, the fact that a public works contract relates to the provision of services cannot remove a clause in an invitation to tender restricting the materials that may be used from the scope of the prohibitions set out in Article 30.

Going on to apply Article 30, the Court noted that the inclusion of such a clause in the invitation to tender might have caused economic operators, who produce or utilise pipes equivalent to pipes certified as complying with Irish standards, to refrain from tendering. Furthermore, the contracting authority's argument that pipes utilised must suit the existing network could not be accepted, since the contracting authority could have verified compliance with the technical conditions without, from the outset, restricting the contract only to tenderers proposing to utilise Irish materials. Accordingly, the court concluded that the form of the specification caused the contracting authority to breach its obligations under Article 30.

In a later case the Court ruled that Article 30 precludes national rules which reserve to undertakings established in particular regions of the national territory a proportion of supply contracts (*Du Pont de Nemours Italiana SpA* v. *Unita Sanitaria Locale* (21/88) [1990] ECR 1-889). It added that although the restrictive effects of a preferential system of that kind might conceivably benefit both domestic and imported goods, the fact was that only domestic goods were benefiting.

Competition

EU competition laws deal with general issues, which encompass the specific objectives laid down in the procurement requirements. In other words, the procurement laws are not an alternative to, nor do they derogate from, the laws of competition. By virtue of Article 90 TEU, the competition laws are expressly extended to cover public undertakings. Moreover, the Court has ruled that provisions in the Treaty on state aid cannot be used to frustrate rules on the free movement of goods. In *Du Pont de Nemours Italiana* (see above) the local health authority had extended to all public bodies and authorities, the obligation to obtain at least 30% of their supplies from industrial and agricultural undertakings and small businesses established in southern Italy. The Court observed that in such cases it is not necessary to examine the possibility that these measures might constitute aid because Article 92 was not a sufficient reason to exempt national measures from the prohibition in Article 30.

Elsewhere, the Court of Justice has preferred to rely on free movement provisions to ensure compliance with the principles if the single market. In *Commission* v. *Italian Republic* (3/88) [1989] ECR 4035 it held that a member state which provides that only companies with a majority of the shares or in public or state ownership may conclude agreements to develop data-processing systems for public authorities is in breach of its duties under Articles 52 and 59 TEU.

On the other hand, it is not simply public undertakings that must be wary of the competition rules in the sphere of procurement. Private undertakings must do likewise. For example, the construction industry is not without instances of collusive tendering by which a sector can maintain prices and hopefully ensure all participants receive an equal amount of work. Nothing could be more anti-competitive. Collusive tendering is no more than a cartel, because it restricts independence of activity and therefore competition. One only needs to look at the *SPO* case (see Chapter 5) to discover how the Court of Justice has dealt with it.

What, though, of the independent tenderer who seeks to undercut the competition with an abnormally low tender? Is he entitled to be considered and, if the lowest tender is the criterion by which the contract is to be awarded, to be selected? The public sector directives deal with the matter expressly (the Utilities Directive only refers to it in the preamble). If a tender appears to be abnormally low in relation to the contract to be awarded, then the contracting authority cannot reject it before asking the tenderer for details of the constituent elements of the tender which it considers relevant, and shall verify those constituent elements taking account of the explanations received. The contracting authority may take into consideration any explanation which is justified on objective grounds including:

- the economy of the working method proposed;
- the technical solution chosen;
- the exceptionally favourable conditions available to the tenderer for the execution of the work; or
- the originality of the work proposed by the tenderer.

In addition the Court dealt with this issue in *SA Transporoute* v. *Minister of Public Works* (Case 76/81, [1982] ECR 417). In this case, a dispute arose in respect of a notice of invitation to tender issued by a bridges and highways authority in Luxembourg, in response to which Transporoute had submitted the lowest tender. The tender was rejected, *inter alia*, by the minister of public works because the prices in Transporoute's tender were considered by the minister of public works to be abnormally low. As a result, the minister awarded the contract to a consortium of Luxembourg contractors whose tender was considered to be economically the most advantageous. Transporoute brought an action for the annulment of the decision.

The Court was asked to examine Article 29(5) of the Works Directive, but there are similar provisions in the other two public sector directives. The Court noted that the fact that the provision expressly empowers the awarding authority to establish whether the explanations are acceptable does not under any circumstances authorise it to decide in advance that no acceptable explanation could be given. It ruled that the aim of the provision was to protect tenderers against arbitrariness on the part of the authority awarding contracts, and this would not be achieved if it were left to that authority to judge whether or not it was appropriate to seek explanations. The Court concluded that it was compulsory (and therefore a directly enforceable right) to require the authority to seek from the tenderer an explanation of the prices, or to inform the tenderer which aspect of the tender appears to be abnormal and allow a reasonable time within which to submit further details.

Choice of procedure

The issue to be determined here is whether a contracting authority is bound to observe exceptions once chosen. For instance, where a contract which the authority seeks to award comes within the negotiated procedure, is the choice of procedure binding in its entirety, preventing the authority from being more open in the procedures than the directive provides?

The problem is not so much the direct issue of whether or not to elect to make use of an exception, but rather, if that exception is chosen, what are the consequences of the contracting authority not fully observing the full application of that exception? For example, a contracting authority which lawfully elects to make use of the restricted procedure would have published a Notice in the appropriate Model Form. However, if it then proceeds to carry out a far more open procedure than the restricted procedure requires then, given that the underlying purpose of the procurement regime is to ensure transparency in the award of public contracts, the persistent uncertainty may result in prospective tenderers being confused as to the definitive choice of procedure. This could place the contracting authority in breach of its duty not to discriminate between different service providers. Some tenderers may judge the conduct of the award process to indicate an open procedure, whilst others may rely on the notices as published. This is of greater concern than the issue of the choice of procedure. In respect of that choice what needs to be determined is whether the choice of procedure (or any other use of a discretion) is mandatory. The negotiated procedure will be examined as an example.

Is use of the negotiated procedure compulsory?

Under the directives, unless the authority can establish grounds for employing the negotiated procedure (with or without publication) then it should award its public service contracts by the open or restricted procedure. It is assumed that a given project offers objective justification for using the negotiated procedure (with prior publication) if the nature of the services does not permit prior overall pricing. However the contracting authority has a discretion and not an obligation to use the negotiated procedure since all references to its use are prefixed by the word 'may'.

Is the choice of the negotiated procedure binding?

Must a contracting authority which elects to make use of an exception comply with all aspects of that procedure, or are the procedures divisible? On this the Court of Justice offers some guidance. In *Commission* v. *Ireland (45/87)* ('*Dundalk*') referred to above, the Court ruled that if, pursuant to a procurement directive, a contracting authority chooses to publish or mistakenly publishes a contract notice in respect of works which are in fact unambiguously excluded from the scope of that directive, then that step does not cause the exception to cease to apply. With that reasoning the Court concluded that the contracting authority in *Dundalk* was not in breach of the directive in making a reference to specific non-equivalent technical specifications.

On the basis of *Dundalk* one can begin to distil the principle that, where a contracting authority elects to award a contract according to a procurement directive when technically it is not obliged to, then it is not bound by the other provisions of the directive, but may respect them if it wishes. Whether a contract comes within the scope of a directive or not depends on its object and not on the conduct or policy decisions of the contracting authority.

It would therefore be open to a contracting authority to argue that by justifying recourse to the negotiated procedure they are not bound to comply with the open and restricted procedural rules, but that, on the basis of *Dundalk*, they may respect them if they wish. One could further argue that a contracting authority may make selective use of a directive that it is not bound by, since in *Dundalk* the contracting authority did just that, choosing to define a technical specification by reference to a national standard when the directive required it only to accept equivalents. Equally, the directive expressly permits changing from one procedure (open) to the negotiated procedure, albeit on specific grounds.

The issue is not whether a contracting authority has made full or selective use of an exception, but rather has it complied with the duties and requirements which it is bound by? This was the approach of the Court in *Dundalk* because, having rejected the alleged breach of the works directive, it then went on to examine the wider and more general duties which the contracting authority was bound by (namely Article 30 – see above). One must contrast the discretion to make selective use of exceptions with the broader duty to not discriminate between tenderers (derived from the directive) plus the even broader principles of certainty of legitimate expectations, transparency, etc. (derived from general principles of EC law). Following *Dundalk* and the enduring philosophy of the Court of Justice in such matters, it is almost certain that a national court would have to defer to these general principles if it were established in a given case that selective use of procurement procedures was directly or indirectly discriminatory, undermined the principle of certainty of legitimate expectations or was not transparent.

Partnering

In principle, since public undertakings are no less participants in the market place than private undertakings, they have just as much freedom to enter into agreements as their private counterparts do. Entering into a partnering agreement does not, in itself and subject to the laws of competition, cause any difficulties. On the contrary, it can be highly desirable for public authorities to minimise their expenditure through the development of constructive, cost-cutting relationships with their suppliers.

On the other hand, the duties placed on public authorities in procurement matter mean that closed but fruitful relationships with select undertakings would ultimately be contrary to the spirit of the directives. Therefore one can cite another principle that a public undertaking should not look to satisfy its procurement needs through the process of partnering. Between these two principles, though lies a grey area. What scope is there within the procurement directives for partnering to take place?

The closest approximation to partnering that one will find in EC procurement legislation (although the extent to which it may be employed is uncertain) is known as the framework agreement and is a feature of the EC Utilities Directive (93/38/EEC, [1993] OJ L199). There is no counterpart to be found in the public sector directives.

The Utilities Directive

Framework agreements are specifically mentioned in the Utilities Directive. This lays down procurement procedures for contracts concluded by entities which are either public authorities responsible for, or undertakings endowed with, special or exclusive rights in relation to activities in the sectors of water, energy, transport and telecommunications.

In the context of partnering, the single most compatible feature of the Utilities Directive is the use of the framework agreement. This is defined as:

'an agreement between a contracting authority and *one or more suppliers or contractors*, the purpose of which is to establish the terms, in particular with regard to the prices and, where appropriate, the quantity envisaged, governing the contracts to be awarded during a given period' (Article 1(5) Utilities).

As the author's emphasis indicates, the framework agreement establishes a basis for negotiations with a limited band of tenderers, and thus it would seem immediately to meet the requirements for partnering. It also appears to permit future contracts to be awarded (but the observation is a qualified one). The imprecise wording of the provision, however, leaves considerable uncertainty as to how far such an agreement may legitimately be taken, and there is yet to be any elucidation by the European Court. Trepte, in *Public Procurement in the EC* (1993, CCED) asserts that framework agreements, as intended by the directive, do not imply binding obligations and are to be seen in contrast to framework *contracts*. The inference is that the latter are outside the scope of the directive.

The Commission's draft policy guidelines put it differently. The guidelines identify three different types of possible framework arrangements:

- written information relating to the general terms and conditions applicable to all future contracts drawn up by a supplier on the request of a public purchaser;
- written agreements relating to the general terms, etc. but the where purchaser makes a down payment or pays a retainer in order to have the guarantee of the supply or service in question; and
- framework contracts which bind both parties even if the quantities to be purchased are unspecified.

The guidelines go on to say:

'It is only the arrangements described in [the first two options above] that fall within the definition of framework agreements provided in Article 1(5) of the directive. Framework contracts, on the other hand, are to be considered as binding contracts which fall under the general provisions of the directive, including the specific provisions concerning contracts with options, provided for under Article 14(6).'

However, it is only later that the guidelines become more emphatic:

'It is to be understood that framework agreements are neither binding contractual agreements nor even the promise of a contract.'

Instead, they can be regarded as standing offers which remain valid during the life of the agreements, of which the contracting entity may avail itself if it chooses. Interestingly, they may also cover the needs of more than one contracting entity.

Contracts intended to be binding and enforceable may nevertheless be awarded, but cannot be considered as framework agreements *per se*. What this appears to mean is that contracting authorities cannot enter into framework contracts with more than one supplier or contractor, nor avail themselves of the following discretionary power. Article 5 of the Directive provides that contracting entities '*may* regard a framework agreement as a contract within the meaning [the Directive] and award it in accordance with [it]'. The direction is discretionary and jurisprudence on this matter does not suggest any other interpretation. Thus a contracting entity is given the option to treat a framework agreement as if it was a substantive supply or works contract itself. Where it does so, then individual, above-threshold contracts may be awarded without resorting to a prior call for competition (although the actual awards must still be published by way of notice in the *Official Journal*). Note the use of the word 'may'. Despite the existence of a framework agreement, the contracting authority may opt to award a contract which was initially covered by the agreement by way of a separate contract. It is this facility that necessarily distinguishes non-binding agreements and binding and enforceable contracts.

On the other hand, where a contracting authority chooses not to treat an agreement as a substantive contract then individual contracts are subject to the normal rules. Despite the apparent choice there is a working presumption that, unless a framework agreement is concluded in accordance with the directive, individual contracts will be treated as separate and thus subject to a prior call for competition. However, the directive is silent on how well, or indeed whether, the individual contracts which are to be awarded under the framework agreement should be identified. Instead it crystallises the otherwise implied rule that contracting authorities may not misuse framework agreements in order to hinder, limit or distort competition. With the above presumption and this express rule, together with the principles of transparency and non-discrimination, there is effectively only one course a contracting authority can take when it is drawing up its framework agreement: to state the object and scope of the framework agreement by reference to the project or projects envisaged and the works or services required. Failure to do so will jeopardise the framework agreement itself and the immunity from challenge it offers. If any of the individual contracts are challenged, then the contracting entity needs to show that the framework agreement was one which falls within the definition contained in the directive.

In the context of partnering, a Utilities Directive framework agreement offers some scope for co-operation between purchaser and supplier on future purchasing requirements, although the natural flexibility of partnering is slightly restricted in terms of duration, selection of partners, etc. By treating a partnering arrangement as a contract for the purposes of the directive and inviting tenders, it would be open to a contracting entity to enter into a framework agreement for negotiations with a limited band of tenderers. Subsequent contracts could therefore be awarded under the terms of the agreement, avoiding the need for them to be put out to tender.

As for the award of future contracts, the obligatory time limit and the duty not to distort competition mean that framework agreements cannot be open-ended, indeterminate or vague, since this may imply exclusivity. The directive refers to 'a given period' of time but it is unclear how this period should be defined. However, given the nature of the sectors and contracts the directive was intended to cover, it would be reasonable to suppose that the conclusion of a specific contract should be sufficiently definite for a given period to be inferred.

As for *de facto* indeterminate or exclusive commitments, then these may infringe the directive since the scope of the award of subsequent contracts would be limited to the partners, breaching the basic premise of the directive. Overall, it is clear these framework agreements need to be established very carefully in order to avoid any possibility of infringement. Understandably, the Commission services treat them with caution because of the possibilities of misuse.

Partnering and the Public Sector Directives

It is only in the Utilities Directive that the use of framework agreements is sanctioned. No mention is made of them in the public sector directives, but this does not mean they have not been considered. In its original proposal to amend the Supplies Directive, the Commission included a provision for framework agreements, but this article was removed by the time the proposal was formally put forward in October 1992. However, it has been suggested (Brown, *The Utilities Directive* [1993] CML Rev. 733) that a sufficiently precise framework agreement is allowable under the Supplies Directive provided it is publicised in accordance with the directive's rules. This means that rather than relying on a specific loop-hole in the directive, if a contracting authority is 'sufficiently precise' in ascertaining its requirements over the medium to long term, then this would form a feasible basis to advertise and award a single contract to one supplier, and thus provide a 'framework' in which authority and supplier could concentrate on their working relationship.

The problem is that the scheme could only work with a single supplier and not with a number of suppliers. Brown's suggestion mentions only the Supplies Directive but is not tied to any particular article of the Supplies Directive. Therefore there is nothing in principle to preclude the same scheme being invoked in respect of the Public Works and Services Directives, so long as (and this is the issue) the agreement is 'sufficiently precise'. Looking again at the three public sector directives, one cannot use a specific article therein to provide the institutional foundation for partnering; it is necessary to run the gauntlet of the general approach.

There may, however, be an alternative. Each directive includes the facility to 'split' contracts. Any project can often be divided down into sections, and so, to give contracting authorities the necessary flexibility to contract accordingly, contracts pertaining to one identifiable project can be awarded separately. In this regard there is a difference in style and substance in the Works Directive compared to the Supplies and Services Directives.

The Works Directive (Article 6.3) refers to the sub-division of work into several lots. When this option is chosen:

'The value of each lot must be taken into account for the purpose of calculating the amounts referred to in paragraph 1 [i.e. the threshold of ECU 5 000 000]. Where the aggregate value of the lots is not less that the amount referred to in paragraph 1, the provisions of that paragraph shall apply to all lots. Contracting authorities shall be permitted to depart from this provision for lots whose estimated value net of VAT is less that ECU 1 000 000, provided that the total estimated value of all the lots exempted does not, in consequence, exceed 20% of the total estimated value of all lots.'

This facility is open to abuse with contracting authorities attempting to split contracts or work too far (which is prohibited by Article 6.4). However, on the assumption that the objective here is to devise a common system that maybe employed either within or without the procurement process, and further that it would not be in the contracting authority's interest to abuse the procedure, the authority can begin to concentrate on being able to satisfy its public purchasing needs under the aegis of a *de facto* framework/ approximated partnering agreement.

As for the Services and Supplies Directives, these refer (at Article 5.3 and 7.6 respectively) to the award of regular contracts and contracts which are to be reviewed within a given time. In such situations (the Articles being virtually identical):

'the estimated contract value shall be established on the basis of either the actual aggregate [value of similar contracts concluded/cost for the same category of services awarded] over the previous fiscal year or 12 months, adjusted where possible, for anticipated changes in quantity or value over the 12 months following the initial contract; or the estimated aggregate value during the 12 months following the first [delivery/service performed] or during the term of the contract, where this is greater than 12 months.'

Similarly, both the Services and Supplies Directives caution against sub-dividing contracts with the intention of avoiding the application of the directive in question. Once again, if a contracting authority concentrates on exploiting rather than avoiding the directives, it can begin to think in terms of using partnering, or at least an approximation of it.

Before doing so, it is necessary to clear two further obstacles. First, it was mentioned earlier that even if a contracting authority was sufficiently precise in drawing up a framework agreement in the context of the Supplies Directive, there still appears to be the limitation that it is restricted to concluding one contract with one supplier. However this is not necessarily so. Contracts may also be awarded to a group of suppliers/contractors/service providers who submit a joint tender, since group tenders are permissible under all three directives. It would therefore be possible for a contracting authority to negotiate with a number of contractors/suppliers/service providers, even though they are not separate and independent tenderers. Whilst this is a solution, it is convoluted and requires the contracting authority to act sufficiently precisely in determining its future needs.

The second problem arises out the first, but lies in the limitations inherent in the fields of application of the three public sector directives. Whereas the Utilities Directive is, by its very nature, designed to embrace the disciplines of contracting (in the building sense), supply and service provision, the public sector directives are, again by their respective natures, mutually exclusive. In the public sector domain authorities therefore have to contend with the problems of trying to award mixed contracts. Mixed contracts are not in themselves unlawful, but problems have arisen with some contracting authorities attempting to pass off one activity as incidental to another.

In this respect, the European Court of Justice has learnt to look beyond the form of words and consider the real object of the tender contract. For example, in *Gestion Hotelera Internacional SA* v. *Comunidad Autonoma de Canarias and Others* (Case 331/92) the Court held, *inter alia*, that a mixed contract relating to the performance of works and the assignment of property does not fall within the scope of the Works Directive if the performance of the works is merely incidental to the assignment of the property.

On the assumption that no properly advised authority would attempt to evade the advertising rules, there can be no objection to awarding a mixed contract so long as all relevant procedures are complied with.

Conclusion

In the final analysis, it needs to be decided whether partnering can be made to work in the context of the procurement regime.

It is generally accepted that a contracting authority must award contracts by one of three procedures. The only possible way a contracting authority could negotiate with a limited band of tenderers is by choosing either the restricted or negotiated procedures. These procedures obviously involve a large element of discretion and so it would seem to give the authority scope to choose the tenderers it believes would fit its requirements, including the style of project management. This element of discretion would be sufficient to enable a contracting authority to pre-select a band of suitable and potential tenderers by drawing up an Expression of Interest List. Presuming that this list is manageable, it would be open to the contracting authority to negotiate with these contractors along the lines of partnering. However, if competition between the participants is too fierce, this could undermine the open and harmonious relationship established through the partnering technique.

In respect of contracts awarded under the negotiated procedure, it should be noted that the three reasons for using that procedure (irregular tenders received, non-commercial research, or exceptional risks precluding overall pricing) still require prior publication of a contract in the *Official Journal*. In any event, it is clearly open to and in the interests of contracting authorities to enter into appropriate arrangements with contractors of their choice in these special circumstances. Accordingly, it may be possible to negotiate with a limited band of tendererers, assuming that, when there is more than one, the contracting authority sets out the terms upon which it wishes to contract, giving each tenderer an equal opportunity to bid for the contract, and finally awards the contract either on price or to the most advantageously economical tender. In this respect, the negotiated procedure does not give the contracting authority any more freedom than in normal circumstances. Moreover, the authority must first ensure that it is correctly invoking the negotiated procedure and is only commissioning work/supplies/services which have been pre-determined; it is not possible for a contracting authority to provide for future contracts, for these, by definition, are outside the intended scope of the negotiated procedure.

However, this does not take account of the range of possibilities in which a contracting authority might first enter into a partnering arrangement with a given supplier outside the context of a specific award. Does this preclude the supplier from participating in the procedure? There are three possible answers.

- First, if there is no likelihood of a private undertaking party to a partnering agreement participating in any subsequent procurement procedure, then the parties are unrestricted in what they do.
- Second, if it is likely that a private undertaking party to a partnering agreement might want to participate in any subsequent procurement procedure, then the parties should ensure that the relationship is purposely kept to only those matters and contracts which will not exceed the procurement thresholds. This can be very difficult and it means the benefits will be very hard to achieve.

● Third, where the parties come into contact with each other within the context of an award procedure for a contract that exceeds the threshold, then the risk of a conventional one-to-one partnering agreement interfering with the subsequent award is too great to make a partnering arrangement worthwhile to the authority.

Instead, if a public undertaking is to make the most out of partnering and stay within the confines of the law, then it might take the initiative from within the procurement process itself and look towards achieving a partnering environment in the long term. Rather than conclude a partnering agreement and then run the risk of it spoiling a subsequent process, it could instead incorporate a framework for partnering within its procedures for awarding contracts that will welcome any successful tenderer. It is vital for the public authority to take the initiative because, by doing so, it will be able to maintain control and observe its duties for the correct application of the procurement laws.

The public undertaking should invest in establishing a structure to which any and all contractors can subscribe. This would entail developing an action plan, drawing up criteria for selecting partners, creating a framework for assessing and understanding policies and strategies and focusing on a mission statement.

It is obvious that this is not what is commonly understood by 'partnering' in that is not a long-term commitment between two or more organisations for the purpose of achieving specific business objectives, etc. However, it is possible, with a properly-prepared partnering framework and with the help of a compliant contractor, to prepare the ground work for the significant saving in costs in the future. Alternatively, if there is only one reliable contractor on the market it does not matter that the 'partnering agreement' is not as concrete as it would be if the parties entered into a contract.

This process hinges on the participation of a compliant contractor. Clearly this is the unavoidable weak link in the theory. Whilst those who comply no doubt have their own best interests at heart, there will also be those who fail to see the advantages of co-operation. In this case there is no answer. Every agreement, especially partnering, requires the willingness of all parties concerned, and the law can only enforce rights and duties, not co-operation.

This brings about a circular argument in that, if it is assumed that the purpose of partnering is to reduce prices through reducing costs by developing partnering techniques with one or several contractors then this gives those contractors a possibly unfair competitive edge. That may be true, but in the final analysis there is only one answer: to allow contractors and public undertakings to practise partnering techniques is a *policy issue*, and as such requires the EU in consultation with the industry to give a ruling. On the question of lawfulness, in my opinion, the rights and wrongs of this are equally balanced. On the one hand, it cannot be said to be the purest form of competition, but on the other it brings about the most economically advantageous tender solely by indirect, incidental, and, to a large extent, indiscriminate means, which are not themselves anti-competitive.

Group tenders

In large, multi-faceted projects for which the contracting authority has a range of needs, it is often the case that one undertaking will be unable to meet them all. Clearly then the alternative will be to make a group bid. At what point should a group be formed? In these large projects, it is normal (although not a legal requirement) to invite 'expressions of interest' from individual parties with a view to issuing them full contract specifications, so that they may then decide whether or not to submit a formal bid. Invariably there will be a deadline by which expressions of interest are to be received. In large projects it will often be impossible for a prudent prospective tenderer to determine, prior to that deadline, the scope and need for partners. Even if this can be established, if the tendering process is drawn out because of the complexity of the project it may be the case that the group is joined or even led by undertakings which did not respond to the original invitation to express an interest. Would this be unfair to those parties who did express an interest or were able to prepare themselves ahead of the deadline by forming a definitive group? The question to be answered is whether the composition and structure of such a group need to be definitively formed prior to expression of interest, or if not, what is the latest point at which change is acceptable.

The public sector directives provide that tenders may be submitted by groups of tenderers. They state:

> 'These groups may not be required to assume a specific legal form in order to submit the tender, however the group selected may be required to do so when it has been awarded the contract.'

The provisions are silent on whether the group should (at the very least) be in exactly or substantially the same form as when it expressed an interest (if at all). To decide this the legal significance of the deadline for receipt of applications must first be determined, before then deciding how much continuity there must be in the identity and composition of a group between expression of interest and submission of tender, and whether in particular a pre-qualification questionnaire (PQQ) can be completed by a prospective tenderer which did not express an interest in the contract before the deadline.

The significance of deadlines

It is minimum time limits that are set in the directives. Therefore deadlines beyond these can be set by the contracting authority at its discretion. Clearly there has to be some deadline otherwise it would be impossible for a contracting authority to declare to the market when it proposes to examine expressions of interests received. To some extent, therefore, its decision is an administrative/commercial one, but undoubtedly the authority will be guided by statutory and common law duties involving the use of public finances and the need to achieve the objectives of the project.

The Court of Justice has repeatedly ruled that these commercial, administrative, statutory and political choices are within the competence of national authorities to exercise, subject only to the overriding duties in the Treaty (set out elsewhere in this book) and specific legislation, such as the procurement directives, where the primary duty is not to discriminate between prospective tenderers. This duty is perhaps even more fundamental than the duty to advertise. Where there is a breach of the Procurement Directive the Court usually has no hesitation in ruling against a member state. Therefore there is some force in the argument that to admit an expression of interest after the deadline has passed is a breach of that fundamental duty, because it discriminates against other would-be tenderers who saw no merit in expressing an interest because the deadline had passed.

If there is a requirement to observe pre-determined deadlines in the interests of non-discrimination, then there must be a like duty to set a reasonable deadline so that prospective tenderers from anywhere in the Union have an opportunity to make an informed and if necessary prepared expression of interest. Therefore, in principle, any prospective tenderer may lawfully claim if it believes that the deadline is unreasonable. Of course to do so it would have to demonstrate discrimination (or a breach of a particular provision).

Continuity in the identity and participation of the prospective tenderer

Subject to certain fundamental safeguards in the procurement directives, it is strongly arguable that there is no prohibition against changes in the structure, composition and presentation of prospective tenderers, even if this involves the addition of members who did not respond to the original notice. In the absence of specific authority, this opinion is based on the formative arguments explained below.

Both the relevant provisions in the procurement directives which permit groups and the model forms annexed to them refer to 'tenders' or 'bids'. In contrast they do not mention expressions of interest. It can be argued that an expression of interest is not binding, either on the prospective bidder or the contracting authority. One might suggest that it is simply a method for interested parties to make themselves known to the contracting authority and to obtain further details upon which a binding tender might be submitted. Furthermore, it would be anti-competitive and counter to the useful effect of the procurement process if prospective tenderers were prevented from adapting themselves, alone or in conjunction with others, to the exact requirements of the bid. If this were not possible then contracting authorities would simply not receive tenders of a sufficient number or calibre to ensure genuine competition and allow them to make an effective choice – as required by all procurement directives.

The standard form of wording in the model forms for dealing with group bids is simply not sufficiently flexible or commercially sophisticated to cope with large complex projects. It is unrealistic for a defined group submitting an expression of interest in any particular case to retain its exact status and composition throughout the tender process. On the other hand, it must be borne in mind that the procurement procedures provide a general frame-work to co-ordinate (as opposed to regulate) the award of public contracts but they also contain certain fundamental safeguards which must be respected, and it is incumbent on a contracting authority to adapt its requirements to that framework.

The directives do not lay down a uniform and exhaustive body of community rules. Within the framework of the common rules which contain the directives the member states remain free to maintain or adopt sub-stantive and procedural rules in regard to public contracts on condition that they comply with all the relevant provisions of Union law (in particular the prohibitions flowing from the principles laid down in the Treaty on the right of establishment and the freedom to provide services) and other specific requirements as to time limits and number of tenders to be considered, etc. (See *Gebroeders Beentjes BV* v. *The Netherlands* (31/87) and copious authority for the proposition that, insofar as the Community has not adopted common rule in relation to any field of activity, then member states (including national authorities) remain free to regulate themselves subject to their general duties under the EC Treaty (for example *Commission* v. *Germany* (178/84) [1988] ECR 1227.) Therefore, the lawfulness of any procurement will often ultimately turn on whether the notice was adequate.

In the meantime, assuming that the notice is adequate in terms of timing, the period of concern regarding changes in composition is between the deadline for expressions of interest and the point at which formal tenders, upon the basis of which the contracting authority will award the contract, are submitted. It is clear that once this penultimate stage has been reached the authority may not enter into further negotiations but must decide the qualifying proposals on the basis of lowest price or most economically advantageous tender. In contrast there is no restriction on the conduct of negotiations at any pre-qualification stages prior to this point, so long as all prospective tenderers are treated equally in accordance with the selection criteria. The point is whether this flexibility will permit variations in the structure, composition and identity of the prospective bidder from its form when the expression of interest was submitted. If this rationale is applied in practice then it would suggest that, so long as one member of the consortium has responded to the notice (and one might query whether this should be the prime contractor), then the contracting authority is not acting unlawfully by admitting structural and compositional changes to the group.

The adequacy of contract notices

The extent to which a problem will arise in coping with changes in the identity and composition of a group tender will depend partly upon the adequacy of the contract notice and on whether there was sufficient detail to indicate the range of expertise that was required.

In general, imperfections in the notice which are minor will not affect the validity of the eventual award if they do not place any individual tenderer at either an unfair advantage or disadvantage. Errors in the notice which might cause confusion but which are corrected by way of a corrigendum should not affect validity if any conceivable disadvantage of significance is compensated for, for example by extending the date for receipt of tenders. However, in some cases this may not be necessary. For instance, the post contract notice procedure in Article 19 of the Services Directive deals with both restricted and negotiated procedures. Mis-describing the procedure as 'negotiated' when it was intended to be restricted should not necessitate an extension of time since the deadlines are identical for each. Accordingly, such a misdescription would not in itself invalidate the award. However one must again have regard to the implications of the contracting authority's duty under Article 3(2) and the general principles already referred to.

In the context of group tenders then it is submitted (relying on *Dundalk* and other authorities such as *Commission* v. *Portuguese Republic* (C-247/89)) that within the general framework of the public sector directives, a contracting authority has a fair amount of discretion to design a tender process which is most appropriate to its current needs. Clearly, the greater the project the greater the need to design a tender process which is appropriate. In order to do so it has to set the general parameters in the contract notice. These need only be general because the object of the whole procurement regime is the adequacy of the advertising for individual contracts and the avoidance of undisclosed invitations to tender. In practice this involves a requirement to advertise the existence of proposed contracts and not their finite details, other than the minimum requirements which are reflected in the model forms annexed to each of the directives.

On the other hand, given that the contracting authority is to be permitted some flexibility in contract notices over their content it cannot then insist on strict observance of the notice's conditions where this too is not really necessary. For instance, in the case of a project which, in view of its size and special considerations, requires substantial (even unique) strategic, managerial, operational and commercial planning, which can only be delivered by a group of contractors, then it must be envisaged that many if not most prospective tenderers would make an initial request for information in their own name but not rule out submitting a substantive tender in the name of a group once they have obtained and digested the information offered by the contracting authority. If a contracting authority did indeed refuse a tender submitted by such a group on the ground that groups were invited by the contract notice to express an interest, and the group so named had not submitted an expression of interest, it could be very forcefully argued that no informed and prudent service provider would realistically anticipate submitting a tender on the basis of a preliminary view formed prior to expressing an interest, and nor should it be required to because, given the objects of the procurement regime, that could be considered uncompetitive and possibly a breach of the principles of free movement on the ground that only 'local' businesses would have the requisite knowledge to understand the full implications of the proposed contract.

Selection and award criteria

Selection of suitable candidates lies at the heart of the EU procurement regime. It is considered vital that there are objective criteria for participation and accordingly each directive lays down the conditions for the exclusion as well as the selection of prospective tenderers. The system is open to abuse (even unintentionally), not least because the legislation simply co-ordinates procedures. Therefore it has been left to the Court of Justice to provide a fuller picture.

It should be noted that the form of references which a tenderer may adduce in order to provide proof of its financial and economic standing is not exhaustive (*SA CEI* v. *Fond des Routes* (27/86)). On the other hand, a contracting authority may not require a tenderer from another member state to furnish proof of good standing by any means other than those contained in the relevant provisions of the directive (*SA Transporoute* v. *Minister for Public Works* (76/81)).

One case which is worthy of some detailed attention is *Gebroeders Beentjes BV* v. *The Netherlands* (Case 31/87) since it provides an in-depth guidance about assessing a tenderer's past work experience in contracts which are to be awarded. In this case, Beentjes' tender had been rejected by the contracting authority even though it was the lowest. The authority asserted that Beentjes lacked sufficient specific experience for the work in question even though the invitation did not lay down any qualitative criteria but in fact referred to general conditions containing a general reservation relied upon by the state in this case.

The Court observed that the examination of the suitability of contractors to carry out the contract to be awarded and the awarding of the contract are two different operations in the procedure. Whilst the directives do not rule out the possibility that examination of the tenderer's suitability and the award of the contract may take place simultaneously, the award should take place after suitability has been checked. The reason for this order is not to limit the power of a member state to fix the level of a contractor's financial and economic standing and technical knowledge required before it can take part in procedures for the award of public works contracts, but to determine the references or evidence which may be furnished in order to establish such standing, knowledge or ability.

As regards assessing specific experience relating to the work to be carried out, the Court confirmed that this is a legitimate criterion for checking contractors' suitability. What was more significant was its guidance on whether the authority had to disclose the fact that this would form part of the selection criteria. The Court said that, although the directives require the authorities contracts to specify in the contract notice which references concerning the contractor's technical knowledge and ability are to be produced, it does not require them to list in the notice the criteria on which they propose to base their assessment of the contractors' suitability.

However, it added that, in order for the notice to fulfil its role of enabling contractors in the community to determine whether a contract is of interest to them, it must contain at least some mention of the specific conditions which a contractor must meet in order to be considered suitable to tender for the contract in question. On the other hand, the Court did not offer any guidance on what difference this ruling would make on the use of pre-qualification questionnaires. In principle, the use of PQQs will indicate an extensive or detailed selection process which it would be extremely difficult to summarise in the contract notice. However, where contract notice invites expressions of interest subject to fuller information being provided in response to such, at which time the authority will also be supplying a PQQ, a sufficiently detailed indication of the object of the contract, plus a reference to the delivery of a PQQ should satisfy the advertising rules.

As for the criteria for the award of contracts, the Court ruled that the directives provided that the authorities awarding contracts must base their decision either on the lowest price only or, when the award is made, on various criteria according to the contract: e.g. price, period for completion, running costs, profitability or technical merit. However, although the most economically advantageous tender alternative leaves the authority free to choose the criteria on which they propose to base their award of the contract, they cannot at this point introduce criteria which should really form part of the tender specification: for instance an authority cannot use environmental concerns as the overriding criterion. Their choice is limited to criteria which identify the offer which is economically the most advantageous.

Chapter 8
Public Procurement in International Law

The Agreement on government procurement

Within the context of the General Agreement of Tariffs and Trade (GATT) procurement is singled out for special treatment because of the considerable wealth it creates. In command and capital economies alike, the state is the single biggest purchaser of goods and services, thus procurement rules have become an important feature of the rounds of talks. The Government Procurement Agreement of 1983 brought about ECU 30 million additional public business. The 1994 one is expected to engender ECU 350 billion as well as major savings through economies of scale, greater efficiency and more competitive bidding. The regime mirrors the one operating in the EU.

The Agreement of Government Procurement ('GPA') was originally drawn up because it was recognised that there was a need for an effective multilateral framework of rights and obligations in respect of laws, regulations, procedures and practices regarding government procurement, with a view to achieving greater liberalisation and expansion of world trade and improving the international framework for its conduct.

It was also recognised that governments should not maintain laws which afford protection to domestic products and services at the expense of foreign ones, nor should they discriminate between different foreign products, services or suppliers.

The agreement of 1994 was signed by twenty-three nations: Austria, Canada, the EC twelve, Finland, Hong Kong, Israel, Japan, Korea, Norway, Sweden, Switzerland, and the USA. Other parties are free to join at any time. Particular note should be taken of the application of the GPA as regards the US and the EU. Under a separate agreement on government procurement, concluded in the form of an exchange of letters, the EC and the US have agreed that their respective Appendix 1 entries (see below) in the GPA should be amended as between each other. Essentially the agreement extends the principles of the GPA to certain states and cities in the US otherwise not included in the GPA for the exclusive benefit of EC undertakings. As a side note, it is nowhere suggested that these concessions breach the fundamental rules central to the GPA and mentioned below.

Scope

The Agreement applies to any law, regulation, procedure or practice regarding any procurement achieved by any contractual means. It covers both services (including construction) and supplies in the five utility sectors – water, ports, airports, electricity and urban transport.

The GPA also provides for the enforcement of remedies. Yet these relate solely to those rights and procedures which it itself creates. It is therefore a stand-alone regime. Countries that sign up to the GPA agree to adapt their internal procurement procedures to those of the GPA. Whilst this may lead to improved enforcement procedures at a national (or European) level those changes should be seen purely in their domestic context, for they neither preclude nor usurp the role of the GPA as a conduit for resolving disputes.

For a complaint to be brought under the aegis of the GPA there are two important pre-conditions.

- Firstly the purchasing entity must be one covered by the agreement.
- Secondly, the procurement contract in question must be of a value which is not less than the relevant threshold.

The type of entities covered by the GPA (and listed in Appendix 1 therein) are too numerous and diverse to list here. Each contracting state has put forward those entities which it is willing to be subject to the GPA regime. These are grouped into three categories:

- central government entities,
- sub-central government entities, and
- other entities.

Likewise with regard to the types of contract which are covered (on condition that is that they are offered by a listed procuring entity), each state has drawn from a Universal List of Services those services which it is content to expose to the rigour of the GPA. It will be noted that the GPA only refers to services, but this includes construction services, which of course relate to works contracts.

Finally, thresholds have been assigned to each category of entity and service. These are expressed as Special Drawing Rights (SDR 1 = ECU 1.1). The GPA thresholds are slightly less than them in the EU directives by about one percent. A directive giving effect to these changes has been proposed. At the time of writing there is some dispute as to whether the proposed directive will actually take EC law further than required by GATT/WTO. One school of thought is that the EC procurement directives already provide for the fundamental principles of the directive.

The thresholds used in the GPA are as follows:

- Central government: services –SDR 130 000
                             works   –SDR 5 000 000

- Sub-central government: services –SDR 200 000
                             works   –SDR 5 000 000

- Other entities   services –SDR 400 000
                             works   –SDR 5 000 000

In determining the value of contracts it is necessary to take into account all forms of remuneration, including any premiums, fees, commission and interest receivable. States expressly declare that selection of the valuation method by the entity will not be used with the intention of avoiding the application of the GPA. Special provision is made for the award of more than one contract, contracts in parts and fixed-term contracts.

Grounds for complaint

The two most central features of the agreement are the fundamental principles of 'national treatment and non-discrimination' and 'rules of origin' If experience of the old regime is anything to go by, these will often form the basis of a 'cause of action' under the aegis of the GPA. This said, the Agreement envisages that these are not the sole grounds for complaint by providing that the challenge procedures explained below can be invoked for any 'breach of this Agreement'. Thus, one should also have in mind breaches of procedure (mentioned briefly below), including failing to award a contract according to the GPA regime.

In respect of non-discrimination Article III provides:

'Each Party [i.e. each state signatory] shall provide immediately and unconditionally to the products, services and suppliers of other Parties offering products or services of the Parties, treatment no less favourable than that accorded to domestic products, services and suppliers, or that accorded to products, services and suppliers of any other Party.'

By extension, locally-established suppliers are not to be discriminated against on the grounds that they either have foreign affiliation or ownership or on the basis of the country of production of the goods or service being supplied. As for local enterprises without any foreign connection, their interests are not expressly provided for, thus, technically, reverse discrimination could be said to exist under the GPA. For a remedy in such a situation then recourse should be had to those remedies under European and national law.

The term 'rules of origin' refers to provisions which serve to distinguish foreign products or services from domestic ones for a variety of reasons when a state does not want to give equal treatment to foreign products and services. It is to overcome these rules of origin that the 'most favoured nation clause' concept was devised to ensure that every state was treated on the same terms as a state's most favoured trading partner.

Rules of origin can manifest themselves as technical requirements, economic evaluations or customs classifications – or any combination of these. However so defined or applied it is requirements of this type which often come under the category of quantitative restrictions and measures having equivalent effect under Article 30 of the EC Treaty, which are of course prohibited.

Under Article IV of the GPA

'A Party shall not apply rules of origin to products or services imported or supplied for different purposes of government covered by this Agreement from other Parties, which are different from the rules of origin applied in the normal course of trade to imports or supplies of the same products or services from the same Parties.'

which means a nation's rules of origin (by which it identifies which state imports originate from) must be those it applies in the normal course of trade. It must not draw up special rules to be more (or less) fair to any party to the GPA.

These two principles, fundamental as they are, permeate all aspects of the Agreement. To wit:

- technical specifications must not create obstacles to international trade;
- tendering procedures much not be applied in a discriminatory manner;
- in the process of qualifying suppliers, entities shall not discriminate among suppliers of other parties or between domestic suppliers and suppliers of other parties;
- to ensure optimum effective international competition under selective tendering procedures entities shall invite tenders from the maximum number of domestic and foreign suppliers;
- in determining the time limit for the preparation of tenders, entities shall take account of the normal time for transmitting tenders by mail from foreign points.

These rules are, however, not without exceptions: under the GPA, special or differential treatment may be applied for developing countries.

Thereafter tendering procedures under the GPA are similar to the ones under European Union law. Thus, contracts can be awarded by way of open, selective or limited procedures. Invitations to participate have to be published, but may take only the form set out in the GPA. Entities may be permitted to negotiate in order to identify the strengths and weaknesses of particular tenderers, but all aspects of the tender process must be regular and transparent.

These then are the parameters and ground rules which contracting states must implement into their national laws and regulations and breach of which will form substantive grounds for complaint. If implemented properly by the contracting states then the regime established by the GPA should lead to an open and competitive world market for all government contracts over the financial thresholds. However, for those who come across difficulties or who wish to challenge the award of a government contract then they may avail themselves of the challenge procedures which the GPA provides.

There are two forms of challenge procedures which will be looked at. Firstly the Dispute Resolution System for contracting states, and secondly the challenge system for suppliers. The second form will be looked at from a national and EC perspective.

Challenging GPA contracts at the international level

There is no direct right of recourse or *locus standi* for private individuals and undertakings within the legal structure established under the GPA or the WTO. The WTO is a forum for contracting states to air their grievances and seek dispute resolution and compensation.

Article XXII

Under the GPA:

'If any Party [that is a contracting state] considers that any benefit accruing to it, directly or indirectly, under this Agreement is being nullified or impaired, or that the attainment of any objective of this Agreement is being impeded as a result of the failure of another Party or Parties to carry out its obligations under the Agreement, or the application by another Party or Parties of any measure, whether or not it conflicts with the provisions of the Agreement, it may with a view to reaching mutually satisfactory resolution of the matter, make written representation or proposals to the other Party or Parties which it considers to be concerned. Such action will be promptly notified to the Dispute Settlement Body of the DSU [Dispute Settlement Understanding]. Any Party thus approached shall give sympathetic consideration to the representation or proposals made to it' (Article XXII GPA).

In short, this clause enables a member state not only to raise complaints of a general nature, about either the application or implementation of the GPA, but also (by virtue of the words 'directly or indirectly') complaints about a specific award by a procuring entity in another contracting state. In this latter scenario the state can pursue a complaint on behalf of an aggrieved supplier.

The DSU

The form and procedure for this means of redress is contained in Article XXII of the GPA, above. This provision begins with a reminder of the fact that this level of dispute resolution is very much for states alone in that the specific dispute resolution rules found in the GPA are subject to the Understanding on Rules and Procedures Governing the Settlement of Disputes under the WTO Agreement (the Dispute Settlement Understanding (DSU)) – the dispute resolution procedure under the parent agreement.

The DSU is conventionally regarded as a two-stage procedure. To confuse matters the stages are sometimes referred to in parallel, and sometimes separately. Either way the two components are:

- consultation, good office, conciliation and mediation – which is often described as the conciliation and negotiation approach; and
- panel proceedings – often described as the adjudication approach. Purists would argue that a real dispute resolution procedure is only to be found in panel proceedings. Whilst in theory that might be correct, it should not be forgotten that disputes at the international level are just as much resolved through diplomacy and negotiation (colloquially termed 'horsetrading') as by open argument. In this light the conciliation/negotiation stage is equal in its importance and role with the second stage.

The DSB

The DSU system serves to preserve the rights and obligations of the WTO members under the WTO Agreements and is administered by the Dispute Settlement Body. Its first priority is to bring about the withdrawal of measures inconsistent with these agreements, an objective which is reinforced by the sanctions of compensation and suspension of obligations. Thus, in the context of the GPA, a contracting state which is particularly flagrant and repetitive in its breaches of the principle of open and fair competition in the awarding of procurement matters may ultimately face suspension from not just the GPA but also the WTO as well.

Lobbying

A complaint must in the first instance be raised with the relevant party. That may be easier said than done because bringing a complaint to the attention of an allegedly errant state involves two significant assumptions. It implies that the aggrieved supplier has:

- firstly, the wherewithal to approach its home state – that is the state in which it is established; and
- secondly, the ability and the case to convince its home state that it has been discriminated against in a tender administered by a procuring entity of another contracting state.

The art of persuading government ministers to take up a particular cause has become known as lobbying. As a service lobbying has always existed but only recently, in Europe, has it become an acceptable, even fashionable, profession. There is not room enough here to explain the art in detail, but it is essentially litigation by more subtle and informal means – the government official might be regarded as a judge who needs to be convinced of the merits of a case. Fortunately, however, the official is not there to adjudicate but simply to judge whether a supplier has a grievance that the state should take up. In this regard it might be said that a state has a vested interest in taking up complaints on behalf of aggrieved suppliers against other contracting states to the GPA since it is in its interests that its own suppliers win contracts in other states, if necessary by challenging awards believed to be irregular. That is not to say that advice and representation should not be sought from professionals with experience (and connections) in handling cases before government officials.

Thereafter, once the case has been taken up by the home state the matter should be brought to the attention of the contracting state whose procuring entity is said to have acted irregularly. A complaining supplier is likely to have little or no involvement in the dialogue between states, but at the very least it should keep in close touch with its home government department, supplying it with the information and documentation necessary to prosecute the complaint. As required by Article XXII the contracting state alleged to be in breach of the GPA should give 'sympathetic consideration to the representations or proposals made to it'. Clearly, this offers no guarantee of a solution and will depend upon the extent to which the state supports and defends the way in which its procuring entity handled the tender in issue. Assuming that this fails then it is open to the state of the aggrieved supplier to initiate proceedings before a panel of experts in government procurement.

Panel procedure

These proceedings are initiated by way of request made to the DSB. The DSB has sole authority to establish panels and adopt reports made thereby or by an Appellate Body also established by itself. It can also make recommendations or give rulings on a matter and maintain surveillance of rulings and recommendations being implemented. Finally it can authorise suspension of concessions and other obligations under the GPA or award compensation when withdrawal of measures found to be in contravention of the GPA is not possible.

The DSB will establish a panel by appointing (usually three) persons qualified in the area of government procurement and issuing its terms of reference. The GPA provides that the terms of reference should be:

'To examine, in the light of the relevant provisions of this agreement and of [any other Agreement cited by the parties to the dispute], the matter referred to the DSB by [name of party] in document ... and to make such findings as will assist the DSB in making the recommendations or in giving the rulings provided for in the Agreement.'

Under the old GATT, panels were convened in just three cases. The first, in 1984, arose out of a complaint from the USA against the EEC about the latter's practice of excluding value-added tax from the contract price of EC member state government purchases in relation to the determination of whether such purchases fell under the GPA (Panel on Value-Added Tax and Threshold, Ref. GPR/21 26 June 1984). In that case the Panel found against the EEC. In the second, the EC complained against the US about the latter's Buy America policy and the manner in which the US National Science Foundation procured a sonar mapping system (United States – Procurement of a Sonar Mapping System, Ref. GPR.DS1/R 23 April 1992). Again the Panel found for the complainant. In the final case, the US successfully complained that Norway had violated the GPA in the way the city of Trondheim procured toll collection equipment (Norway – Procurement of Toll Collection Equipment for the City of Trondheim, Ref. GPR.DS2/R 28 April 1992). (For a study of the Trondheim case see 'Government Procurement Agreement. The Trondheim case: the remedies issue' by Dr. Petro C. Mavrodis, Aussenwirtschaft (1993) 48/01)

Clearly, examples of the panel in action are few and far between and so those interested in knowing more of how a panel deals with particular arguments (not that its treatment of the law is binding) are confined to reading these three cases.

The panel acts as a tribunal of fact, whose findings are delivered to the DSB to act upon. It should must be kept well in mind that, just as with the appointment of an arbitrator, the panel is bound to act within its terms of reference. Thus an aggrieved supplier must ensure that it makes clear from the start the full extent of its grievances so that all allegations are included amongst the issues the panel must enquire into.

Once the panel is appointed and its terms of reference known it will receive a document with details of the matter referred to it. It will then meet with the parties, and meet again as often as it requires, although the need to report within four months (or if there is a delay then within seven months) will naturally limit the number of times it can meet. In any event, panels will usually be required to give the fullest possible opportunity for the parties to present their evidence and arguments, be consulted, and, if possible, develop a mutually satisfactory solution, but at the same time it should make every effort to accelerate the proceedings to the greatest extent possible.

Once all argument has been heard the panel will deliberate in private and then draw up its report. This is divided into five parts:

- the introduction (comprising terms of reference, the basic allegations, and the dates when the panel met with the parties);
- the factual aspects based on respective versions presented to the panel by the parties;
- the main arguments in law and fact of the parties;
- the findings of the panel in fact with reference to the GPA supported by its own reasoning; and finally,
- the panel's conclusions on whether the procuring entity did or did not comply with the GPA, and if not, to what extent the complaint has been proved.

It will then recommend to the DSB to take the measures necessary to ensure that the entity concerned conducts government procurement in accordance with its findings. It appears to be standard practice for the panel to make this general recommendation rather than particularise measures which should be taken. The specifics are left to the DSB to which the report is submitted.

Unfortunately, if past performance of the GPA is anything to go by, the availability of remedial measures is likely to be less than desired. Nowhere in the GPA are the applicable remedies in cases of violations enumerated, and it appears that complainants must look to private international law for a remedy because the GATT/WTO as a whole does not provide anything more effective. The DSB might order reparation and *restitutio in integrum*, but these depend upon compliance by the state concerned which will only be forthcoming if the ultimate threat of suspension is itself likely to be enforced. Alternatively, a possible way of overcoming the shortage of defined remedies in international law is for the complaining state to ask for specific or sufficient remedies. Otherwise the very least that the DSB can do is to guarantee the non-repetition of a violation by the state in breach, which, for the supplier hoping for more opportunities to tender in the state concerned, may be something worth having.

Challenging GPA contracts at the national level

Article XX

In the past, dispute resolution under the GATT and GPA was an international affair. Certainly the few cases heard under the old regime witnessed complaints on the part of aggrieved suppliers or prospective suppliers being brought before a specially constituted *ad hoc* panel by the supplier's home state against the host state said to have been in breach of the terms of the previous GPA.

The new regime is much more sophisticated in that it is envisages that a claim or complaint can be brought by the aggrieved supplier against the procuring entity before a local court or tribunal of that entity, in addition to the forum for disputes between contracting states.

These national challenge procedures are not spelt out in detail in the GPA. It merely provides for the framework which contracting states must apply and meet within their own jurisdictions. The GPA does, however, envisage two stages to the resolution of a complaint under the aegis of the Agreement. The first stage is consultation:

> 'In the event of a complaint by a supplier that there has been a breach of the Agreement in the context of a procurement, each Party shall encourage the supplier to seek resolution of its complaint in consultation with the procuring entity. In such instances the procuring entity shall accord impartial and timely consideration to any such complaint, in a manner that is not prejudicial to obtaining corrective measures under the challenge system.' (Article XX)

There is nothing to indicate that consultation is a pre-requisite to a challenge – least of all on the part of the supplier who, it seems, can proceed to direct action straight away. It leaves the supplier with the option of seeking amicable redress at a local level – with the added attraction that such consultation is without prejudice to later action.

The challenge procedure itself is contained in Article XX of the GPA. This states that each Party shall provide non-discriminatory, timely, transparent and effective procedures enabling suppliers to challenge alleged breaches of the Agreement arising in the context of procurement in which they have, or have had, an interest. Each party is to provide its challenge procedures in writing and make them generally available.

The procedure

To that single requirement are added certain other conditions with regard to initiating a procedure, the composition and procedures of the court and the available remedies.

Firstly, contracting states are left the option to require that a supplier initiate the challenge procedure and notify the procuring entity within specified time limits, although these time limits must run from the time when the basis of the complaint is known or reasonably should have been known and should not be less than 10 days.

Secondly, the challenge should be heard by a court or 'impartial and independent review body with no interest in the outcome of the procurement and the members of which are secure from external influence during the term of the appointment'. 'Court' implies one which is properly constituted by law with the powers of such, whereas the facility of creating a review body enables contracting states to cordon off GPA disputes in a special forum. However, Article XX adds that this review body must observe certain characteristics. These characteristics are essentially devised to make the tribunal accountable and observe the principles of natural justice. Hence, participants must have a right to be heard or be represented, present witnesses and documents, have access to all proceedings which can take place in public and have the tribunal put into writing the reasons for its opinion or decision.

Finally, the challenge procedures must provide for:

- rapid interim measures to correct breaches of the Agreement and to preserve commercial opportunities;
- an assessment and a possibility for a decision on the justification of the challenge; and
- correction of the breach of the Agreement or compensation for the loss or damages suffered, which may be limited to the costs for tender preparation or the protest.

The contracting state has an overall duty to give effect to these requirements in national law. In the case of the EC this is brought about through amendment of existing directives, which in turn must be implemented into the national laws of the member states. Nevertheless, since the member states have signed up to the GPA in their own right, it could be argued that this duty impacts on them directly.

'Direct effect' of the GPA

The question remains whether the GPA itself is of any legal relevance in what will otherwise be national proceedings. In other words, do the provisions have direct effect – to borrow the terminology of the Court of Justice of the European Community.

In this regard, the answer turns on how national law treats international agreements and in particular whether the legal tradition of the state in question is monist or dualist. That is to say does an international agreement to which the state is a party to become 'law' simply on accession or signature (the monist doctrine) or does it need to be ratified as a piece of substantive legislation in the normal way before it can become law (the dualist approach). International law recognises both approaches and it cannot be argued that suppliers in a dualist state are being disadvantaged compared to those in a monist state. The question is of particular relevance, however, should a contracting state fail to facilitate an accessible and effective remedy. In this situation then the only course open to the aggrieved supplier is to have the host state take the dispute to the DSB.

In conclusion, therefore, an aggrieved supplier must look for a remedy to national provisions implementing the essence of Article XX. Should this fail to bring satisfaction then there may be an avenue to pursue a claim indirectly through the Dispute Settlement Procedures.

Challenging GPA procurement procedures – EC

European Community membership of the WTO arises out of its exclusive competence to deal with common commercial policy (under Article 113 of the EC Treaty). It was therefore the European Commission which participated in negotiations and signed on the Community's behalf, although representatives of the member states also signed. Under Article IX of the GATT Final Act, the EC may vote on behalf of its member states in the Ministerial Council and the General Council of the WTO. In these forums, as an exception to the principle that each member of the WTO have one vote, the EC 'shall have a number of votes equal to the number of the member states which are members of the WTO'.

The participation of the EC in the WTO and GPA offers an interesting and useful dimension. As the richest trading block involved and with *locus standi* before the institutions of the GATT and WTO, the EC offers considerable weight and influence in the determination of disputes under the GPA

Dispute Settlement Procedures. If its support is forthcoming, this will be additional to the support which will hopefully be available to a complainant from its own national government. The way to enlist the support of the Community would be to contact the Commission directly. A complaint should be directed to the Secretariat-General, but any action taken would be by the External Affairs Directorate General of the Commission, via the Delegation Office in the state concerned.

However, the EC's participation is also interesting in that a complaint falling to be resolved by a national court concerning an award covered by the GPA might actually fall to be considered by the European Community institutions. Here one must briefly consider whether the normal openings available can be accessed here.

Although the GPA has not been formally entered into Community law the Court has ruled (in *International Fruit Company & Others*. v. *Commission* (ECR [1971] 421)) that the Community is bound by GATT. However, this is not to say that the GPA or any provision in the GATT/WTO Agreement has direct effect. The Court has consistently held (most recently in Case C-469/93 *Amministrazione delle Finanze dello Stato* v. *Chiquita Italia SpA*, 12 December 1995, ECJ, not yet reported) that GATT does not contain provisions of such a nature as to confer rights on individuals which they can rely on before national courts in order to challenge the application of conflicting national provisions. This is because it takes the view that GATT is based on the principle of negotiations undertaken on the basis of reciprocal and mutually advantageous arrangements, characterised by the great flexibility of its provisions, in particular those conferring the possibility of derogation, the measures to be taken when confronted with exceptional difficulties and the settlement of conflicts between the contracting states. Most of all the possibility of a contracting party withdrawing or being suspended from the agreement ultimately renders it conditional and insufficiently precise for the purposes of direct effect.

On the other hand, the Court has also held that it has exclusive jurisdiction to interpret GATT in EC law (see Case 267-269/91 *Amminstrazione delle Finanze dello Stato* v. *Societa Petrolfera Italiana SpA* [1983] SPA 801 [1993] ECR 801) and the lack of direct effect does not affect the EC's obligation to ensure that the provisions of GATT are observed in its relationship with non-member States which are parties to GATT (see Case 266/81 *Societa Italiana per l'Oleodotto Trasalpino* v. *Ministerio delle Finanze & Ors* ECR [1983] ECR 731).

From the jurisprudence it is established that a national court can refer a case to the ECJ for a preliminary ruling on the interpretation of a GATT/WTO Agreement/GPA provision. However it is uncertain whether an aggrieved supplier from outside the EC could bring a direct action against a Community institution before the Court of Justice, bearing in mind that the EC institutions are also covered by the GPA. There is no precedent directly on this point, but it has been given a significant amount of academic thought (for an overview see 'The Status of GATT in EC Law, Revisited', Fernando Castillo de La Torre, *J.W.T.* 53, 1994) and on balance it must be considered that it is arguable that a direct action would lie before the Court of Justice.

Chapter 9
The Principles of Cross-Border Trade

Introduction

The European Community is not anything if it is not a trading block with measures to free up the movement of goods and services between different sovereign states just as we take such freedom for granted between England and Scotland.

This chapter will therefore focus on the trade dimension of the European Community and will be followed by chapters focusing on how these trade aspects have been applied in the context of the construction industry.

By referring to the fundamental freedoms, we come to the very *raison d'être* of the European Community. This book initially considered competition and public procurement, but neither would be relevant without the basic principle of free trade across national borders.

Basic principles of free movement

Free movement is invariably one of the first significant consequences of a international pact between two sovereign states. There are examples in the Roman Empire, the Hanseatic League (in Germanic Europe during the Middle Ages), and in the Treaty of Union between England and Scotland in 1707.

The same is true for the European Community. In 1957, the Community set about establishing a Common Market in which the free movement of goods, workers, services, and capital could be assured. Today it is more usual to speak of the Internal or Single Market which was put in place from 1 January 1993. The internal market – styled as an area without internal frontiers – differs slightly from its common market predecessor in that it confers free movement on 'persons' and not merely 'workers'. 'Free movement' is characterised by the means to move factors of production and pursue all kinds of economic activity across national borders without direct and indirect restrictions, or direct or indirect financial charges, and free from all direct, indirect or disguised discrimination on grounds of nationality.

To exercise the right to free movement in a transaction, it has to be shown to meet certain requirements relevant to that right; individuals or companies must first demonstrate that they are in a position to exercise rights in European law by reference to the activities they pursue:

- a trader seeking to import or export goods into one member state must first show that the goods *originate* from a member state within the Union;
- an individual seeking work or a professional seeking to set up business in one member state must first show he or she is a *national* of another member state (and therefore a citizen of the Union); or,
- a company or self-employed person seeking either to offer services or to establish a branch, agency or other secondary office in one member state must first demonstrate *establishment* in another member state.

Each of these notions will be explained within the context of the legal right to which they belong. However, it will be observed that each transaction is set in a cross-border situation featuring a *host* state (the state towards which the transaction is directed) and a *home* state (the state of origin, nationality or establishment). This is no accident but serves to delineate the jurisdictional boundaries of European law relating to free movement (cf. other disciplines such as competition, procurement, employment, etc.). So entrenched is this requirement that the 'principle of reverse discrimination' has emerged preventing persons or companies that have never exercised their right to free movement from enforcing those rights against the authorities of the member state where they are national or established (*Knoors* v. *SS for Economic Affairs* (115/78) [1979] ECR 399). The principle of reverse discrimination should therefore be regarded as a major limitation to the right of free movement (see also Chapter 2).

Nevertheless, the basic principles of free movement are to be found in the Treaty of European Union, supplemented by several pieces of secondary legislation, and given considerable impetus by the Court of Justice in its rulings.

Free movement of goods

Trade in goods is the cornerstone of any free market economy and, reflecting its importance, the free movement of goods features as the first community policy to be dealt with in the EC Treaty.

The Community has sought to achieve free movement in goods by basing itself on a customs union. A customs union is, short of full economic and monetary union, the most advanced form of economic integration between sovereign states, and consists of two dimensions, one external and one internal.

The external dimension is characterised by a common external tariff. In spite of the ever-increasing globalisation of trade and economies and not-withstanding the work of GATT and now the World Trade Organisation in reducing barriers to trade, there comes a point in any trading block in which a distinction has to be drawn between goods originating from a member of that block and goods originating elsewhere. That distinction is marked by a common external tariff. Hence, any goods being imported into (or exported from) the European Community, that is to say between the territories of any of the member states and a nation outside, will attract the Common Customs Tariff (CCT).

Article 9 TEU establishes the customs union and the common external tariff. However detailed implementation of the CCT, including the nomenclature of goods, tariff rates, and all procedural aspects will be found in Regulation 2913/92 of the Community Customs Code – to which reference should be made in the first instance.

'Goods' are anything which has commercial value or can be made the subject matter of a transaction (*R* v. *Thompson* [1978] ECR 2247). They will be regarded as originating within the European Union if they are produced or manufactured in one of the member states or in any of the colonial territories with special arrangements with the Union. Note that parts which are incorporated into goods or are assembled within the EU, or goods which are processed here, will be regarded as originating within the EU. Products coming from a third country shall be considered to be entering into free circulation (which is equivalent to originating in) in a member state if the import formalities have been complied with and any custom duties or charges payable have been levied in that member state and paid (Article 10 TEU).

The internal dimension of the customs union is characterised by three prohibitions. These impact on the tools and mechanisms which nation states employ to protect domestic industries or to raise revenue: customs duties, quotas, and import taxes.

Customs duties

A customs duty is a financial charge which is levied on goods by virtue of the fact that they have crossed a border (Cases 2 & 3/69 *Sociaal Fonds voor de Diamantarbeiders* v. *SA Ch Brachfeld & Sons and Chougal Diamond Co.* [1969] ECR 211).

By Article 12 TEU (reinforced by Article 9 TEU) member states are prohibited as between each other from introducing new customs duties on imports and exports, or charges having equivalent effect. This is supplemented by the requirement progressively to abolish custom duties on imports (Article 13 TEU) and exports (Article 16 TEU). The last two requirements are, in essence, 'spent' in that they have achieved their objective, so today one need only refer to Article 12 TEU and this is likely to be infrequent since the prohibition on customs duties is so well established. They may, however, arise from time to time, (especially in connection with the prohibition on import taxes) and when they do may be challenged by relying directly on Article 12, since this provision has direct effect (*van Gend en Loos* [1963] ECR 1).

The charge need not have been levied 'at the border', but at any place where inspections or formalities of a customs nature are carried out. This could be well within the member state at an airport or customs warehouse. The purpose or reason for the charge is irrelevant, as is its size. Thus a nominal, but compulsory administrative charge for monitoring imports would be unlawful (*Commission* v. *Italy (Statistical Levy)* (24/68) [1969] ECR 193), even if is not imposed for the benefit of the state, is not discriminatory or protective, and if the product on which the charge is imposed is not in competition with any domestic product.

The only charges which can be imposed by virtue of the fact that goods have crossed a border are those which are made for the benefit of an importer (e.g. certifying that goods meet a quality standard). However, it would be wrong to describe these as customs duties, so therefore prohibition remains complete and intact. Service charges can be imposed if they are mandatory as part of an EC or international regime (in which case the cost can be recovered) or when they give an optional tangible benefit to the importer or the goods and are not imposed on him (in which case value is received). Examples of the former could be health or security controls, and of the latter, the supply of packaging for particular goods.

Quantitative restrictions

Introduction

As the Court of Justice has observed, it is the basic right of an importer to be able to introduce goods into one member state if they have been lawfully produced and marketed in another (*Rewe-Zentral AG* v. *Bundesmono-polverwaltung für Branntwein* ('*Cassis de Dijon*') (120/78) [1979] ECR 649) where a German prohibition on the marketing of liqueurs with an alcoholic strength of less than 25% made it impossible for the plaintiff to import a consignment of Cassis de Dijon, a French liqueur with a strength of 15–20% into the Federal Republic. The rule was challenged in the national courts which made a reference to the Court of Justice. Any national measure which in fact prevents, restricts or hinders that right therefore falls to be considered under Article 30 (in the case of imports) and Article 34 EC (in the case of exports). These Articles contain the basic prohibition against quantitative restrictions and measures having equivalent effect.

Quantitative restrictions are measures which restrict or hinder the amount of imports or exports which would otherwise take place. Ordinarily there are quotas – both minimum and maximum – but one should also include in this category any measure which makes the cross-border movement of goods subject to technical or commercial rules that act as barriers to trade.

In fact, quantitative restrictions, that is to say *de facto* quotas or other total or partial restraints or bans on the quantities that can be moved, had in the main been removed before the EC Treaty came into force. Thus the ambit of Article 30 EC has focused on what trading rules can firstly be considered as constituting measures equivalent to a quantitative restriction (in that they restrict the quantity of goods that can be moved across a border) and secondly, in cases where a rule can be so construed, whether a recognised exception can be applied to justify its continued application.

Measures coming within the prohibition

In short, an importer should be able successfully to challenge any obstacle to the free movement of goods if it is capable of 'hindering, directly or indirectly, actually or potentially, imports between member states'. This test was handed down by the Court of Justice in the landmark ruling of *Procurer du Roi* v. *Dassonville* (8/74) [1974] ECR 837 at 852.

By 'any obstacle' one can refer to any national legislative act, regulatory measure, or administrative practice the effect of which is to hinder imports. Thus it covers direct, binding measures which are themselves a breach of Article 30 or which appear to be compatible with that provision but are applied in a discriminatory way. It also covers direct, non-binding measures such as recommendations or advertising campaigns which either deter imports or encourage the purchase or consumption of domestically produced goods. Furthermore, it will cover any measure or practice which indirectly brings about the same result.

Thus the definition of measures having equivalent effect to quantitative restrictions is a very wide one. What is more, there is no *de minimis* rule automatically excluding cases where the restrictive effects are negligible, nor can a member state provide any exceptions or procedures for exemption which might negate or attempt to neutralise the effects of the basic restriction. In this sense it is a rule of strict application which can be invoked by any trader at any stage of the production process, from the supply of raw materials or manufacturing, through chains of distribution and transit, to final use or consumption.

In any particular situation, however, one might be faced with a rule which is distinctly applicable, in that it only applies to imports, or is indistinctly applicable, in that it applies to domestic and imported products alike. It will be noted that the *Dassonville* formula applies Article 30 EC to 'all trading rules' thus including both types of measures cited here. However, they are treated differently under Article 30 TEU.

Distinctly applicable measures (affecting only imports, making them more costly or difficult or subjecting them to unique or different conditions) are automatically considered as measures of equivalent effect and unlawful, but indistinctly applicable measures (affecting domestic and imported products alike) pose a particular problem since the element of discrimination is not overt. Suffice it to say that in the case of indistinctly applicable measures a line is drawn between, on the one hand, rules laying down manufacturing and presentation requirements to be met by goods and, on the other hand, rules governing selling and marketing arrangements. Only the former can be considered as coming within the scope of Article 30. The latter do not.

The kind of indistinct requirements which are covered by Article 30 are those relating to designation, form, size, weight, composition, presentation, labelling and packaging, as in the *Cassis de Dijon* case. The reason is that if such goods have been lawfully manufactured and marketed in the member state of origin, they should be lawful in the state of import. On the other hand, indistinct arrangements which fall outside Article 30 are rules which restrict or prohibit the marketing of domestic or imported goods and apply to all affected traders operating within the same national territory and in the same manner, in law and in fact (*Keck & Mithouard* (C-267 & 268/91) [1993] ECR I 6097). Thus, shop opening hours is an example of lawful selling arrangements and not unlawful product specifications.

Having dealt with imports, one can complete the study on quantitative restrictions by adding that, in the case of exports (covered by Article 34), the prohibition only applies to distinctly applicable measures.

Exceptions

The rule that any trading measure (as defined above) which restricts trade is unlawful is subject to two sets of exceptions. One set was provided by the EC Treaty and the other developed in the case law of the Court of Justice. There are two lists because the one developed by the Court was devised to deal only with indistinctly applicable trading rules.

The Treaty list applies in any trading rule covered by the ambit of Article 30. It is set out Article 36 which provides that the prohibitions in Articles 30 (imports) and 34 (exports) shall not preclude restrictions on imports, exports or goods in transit justified on the following grounds:

- public morality, public policy or public security;
- the protection of health and life of humans, animals or plants;
- the protection of national treasures possessing artistic, historic or archaeological value;
- the protection of industrial and commercial property.

Of these the last chiefly concerns intellectual property law which will possibly be of most significance. In short, IP rights, as a product of legislation in an advanced and sophisticated economy, hinder trade. Yet so vital are they in protecting investment (without which there would be no technological development and innovation) that they are excepted from Articles 30 and 34 by Article 36. Given that European IP law is still in its formative stages the present situation is that the Court of Justice is prepared to fragment the single market in so far as this assists in preserving the basic protection that IP rights offer. Accordingly, the exception permits an IP rights holder to prevent any third party from interfering or threatening to interfere with the specific subject matter of a particular IP right (whether it be patent, trade mark, copyright, etc.) but limits the absolute protection to control goods subject to an IP right to allowing the owner to place goods on to the market for the first time. Thereafter, and subject to protecting the specific subject matter of the IP right, those goods placed onto the market are then in free circulation and no further restrictions on their movement may be imposed by national law.

The list comes with two *caveats*. Firstly, as Article 36 itself states, these permitted restrictions cannot used in an arbitrarily discriminatory way (i.e.

they must be objectively justified) nor act as a disguised restriction on trade between member states (i.e. they must be proportional and not too restrictive in achieving the desired objective). Secondly, the list as a whole is exhaustive and is to be construed strictly (as must all exceptions to basic rules in EC law).

The case law list, applying only to trading rules which themselves apply to both domestic and imported products, was drawn up by the Court of Justice in the landmark ruling of *Cassis de Dijon* (cited earlier). The Court recognised that certain rules fulfil objectives which have to be accepted on grounds that they are reasonable and necessary. The Court in *Cassis de Dijon* identified that these 'mandatory requirements' related to the effectiveness of fiscal supervision, the protection of public health, the fairness of commercial transactions, and the defence of consumer protection. Unlike Article 36, the case law list is not exhaustive, and has been added to, in respect of the protection of the environment (*Commission* v. *Denmark* (302/86) [1988] ECR 4607, [1989] 1 CMLR 619), and development of the arts (*Cinéthèque* (60 and 61/84) [1985] ECR 2605, [1986] 1 CMLR 365). In addition the Court has also recognised that certain differences between the laws of member states may be justified on account of the fact that they represent the social, cultural or political choices each will make (*Torfaen* (145/88) [1989] 3851, *Semararo Casa Uno Srl* v. *Sindaco Del Comune Di Erbusco* (C-418/93) (not yet reported)).

Finally to the list could be added national laws relating to product selling and marketing arrangements, which strictly do not come within the ambit of Article 30 in the first place.

Discriminatory taxation

The third prohibition is not an absolute one like the previous two, but a limited one. Member states do not lose the prerogative to tax products. However, they are required to do so in a way which does not discriminate against imported goods. The reason being that once goods have crossed the border the danger is that they will be singled out for taxation which puts them at a disadvantage compared to competing domestic products.

Thus the prohibition found in Article 95 EC is against discriminatory taxation which is applied in two ways.

- Firstly, member states must not impose on imports, either directly or indirectly, any internal taxation which is in excess of that imposed directly or indirectly on similar domestic products (Article 95(1) EC) – although it is free to do the reverse!
- Secondly, member states must not impose on imports any internal taxation which is of such a nature as to afford indirect protection to other products (Article 95(2)).

Whilst strictly speaking each application is different from the other, there is little differentiation between the two in practice.

Hence, any taxed imported product will be unlawfully discriminated against if the tax on similar domestic products is less or there are other, even possibly dissimilar, products which are being indirectly protected by the tax on the imported product. In either case, the link to be established between the taxed imported product and the lesser taxed or indirectly protected domestic product is one of substitutability. If one product is substitutable for another then they are said to be in competition with each other. Since the aim of the Treaty, and in particular Article 95, is to ensure normal conditions of competition, a higher tax on one than the other is anti-competitive, discriminatory and unlawful. It is in this regard that strict similarity or categorisation is not necessary. All that is necessary is partial, indirect or potential competition between the two, judged on whether the two products in question meet the same consumer or user needs (taking into account future technological advances or changes in consumer or user preferences).

Once a discriminatory tax is identified, an importer can challenge its imposition. No remedy lies to domestic producers even if the tax is truly discriminatory compared to other products. However, if there is no domestic production of a similar or competing product, an importer will have insufficient grounds to launch a challenge under Article 95 EC for the simple reason being that he is not being discriminated against. Furthermore, any challenge under Article 95 could fail in any event if the member state shows that the tax is objectively justified and proportional, is directed at achieving policy objectives acceptable under EC law, and involves no direct or indirect discrimination against imports (*Humblot* v. *Directeur des Services Fisceaux* (112/84) [1985] ECR 1367).

Articles 12, 30 and 95 in context

These three articles characterise the free movement of goods element found in the EC Treaty, and whilst they may appear at different points in the Treaty they stand shoulder to shoulder in eliminating distortions to trade. In this regard, the three prohibitions are mutually exclusive of each other, a factor which can cause some confusion when endeavouring to categorise a financial charge.

To identify the true nature of any financial charge, one needs to look at its name, its origin and the body of law it belongs to, the way in which it is applied and by whom, and its purpose and effect.

For instance, a charge which is only imposed on imported products could well be a customs duty. However, for Article 12, the charge must have been levied by virtue of the fact that the goods have crossed a border. If, in fact, the charge is only imposed on imports because the member state has no domestic production, then the charge could be re-categorised as a tax and member states are not denied the power to tax. In the absence of domestic production it is impossible to mount a claim of discriminatory taxation unless one of the two alternative grounds set out in Article 95 apply. All is not lost, however, if that financial charge could be again re-categorised as unlawful if its incidence is linked to a measure having equivalent effect to a quantitative restriction, in that it hinders trade between member states and cannot be justified by one of the exceptions.

Alternatively, a charge described and generally perceived as a tax, and which is imposed equally on domestic and imported products, could, in fact, be a customs duty if the charge paid by the domestic producer is made up in full later on (see *Cucchi* v. *Avez* (77/76) [1977] ECR 987), the reason being that, in effect, the charge is only being imposed on the importers. If, however, the charge paid by the domestic producers is only partially made up – in cash or in kind – then this could still equate to discriminatory taxation.

Finally, it will be noted that the reimbursing of charges paid by domestic producers, either in full or in part, involves directing state funds to assist private undertakings. Accordingly, in addition to challenging such a financial charge on the basis of Article 12, 30 or 95, an importer might also rely on Article 92, on the ground that the application of such state resources constitutes unlawful state aid (See Chapter 4).

Free movement of services and the right of establishment

Introduction

Combined these rights can be considered as the component parts to the more general right of free movement of 'businesses' since, import/export activities apart, it is through the provision of services or the establishment of subsidiaries, branches and agencies that most cross-border movement is effected.

They are invariably considered in tandem because of they have principles and exceptions in common. However it should not be assumed that only service providers may establish themselves in another member state. On the contrary, any manufacturer, supplier, producer, purchaser, processor, or user of goods *or* services which performs economic activities may exercise the right of establishment. However, insofar as a distinction needs to be need to be made between the two, 'establishment' has been defined as 'the actual pursuit of an economic activity through a fixed establishment in another member state for an indefinite period' (*R* v. *SS for Transport, ex parte Factortame* (C-221/89) [1991] ECR I-3905, para. 20) whereas service-providers actually crossing the border to effect those services will not be considered as being established there if they pursue their activities on a temporary basis (Article 60(3)).

In construction terms, the best way to illustrate the distinction is as follows:

- a contractor based in the UK, which wins a contract to construct a building in France and moves its workforce and equipment on-site simply to perform the contract, will be exercising the right to free movement of services – regardless of the length of the contract;

- a contractor based in the UK which sets up an office in France in order to bid for contracts over an indefinite length of time would be exercising its right of establishment.

The distinction becomes most apparent and significant with regard to compliance with regulatory, technical and company law matters and, in situations where it is uncertain which right is being exercised, the issue often in need of determination is to which national authority (the home or the host) is the operator accountable?

It is proposed to deal with the principles common to both concepts and then to discuss each right in isolation.

Common principles

The principles that follow are common to the free movement of services and the right of establishment. It is important to recognise that each of these primary rights may be exercised by any form of commercial vehicle, from sole trader to publicly quoted company. This results in a contrast between the self-employed professional and the limited company since, whilst they ought to be treated the same they plainly cannot as companies do not have anything other than technical nationality and there are many more ways in which a natural person can suffer discrimination – social, cultural and professional, as well as fiscal and commercial.

The status of companies

Article 58 of the Treaty requires companies or firms to be treated the same way as natural persons who are nationals of member states. For a company or firm to be conferred this equality then it should have been formed in accordance with the law of a member state and have its registered office, central administration or principal place of business within the Community.

The term 'company or firm' means companies or firms constituted under civil or commercial law including co-operative societies and other legal persons governed by public or private law, except those which are non-profit making. However the actual provision is just a little misleading. To avoid the situation in which companies have nothing more than a registered office within the EU but thereby obtain all the benefits under the Treaty, the Court of Justice has added that companies must also have their principal place of business somewhere in the EU (i.e. not necessarily in the same member state) (*Segers* (79/85) [1986] ECR 2375). For firms, including partnerships and self-employed professionals, then it is a requirement that they have their central administration or principal place of business within the EU.

The Union has gone some way to harmonise company law rules. There are now common rules for single-member companies and the publication of accounts. However, proposed instruments which might engender complete and unrestricted movement such as the European Company Statute (Société Europae) are far from being finalised even though they have been discussed for nearly twenty years.

Equality of treatment/non-discrimination

Any trader seeking to open up new markets and therefore compete with domestic operators will sooner or later be forced out unless the legal infrastructure treats him equally. In order to achieve this the constraints which regulate his profession or business should be proportional (that is to say, reasonable), objectively justified, and should not discriminate against him on the grounds of nationality or, in the case of companies, place of primary establishment.

This principle is expressly referred to in both the services and establishment provisions in the Treaty. It can be relied upon to argue the unlawfulness of any requirement which discriminates against a national or company from another member state as well as any requirement which is not in fact discriminatory but nevertheless is contrary to spirit and meaning of the single market, for instance the imposition of a layer of administrative, professional or technical regulation in addition to that required by the home state.

However, the right offers no more than a guarantee to be treated in exactly the same way as a national of a the host state and its scope varies according to whether it is relied upon within the context of the free movement of services or of establishment.

The principle of non-discrimination extends to the cover some of the social rights of individuals and their families. To this end, the Union has adopted Directives on the rights of entry and residence for cross-border service providers, the self-employed and their families (73/148 [1973] OJ 472/14), and on the right of self-employed persons and their families to stay on in a member state on retirement (75/34 [1975] OJ L14/10). Additionally, any self-employed persons are entitled to equality in respect of social and tax advantages.

The right to equality of treatment is subject to several exceptions. Provisions which are discriminatory may yet be justified on grounds of public policy, public security or public health, or that the activities arise from the sovereignty of the state (public service) – these derogations are provided for by the Treaty. Equally provisions which are not actually discriminatory but which distort the single market may be permitted by the wide range of public-interest exceptions which are justified in the 'general good'. Either way, however, they must be objectively justified, be applied according to objective criteria and be proportional. If the service provider or company exercising its right of establishment can show that these requirements are not met then the exception must be set aside by the national court.

Mutual recognition of diplomas

A special issue in ensuring equality of treatment arises with the universal reliance on qualifications to attest ability and experience. Clearly this will concern any self-employed professional seeking to be admitted to an association in a state other than that in which he obtained the qualification, and in this regard it is essentially an 'establishment' issue. However, it will also be relevant to any company which has to rely on the qualifications of its principals, officers and staff to submit tenders or undertake contracts.

It has been held that national requirements concerning qualifications may have the effect of hindering nationals of other member states from exercising their rights (*Vlassopoulou* v. *Ministerium für Justiz* (340/89) [1991] ECR 2357). This could be the case if the national rules took no account of the knowledge and qualifications already acquired by that person elsewhere. The Union has, however, gone some way to level the playing field in this respect and reference will be made to the Architects Directive in Chapter 11. Lawyers, vets and doctors have also undergone similar treatment. For general higher-education diplomas, awarded on completion of professional education and training of at least three years' duration (including degrees which are required for entry to a profession), then Directive 89/48 ([1989] OJ L19/16) introduced a general system of mutual recognition for application (in theory) to any trade or profession. It requires national authorities not to refuse permission to pursue a trade or profession to any persons in possession of diplomas awarded in another member state which satisfy certain conditions as to duration and training. However it does not prevent the authority from refusing permission on other grounds – unlike the sectoral directives as exemplified by that dealing with architects.

A further and similar directive was adopted in 1992 (92/51 [1992] OJ L209/25) to cover all post-secondary diplomas of at least one year in length, as well as educational and vocational training certificates which qualify the holder to take up a regulated profession.

To the extent that the directive does not offer mutual recognition then the Court of Justice has ruled that on an application to join a professional body, the relevant authority must take into account diplomas, certificates and other evidence of qualifications which the applicant has acquired in another member state and make a comparison between the specialised knowledge and abilities certified by those diplomas and the knowledge and qualifications required by the national rules. If they are found to be equivalent then the national authority must recognise the qualification (*Vlassopoulou* v. *Ministerium für Justiz* (340/89) [1991] ECR 2357).

Treaty based exceptions to discriminatory measures

The rights to establishment and free movement of services (as well as the right to free movement of workers (see later)), although extensive, are not absolute. Member states do retain a discretion to limit those rights on grounds of public policy, public security, or public health (Articles 48(3), 56(1), and 66) where the need arises to deal with specific characteristics of particular persons. It will be noted that companies are not included, but they will no doubt be affected since they can only operate through their employees.

The concern here is to ensure that member states deal fairly with individuals whose behaviour or fitness is such that it is likely to threaten (to put it briefly) democratic society and the health of the nation. The only methods which would fall to be considered as specific exceptions are deportation or refusal of entry, since these powers are obviously inapplicable to nationals. In contrast, penal measures would be viewed as equally applicable to both nationals and non-nationals and therefore non-nationals are not discriminated against if this, ultimately, interfered with their economic rights under the Treaty.

As exceptions to primary rights, these claims are construed narrowly, such that the national court should ensure that even if a member state claims grounds of public policy, public security or public health it treats nationals and non-nationals equally, albeit that nationals cannot be deported.

So if a member state considers certain personal conduct to be 'suspect from the point of view of morals' (*Adoui and Cornuaille* v. *Belgian State* (115 & 116/81) [1982] ECR 1665), or that a person's criminal behaviour (even though 'white collar') poses a threat (*R* v. *Bouchereau* (30/77) [1977] ECR 1999), then, so long as the state takes genuine and equally effective repressive measures against its own nationals, and concludes that the behaviour poses an immediate or present threat, then it may exercise its discretion to deport a non-national or refuse entry.

'General good' exceptions to non-discriminatory measures

It became apparent in the free movement of goods that, in order to ensure an efficient and meaningful single market, the prohibition in Article 30 should apply not just to distinctly applicable or discriminatory measures, but also to indistinctly applicable or non-discriminatory measures (unless they were justified by one of the mandatory requirements) on the ground that anything lawfully produced and marketed in one state ought to capable of being introduced and marketed in another member state.

It is also apparent that, in relation to the provision of professional and other services, parallel national regulatory regimes will hinder free movement and establishment since professionals and service providers qualified in one national regime are obviously not authorised to operate in another member state. This is despite the fact that such a regime applies to all professionals or service providers regardless of nationality, thus there is no apparent discrimination.

The Court of Justice is at pains to play down any correlation of treatment between goods and services, but the fact is that it has been willing to extend rules prohibiting discrimination on grounds of nationality – in respect of both the free movement of services and the right of establishment – to apparently non-discriminatory situations. It will do so whenever a particular requirement is:

- firstly, not objectively justified by the public interest;
- secondly, when public interest is not already adequately protected by the rules by which the service provider is already established (i.e. those of the home state); and
- thirdly, the result cannot be achieved by less restrictive means (*Commission* v. *Germany (Insurance Services)* (205/84) [1986] ECR 3755).

Thus, national courts are required to be watchful over equally applicable measures which are in fact not objectively justified. Conversely, any measure which meets these requirements will not be set aside. The sort of measures which would be permitted are those generally relating to the integrity of a profession's title of occupation, professional matters, or the protection of the consumer. No general rule can be given other than the three requirements set out above and so each provision falls to be considered on a case by case basis.

The right of establishment

Article 52 of the Treaty provides that restrictions on the freedom of establishment of nationals of a member state in the territory of another member state are to be abolished. Accordingly, they are therefore prohibited. The prohibition also applies to restrictions on the setting up of agencies, branches and subsidiaries by nationals of any one member state in the territory of another.

Article 52 goes on to state that freedom of establishment shall include the right to take up and pursue activities as self-employed persons and to set up and manage undertakings under the conditions laid down for its own nationals by the law of the state where such establishment is sought.

The Court of Justice has declared Article 52 to be clear, concise and unconditional and it is therefore directly effective (*Reyners* v. *Belgium* (2/74) [1974] ECR 631). The rights are equally conferred on companies and firms to set up agencies, branches and subsidiaries by virtue of Article 58 (see above).

As noted earlier, to be established is to be installed on a permanent basis in the host state. In common with the general scheme of the Treaty, in order to exercise the right at all a person or company must be pursuing economic activities. The right can be exercised in two ways. Nationals (i.e. natural persons) have the right to establish, take over or control a principal establishment in the corporate form permitted by the host state, and to manage that enterprise. Alternatively, nationals or any company with a principal establishment anywhere in the EU (formed in accordance with Article 58) may establish a secondary establishment, by means of an agency, branch or subsidiary in the host state. In either case they are entitled to be treated equally with nationals or companies of the state of establishment – subject to the limitations set out earlier.

Free movement of services

Article 59 of the Treaty provides for the abolition (and therefore prohibition) of all restrictions on the provision of services within the Union in respect of nationals of member states who are established in a member state other than that of the person for whom the services are intended.

The article actually provides for the 'progressive' abolition of restrictions, but the Court has long deemed the transitional stage to have passed. Therefore the right to provide unrestricted cross-border services is directly effective (*Van Binsbergen* v. *Bestuur van de Bedrijfsvereniging voor de Metaal-nijverheid* (33/74) [1974] ECR 1299).

On the other hand there has been no weakening of the requirement that the service-provider and the service-receiver must be in established in different member states. There are three permutations of how such services may be effected

- the service provider can 'move' across border towards the service receiver (e.g. to perform a building contract);
- conversely, the service receiver may move across border towards the service provider (the obvious example being a tourist, but this could cover any commercial service); or
- each party may stay in their respective home states and the service itself 'moves' (e.g. insurance services or, increasingly any advice and information provided on-line).

The first two permutations are expressly (if indirectly) envisaged by the Treaty in that a person providing a service may, in order to do so, temporarily pursue his activity in the state where the service is to be provided, but under the same conditions as are imposed by that state on its own nationals (Article 60(3)).

Notwithstanding the necessity of a cross-border element, the Court of Justice has been mindful not to make this the sole criterion for enforcing the prohibition against indistinctly applicable measures, especially when this results in a service provider abusing the scope and purpose of Article 59. The abuse arises when a service provider seeks to exploit the freedom that Article 59 confers by choosing to establish itself in the state with the most liberal or cost-effective regime, and then seeks in effect to provide services 'back' to the state in which it would ordinarily be established. In these circumstances, the Court has ruled that the fact that the service provider and service receiver are in different states should be disregarded so as to enable the authorities in the state where the service is provided (i.e. the state where the service provider would or should be established) to effect control over that person.

Often the regulatory provision the authorities will seek to enforce is the requirement for certain professionals to be habitually resident in the state where services are to be performed so that proper control and discipline can be effected. It will be observed that a residence requirement would breach Articles 52 and/or 59 since it is indirectly discriminatory over non-nationals. Therefore a residence requirement must first be objectively justified in the general good before the national authorities can insist on enforcing it against an individual or company established in another member state (and therefore technically outside the jurisdiction) for the sole purpose of providing services back to the home state.

As to what is meant by the term 'services', the Treaty provides that they should include activities of an industrial or commercial character, and the activities of craftsmen and the professions. They should also be normally provided for remuneration. The broad nature of the definition does pose problems of distinction with the tasks an employee might perform. Employees (i.e. workers) are not covered by Article 59 but by Article 48. The Court has held that the activities referred to in Article 59 are not to be distinguished by their nature from those in Article 48 but only by the fact that they are performed outside the ties of a contract of employment (*Walrave & Kock* v. *Association Union Cycliste Internationale* (36/74) [1975] 1 CMLR 320, para. 23). However, one activity excluded is transport – covered elsewhere in the Treaty. Note that a service provider may move its workforce and personnel to another member state for the purposes of pursuing its (temporary) services without having to register those workers under the tax and social security regimes of the host state (Article 54(3)(f)) – a point which will be returned to in Chapter 11.

Free movement of workers

As a essential factor of production, the right to freedom of movement of workers forms one of the fundamental aims of the European Community. Only a flexible, mobile labour force of well-trained individuals can strengthen economies and increase wealth.

In this regard, 'worker' is define as one who performs services under the direction of another, the employer, in return for remuneration. That is distinct from the self-employed professional, who simply provides services in return for a fee, who possesses different rights under the Treaty (see above). Likewise, the right of a company to move its workforce, whether large or small, to perform services is covered by Article 59. Thus, in the context of the construction industry and the subject matter of this book, the relevance of the free movement of workers is reduced, although it does pose significant issues.

The right of a worker to look for and take up employment anywhere in the Union is found in Article 48 EC. This is a directly applicable and directly effective right which is enforceable against individual employers and national authorities alike. It entails the right not to be discriminated against on grounds of nationality as regards employment, remuneration and other conditions of work. Once invoked that right becomes a duty on employers not to discriminate, either directly or indirectly, against nationals of another member state in the filling of posts and the paying of wages and salaries. It also extends to the offering of any other benefit or advantage, whether or not it is linked to the contract of employment.

On a practical level this means accepting qualifications or experience acquired in another member state which are equivalent to that which would be required at home. It means treating all workers equally, whether they are part-time or full-time (other than offering wages and advantages which are *pro rata* to employment status). It means offering the same advantages to spouses, children and dependants of a migrant worker as are offered to home-state workers.

The only discrimination EC law condones is in the treatment of home-state workers who have never exercised or attempted to exercise their right to free movement (known as a purely internal situation or reverse discrimination). This category of workers is unable to rely on Article 48 unless they have in the past exercised their right to free movement. Thus there would be nothing against giving foreign EC nationals assistance in re-location which is not available to home-state nationals.

The above (other than the purely internal situation) are examples of the principle of equality of treatment in action. This principle pervades all aspects of employment relations. Yet, as a duty placed on the employer, it is dependent on several conditions being met: firstly, the worker must be an EC national and, secondly, the work he is required to do must be genuine and effective work. That is to say not something which is purely ancillary or marginal to the economic activity the employer pursues. In practice, these conditions will be far more important to the worker than the employer. Nevertheless, it is equally important for the employer to know that he is offering genuine and effective work if he wants to avoid disruption to work in progress by a supposed employee who is under risk of deportation for not having genuine and effective work. Finally, in this culturally diverse continent language ability is a crucial factor to consider. Therefore, where the ability to speak the home state language is necessary for the performance of the tasks to be executed, employers may lawfully refuse to employ an individual without the requisite language ability (*Groener* (379/87) [1989] ECR 3667).

That, in essence, is the relevance of the free movement of workers to the private sector employer. In actual fact, the amount of legislation and case law on the subject is considerable, but both have focused on public (that is national) restrictions on the right of entry into a member state, the right to stay on to look for work, and the right to equality of treatment under national conditions of employment, or the tax and social advantages which are offered. The only justified restrictions on the right to free movement of workers are those based on reasons of public policy, public security and public health, as well as the other major exception in respect of posts which require obedience and loyalty to the state and are involved directly or indirectly with the exercise of powers conferred by public law and duties designed to safeguard the general interest of the state or of other public authorities.

Chapter 10
The Free Movement of Construction Products

The previous chapter gave an overview of the scope and substance of the primary economic rights which characterise the single market. The following two chapters will build on that foundation with details about how the general rules have been applied or adapted to the construction industry. This chapter will deal with the free movement of construction goods and Chapter 11 will focus on the free movement of self-employed professionals and other construction service providers, including contractors. The only aspect which is not treated in any depth is the intrinsic right to freedom of movement for workers.

Introduction

In this chapter we apply the general principles of free movement of goods covered in the previous chapter to the market for construction products.

According to those general principles, all construction material which is lawfully produced, marketed and incorporated into construction and civil engineering projects in one member state ought to be capable of being introduced, marketed and incorporated into construction and civil engineering projects in another member state (*Cassis de Dijon*) (see Chapter 9). That is the primary right of manufacturers, producers, importers, distributors, re-sellers, developers, designers, consultants, contractors, and sub-contractors in undertaking activities in relation to the production, movement, sale, specification or use of construction materials for the purposes of incorporation into private or public project construction or civil engineering projects.

That right entitles any construction participant:

- firstly, not to pay charges which are levied by virtue of the fact the goods have crossed a border (breach of Article 12);
- secondly, not to pay taxes which are either in excess of the taxes on domestically produced materials or afford indirect protection to other available materials in competition with the imported materials (breach of Article 95); and
- thirdly, not to be hindered by any non-pecuniary trading rule which hinders, directly or indirectly, actually or potentially, trade as between

member states in those construction materials (breach of Article 30 as interpreted by *Dassonville* (8/74) [1974] ECR 837).

Where trading rules only apply to imported materials then they can only be justified on one of the grounds set out in Article 36 relating to public policy, security, health, or protection of national treasures or industrial and intellectual property rights. However, the use of such exceptions should not constitute an arbitrary means of discrimination or a disguised restriction on trade.

Where trading rules are indistinctly applicable to domestic and imported materials then such rules will in principle breach Article 30 if they relate to requirements of the product (e.g. size, weight, presentation, etc. *Cassis de Dijon* (120/78) [1979] ECR 649). However, if those requirements can be justified according to one of the mandatory requirements relating to health, the environment, protection of the consumer, then, so long as that requirement is objectively justified, proportional and not already adequately met by regulations in the home state, they will not breach Article 30 (*Cassis de Dijon*). Equally, if the requirements to be met should in fact be considered as selling arrangements then they will also fall outside the scope of Article 30 (*Keck & Mithouard* (C-267 & 268/91) [1993] ECR I 6097).

Finally, any state monopoly which regulates the conditions under which construction materials are procured or marketed should be responsive to commercial realities so as to ensure there is no discrimination between nationals and companies of different member states (Article 37). Likewise, any state or semi-state body or undertaking should not confer any advantage or financial aid so as to favour certain undertakings or the production of certain construction materials without the approval of the Commission (Articles 92 and 93).

Through the application and enforcement of these rights and duties the Union is endeavouring to 'level the playing field' by freeing the market from the influence of the state and national authorities so as to create a single market in which the free movement of goods is assured and competition is not distorted.

The foregoing is laudable if simplistic when it relates to the construction industry, or any other which is technologically-sensitive and in which cost and health and safety are perhaps the two primary concerns. In the construction industry construction materials are, in any member state, subject to individualised specifications which, in the absence of the harmonisation or mutual recognition of standards, can give rise to duplication and therefore discrimination. Thus, achieving a single market in construction materials is really a process of standardisation and not simply of primary rights and duties – relevant and important as they are. What follows, therefore, is how and the extent to which the Union has removed technical barriers to trade in order to standardise the market.

The removal of technical barriers to trade

The working method of the Single Market was the harmonisation of technical standards. Each member state invariably regulates economic activity not just to enable businesses to trade but also ensure a minimum standard of protection for all those who come into contact with those activities. These standards are applied by way of certification. However, laudable as these standards might be, different standards in different member states constitute technical barriers to trade just as obstructive and significant as a complete ban on imports. It is for this reason that Article 30 extends to measures having equivalent effect to quotas and bans. The object of the single market programme is to eliminate these differences through harmonisation of laws, regulations and administrative provisions.

Early on and through the 1970s, the Union believed that it could harmonise these standards in a piecemeal fashion by drawing up independent norms which would be used to adjust or replace the standards that member states had adopted and in fact continue, with technological changes and advancement, to adopt. This process is now known as the 'old approach' to technical harmonisation because it soon transpired that it would become too vast, time consuming and complicated a task, largely because member states were unable to reach agreement on what were extremely detailed provisions. The old approach was therefore discarded in favour of a 'new approach' which centred on the adoption of essential requirements.

The only significant remnant from the old approach is a directive which is still of considerable relevance. Directive 83/189/EEC ([1983] OJ 409/8) lays down a procedure for the provision of information in the field of technical standards and regulations. Each year national authorities for each and every industry or sector are required to inform the Commission of the standards programmes that they have drawn up. More specifically, national authorities must communicate any draft technical regulation which is to be adopted for any reason other than to implement a European standard. A failure to communicate the draft regulation will mean that the national authority will be unable to enforce the adopted regulation against imported products. In addition member states are required to refrain from adopting some technical regulations for a period of twelve months if the Commission has already submitted a proposed directive or regulation on the same subject matter covered by the draft national regulations.

The need for the new approach coincided with and was a major feature of the 1985 White Paper on completing the internal market. Some 200 directives, including the Construction Products Directive, became the subject of the single market programme by which the Commission was directed to bring about technical harmonisation, not through definitive standards but with essential requirements. These essential requirements provide the basis for the preparation of harmonised standards at the European level. However, because this is still evidently such an involved and lengthy process, the essential requirements are also be used, in the absence of harmonised standards, to enable products to be sold in any member state. Such products are presumed to conform with the essential requirements if they comply with national technical specifications which themselves comply with the essential requirements. It will be observed from this that the objective is to achieve a single body of Union-wide technical standards rather than a disparate body of approximated national standards. Accordingly, at the heart of the new approach are fresh standards adopted by the mandated organisations. However, it is envisaged that a combination of factors (including the size of the Union, the continued existence of national accreditation bodies, and the perpetual development of state-of-the-art products) will never eradicate the need for national standards over the long term – although provision is usually made at the European level to deal with such products (see section on European Technical Approvals below).

Finally, it will also be observed that the whole system relies on conformity of standards to requirements. Clearly an indication is needed as to how an assessment is to be carried out, given that a single method of assessment will be unsuitable for all products. To meet this need the Union drew up a series of modules, each of which offered a different mechanism which could be specified for use as a conformity assessment procedure for any directive. These modules consisted of:

- internal production control;
- an EC-type examination;
- conformity to type;
- production quality assurance;
- product quality assurance;
- product verification;
- unit verification; and
- full quality assurance.

Each describes the methods by which a manufacturer will be able to demonstrate that his products conform to the essential requirements of a specific directive. According to general principles adopted in another piece of secondary legislation (Decision 90/683/EEC) each directive should avoid imposing unnecessary procedures for certain products but that the modules to be used should be those which are appropriate to control at both the design and production phase. To this end there is just as much scope for self-attestation as there is for independent inspection, with usually no restriction on the use of self-attestation if the case merits it.

Of the 200 or so directives, several are directly or (more usually) indirectly relevant to the construction industry. The Construction Products Directive is patently of direct relevance, but directives on subjects from the manufacture of machinery to the manufacture of hot-water boilers will be indirectly relevant to operators in these more specific markets. It is only proposed to look at the Construction Products Directive.

The Construction Products Directive

Introduction

The Construction Products Directive (89/106 EEC [1989] OJ 240/12) is three things:

- the facilitator of the free movement of construction products;
- a framework for harmonisation of standards; and
- finally, a basis for ensuring a minimum level of health and safety both in the products themselves and the works into which they are incorporated.

These three functions correspond to the three levels upon which the CPD operates and which together amount to a structure comparable to the properties of any building, for they each support, complement, and depend upon the others. There is firstly the Directive itself which has been transposed into the laws of the Member States. This encapsulates the first objective as a set of Essential Requirements, compliance with which is represented by the CE mark thus establishing the right of access to the market for such products.

The second function – a framework for harmonisation is, to a large extent, set out in Interpretative Documents (IDs) which the Commission has published. The basic principle of harmonisation is found in the CPD, but it is the IDs that 'give concrete form to the CPD'.

The third and final function is manifested in the third and final level of regulation, the technical standards. Again, the principles underpinning these standards are found in the CPD itself, but the standards are the most immediate point of contact at the practical level.

The three levels may be interdependent on each other, but it is the IDs which provide the strategic link between the CPD and the technical standards themselves.

Background to the CPD

In the 1985 White Paper, which set in train the completion of the internal market, the construction industry was singled out (with others) for particular emphasis in efforts to remove technical barriers or, to the extent that they could not be removed, then to diminish their effect by mutual recognition of equivalence of national standards.

It was recognised that member states were responsible for ensuring that building and civil engineering works on their territory were designed and executed in a way that did not endanger the safety of persons, domestic animals or property, while respecting other essential requirements in the interests of general well-being. It was also noted that building regulation in the member states was characterised by provisions relating to safety, energy economy, durability, protection of the environment, aspects of national economy, and other factors important in the public interest. However, it was concluded that since these concerns were reflected in national product standards and other technical specifications, then these national provisions had a direct influence on the nature of the market for construction products and, insofar as there was disparity, hindered trade between member states.

In keeping with the new approach to technical harmonisation, the essential requirements were to constitute both the general and specific criteria with which construction works must comply. However, since a construction product is manufactured for the sole purpose of being incorporated into a building or civil engineering project, it was recognised that the only effective and definitive means of testing or assessing the conformity of a product with the essential requirements is to assess the conformity of the works with the essential requirements.

From this it will be observed that the object of the Construction Products Directive (CPD) is to achieve free movement of goods which are incorporated into construction works by means of the drawing up of minimum standards to ensure the safety and fitness for purpose of the works. Thus the CPD (as well as any other internal market directive) has three dimensions:

- a trade dimension, which will be looked below;
- a contractual liability/fitness for purpose dimension which will be looked at in Chapter 12;
- a tortious liability/health and safety dimension which will be looked at in Chapter 14.

Access to the single market in construction products

There are three provisions in the CPD through which technical barriers to trade have been removed and by virtue of which construction products have access to the single market.

Firstly, by Article 2 of the CPD, member states are required to take all necessary measures to ensure that all construction products which are intended for use in construction works may be placed on the market only if they are fit for this intended use. By construction products, the CPD covers any product which is produced for incorporation in a permanent manner in construction works. Construction works includes buildings and civil engineering works. Products will be fit for their intended use if they have all the characteristics necessary to ensure that the works in which they are to be incorporated, assembled, applied, or installed, can, if properly designed and built, satisfy the essential requirements set out later in the CPD.

Secondly, by Article 6(1) of the CPD, member states are prohibited from impeding the free movement, the placing on the market, or the use in their territory of products which satisfy with the provisions of the CPD. Accordingly, member states are required to ensure that the use of such products, for the purpose for which they were intended, is not impeded by rules or conditions imposed by public bodies or by a private body acting as a public undertaking or body on the basis of a monopoly position.

Thirdly, by Article 4(2) member states are required to presume that products are fit for their intended use if they enable works in which they are employed, provided the latter are properly designed and built, to satisfy the essential requirements, and if those products bear a CE mark. Whilst the first condition is vital, the presumption may only be rebutted if it is shown that when the products are incorporated into the works, the works themselves do not satisfy the essential requirements. On the other hand, as will be revealed, the second condition (that the product bears a CE mark) offers the manufacturer, distributor, importer, or user considerable assistance.

Article 4(2) has been cited non-numerically in third position because of its pivotal role in the operation of the CPD by balancing the duty of member states to ensure that only products which are fit for the purpose are placed on the market (Article 2) with the duty of member states not to impede trade in products which are fit for the purpose (Article 6(1)). The means through which that role is executed is the harmonisation of technical standards, to be achieved in the long term by issuing fresh ones, and in the short to medium term by approving existing national provisions. As is consistent with the emphasis of this Chapter on the application of the principle of the free movement of goods through the elimination of technical barriers to trade, there will be extensive reference to use of technical specifications.

In contrast to the foregoing, the CPD envisages that in some cases a product will not comply with a technical specification which the Union has either issued, approved or harmonised. In these cases then that product may only be placed on the national market if it satisfies national technical specifications consistent with the EU Treaty (Article 6(2)). Effectively such products do not have a automatic right to free movement, but must comply with the relevant provisions for the national market on which they are to be placed. However, the CPD does go some way in order to ensure that these products have a limited right to free movement. Insofar as there are no common or approved technical specifications, a member state into which such products are to be imported must, on request, consider the product to be in conformity with its own provisions if they have satisfied tests and inspection carried out by an approved body in the producing member state similar to the methods in force in the state of destination (Article 16(1)).

Returning to the main thrust of the CPD, even though this envisages the existence of harmonised technical specifications, understandably there are exceptions to these provisions and therefore the primary right of free movement. Under Article 21, where a member state ascertains that a product said to conform with the essential requirements does not so comply, then it shall take all appropriate measures to withdraw that product and further prohibit it being placed on the market. National authorities must additionally take all appropriate action against anyone who has unlawfully placed non-conforming products on the market. Member states usually make use of this duty to include penal sanctions in their implementing instrument, but the use of such sanctions is wholly dependent upon a full and correct implementation of the directive (*Pubblico Minstero* v. *Ratti* (148/78) [1979] ECR 1629).

In addition, in relation to use of the CE mark, Article 15(2) requires member states to ensure that products which bear a CE mark but do not satisfy or no longer satisfy the essential requirements are withdrawn from the market and are not permitted to return until they conform. It could be observed that Article 15(2) is superfluous to the general safeguard clause in Article 21, but the point is perhaps academic. One might also observe that member states thereby impede the movement of products not bearing the CE mark, but such products do not benefit from the primary right in the first place.

Ordinarily, since the Union has legislated in the specific area of construction products, this would wrest from the member states any further sovereign power to act, even under Article 36 TEU which provides exceptions to a primary right of the free movement of goods. However, it will be recalled that in relation to single market directives, such as the CPD, member states retain a residual power to apply national provisions on the grounds of major needs referred to in Article 36 or in respect of the environment or the working environment, but to do so they must notify the Commission of such provisions (Article 100a TEU).

The effective implementation of the CPD falls on national authorities. This in accordance with the nature of a directive which is binding on member states as to the result to be achieved but leaves to them the form of implementation. The relevant national authority is the one notified by each member state to the Commission as required by Article 18 CPD. So in the UK it is the British Board of Agrément which is required to give effect to the CPD by means of applying the Construction Products Regulations, the British instrument implementing the directive.

The main purpose of Article 2, considered in isolation, is to ensure minimum standards rather than freedom of movement. On the other hand, if Article 2 is read in conjunction with Article 4(2), then it is impossible for national authorities to prevent or restrict the using or placing on the market of construction products which are fit for the purpose intended and satisfy the essential requirements and the authority must presume these conditions to have been met if the product bears a CE mark. However, to reinforce the duty of the member state to respect the significance of the CE mark, Article 6(1) expressly forbids interference in trade in construction products which satisfy the foregoing.

At the very least Article 6 appears clear, concise and unconditional – other than the requirement to meet the conditions of the directive. Accordingly, Article 6 is directly effective, enabling manufacturers, users, etc. to rely upon it as against the state or organs of the state. Article 4(2) could likewise have direct effect since national authorities are under a duty to presume fitness for purpose in the conditions referred to. However, any right conferred on individuals is secondary to some other purpose, i.e. acceptance that products comply with the essential requirements or the right to move goods freely – in which case Article 4(2) is in isolation unlikely to confer any directly effective right.

Finally, there is nothing to exclude from the scope of the benefits of the directive transactions for construction products which are not for immediate incorporation into construction works. The definition of 'construction product' and the requirement that member states ensure free movement of the same relates to items which are produced for incorporation or intended for use in construction works. However, to exclude transactions between manufacturer and distributor or distributor and re-seller, where clearly the products are not for immediate incorporation, would counteract the useful effect of the directive since it would exclude several vital stages in the commercialisation process by which the products which leave the factory reach the site.

On the other hand, anyone 'downstream' of the manufacturer (i.e. the distributor, re-seller, designer, contractor, etc.) is dependent on the manufacturer or his agent affixing the CE mark to the product to indicate that it complies with the essential requirements. Thus, without the construction products leaving the factory with the CE mark, or at some point having the CE mark lawfully affixed, then no-one in the commercial chain will be able to rely upon the rights in the directive.

The significance of the CE mark

The CE mark is a symbol which is in general use in single market directives. The mark is composed of a unique design and comprises the semi-circular initials 'CE'. It is used to express a single message: that the natural or legal person who affixed it has ascertained that the product bearing it conforms to all binding Union provisions applicable.

In the context of the CPD therefore the CE mark signifies that the product satisfies the essential requirements and complies with standards which themselves comply with the essential requirements. These standards could be:

* national standards transposing European harmonised standards;
* the subject of a European technical approval; or
* national technical specifications in respect of which the Commission has declared there is a presumption of conformity with the essential requirements.

As explained earlier, under Article 4(2) member states are to presume that products bearing the CE mark are fit for their intended use. Only the additional requirement that they enable the works in which they are incorporated to satisfy the essential requirements qualifies the otherwise unconditional right to move such construction products across borders unhindered – but, as has been observed, only reasonable evidence that a particular product does not enable the works to satisfy the essential requirements can permit member states to impede that free movement. Thus products bearing a CE mark are placed in a considerably advantageous position since ordinarily they should not encounter any impediment to free movement. Or, to put it in the context of the primary right contained in the Treaty, any national rule which requires a national authority to disregard the CE mark and inspect imported construction products in any event would constitute a trading rule directly hindering trade between member states, which would breach Article 30.

It is incumbent on the manufacturers or their agents in the Union to affix the CE mark on the products in some way (by means of labels, packaging, or accompanying documents) (Article 4(6)). The CE mark is to be accompanied by the name or identifying mark of the producer and, where appropriate, indications to identify the characteristics of the products, the year of manufacture (last two digits only), the identification symbol of the inspection body involved, and the number of the EC certificate of conformity (see later).

In the early years of administering the technical implementation of the CPD, doubt was expressed on whether it was compulsory for manufacturers to make use of the CE mark. Note that it is not disputed that the construction products must comply with the essential requirements – that *is* compulsory since, under Article 2(1), member states must take all necessary measures to ensure that all construction products placed on the market do so comply. However, no express mention is made of the need for those products to bear a CE mark. In Article 4(6) the manufacturer or his agent in the EU is to 'take responsibility' for affixing the CE mark, but it was argued that there is no express requirement for the CE mark to be affixed. The question therefore became: is the CE mark compulsory?

A separate legislative instrument provides the answer. Council Directive 93/68 (03L220) concerning the affixing and use of the CE mark makes the manufacturer or importer responsible for ensuring his products bear the CE mark before they are placed onto the market. This measure was proposed as a Regulation but adopted as a Directive designed to amend and clarify the various internal market directives, including the CPD, by making affixation compulsory.

There have not been any further moves to tidy up the technical loopholes in the CPD itself, but it is questionable if this is strictly necessary. Construction products must, because of Article 2(1), comply with the essential requirements to enable the works into which they are incorporated to do likewise. Moreover, the CE mark indicates that the product complies with the relevant standards which themselves comply with the essential requirements and a member state will only presume compliance if the product bears the CE mark. CE marking is not only an option which ensures freedom of movement but is also an intrinsic part of the process of placing products on the market.

That issue aside, if one assumes that the manufacturer must affix the CE mark, it follows that the product must indeed conform to those standards since wrongly to affix the CE mark when the product does not comply with the essential requirements would be misleading. In this regard, member states are not given any specific powers to deal with unlawful use of the CE mark, but they are required to ensure that the CE mark is used correctly and that products wrongly using the mark are withdrawn from the market. This implies that their discretion is unlimited save for the need to employ sanctions which are objectively justified, non-discriminatory and proportionate to the result to be achieved. In the UK and in the Republic of Ireland the ultimate sanction is imprisonment and/or a fine on summary conviction. On consideration, this is unlikely to be considered disproportionate in principle in connection with the construction sector given that construction products are intended for incorporation into construction works which, when properly designed and built, are assumed to satisfy the essential requirements. Clearly then a defective product which intentionally or negligently but still wrongly bears a CE mark has serious implications for the health and safety of construction workers and users of the completed building or civil engineering project. Therefore the benefits that arise from use of a CE mark are conditional on the manufacturer accepting and executing the duty of care which is related to it. The incidence of this duty will be examined in more detail in Chapter 12. The present need is to examine what the manufacturer needs to do in order lawfully to affix the CE mark.

Obtaining a Certificate of Conformity

It will be recalled that it was envisaged by the Union that, in order to achieve free movement of goods which are ordinarily required to be manufactured to a given technical standard, then it was necessary to harmonise those standards. Moreover, it was concluded with the benefit of hindsight that to harmonise standards most effectively a range of mechanisms appropriate to all products had to be made available so that in any market the same products are tested in the same way and according to the same standards. To this end, a number of modules were established some or all of which would be employed in individual technical harmonisation directives for the purposes of attesting the conformity of products to set standards.

The CPD is one of those directives. It provides that construction products subject to an attestation of conformity will benefit from a presumption of conformity with the relevant technical standards; that is to say a presumption that they comply with the essential requirements. Accordingly, products may bear a CE mark and their placement on the single market, movement across borders and use may not be impeded unless a national authority has reason to believe that the CE mark has been unlawfully affixed.

However, since the CPD must also serve health and safety objectives, attestation is not optional. By Article 13(1) of the CPD, the manufacturer or his agent established in the Union is responsible for attestation that products are in conformity with the requirements of the applicable standards. This duty is consistent with the sole right and duty of the manufacturer to affix the CE mark on products, given that this mark indicates that the products are fit for the purpose intended.

The emphasis of the regime employed by the CPD is one of self-attestation by means of a regulated system of factory production control. However, in certain cases it is envisaged that it will be necessary additionally to require assessment and surveillance of the production control or the product itself by an approved certification body. The choice of procedure for a given product or family of products is specified by the Commission on consideration of the following:

- the importance of the part played by the product with respect to the essential requirements, in particular those relating to health and safety;
- the nature of the product i.e. the effect of the variability of the product's characteristics on its serviceability; and
- the product's susceptibility to defects.

In each case the least onerous possible procedure consistent with safety will be chosen and referred to in the technical specifications which will be published and used by manufacturers.

The only exception provided for in this framework is in the case of products which play a minor part with respect to health and safety. Article 4(5) directs the Commission to draw up a list of such products for which the manufacturer need only issue a declaration of compliance with an 'acknowledged rule of technology' in order to obtain authorisation to place such products on the market.

Self-attestation

The ability to self-attest the conformity of products to essential requirements is dependent upon the manufacturer having an appropriate factory production control system. Once in place this procedure enables the manufacturer to demonstrate conformity with a simple declaration on the basis of which he will be entitled to affix the CE mark to his product (Article 14). However the system itself must be approved, but only to a limited extent.

Ordinarily the manufacturer will obtain approval for his factory production control system after completion of two stages. Firstly, by undertaking initial type-testing of the product and possibly testing samples taken at the factory in accordance with a test plan which is itself prescribed; and secondly, by obtaining certification of the factory production control system from an approved body which will inspect the factory and the proposed system and possibly undertake continuous surveillance and assessment of that system (Annex III.2(ii) first possibility).

There are, however, two other possible methods of making use of an approved factory production control system, but these apply in specific circumstances as follows.

Where a product may be released on to the market with a declaration of conformity, but the manufacturer has not applied or has only partly applied the relevant technical specifications in accordance with the first possibility above, then the product's fitness for purpose and the entitlement to affix the

CE mark will depend upon the product undergoing initial type-testing by an approved laboratory and the manufacturer putting in place on his own initiative a factory production control system (even though it is not approved) (Annex III.2(ii) second possibility).

Alternatively, in the case of individual and non-series production, a declaration of conformity will suffice if the product has undergone initial type-testing by the manufacturer and, likewise, the manufacturer has put in place his own factory production control system (Annex III.2(ii) third possibility). However, this final possibility is only available so long as the technical specifications for the product in question do not provide otherwise.

In any event, therefore, the manufacturer cannot avoid type-testing and production control. The type-testing must be undertaken with a view to the product meeting the technical specifications and therefore the essential requirements during its economically reasonable working life by subjecting the product to conditions which simulate the acts and events referred to in the relevant essential requirements.

Factory production control refers to the permanent internal control of production exercised by the manufacturer. All the elements, requirements and provisions adopted by the manufacturer must be documented systematically so as to ensure a 'common understanding of quality assurance' and enable checking of the achievement of the required product characteristics and the effective operation of the production control system. In addition, although the second and third possibilities do not require independent approval of the control system, this would not abrogate the duty of the manufacturer to adopt the main elements of the system featuring in the Union's module referred to earlier. This is to be found in Council Decision (90/686/EEC) and requires a manufacturer to keep technical documentation relating to the design, manufacture and operation of the product for ten years, and to take all measures necessary for the production process to ensure that the product complies with this documentation.

Independent assessment

Given the duty of the Commission to choose the conformity attestation method which is least onerous on the manufacturer, then it is arguable that it will only require attestation of products by an approved certification body it the previous alternative (self-attestation) is not adequately consistent with safety.

Under the independent system of attestation, a product may be affixed with a CE mark and placed on to the market if, in addition to a factory production control system, an approved certification body undertakes an assessment and surveillance of the production control or the product itself.

Thus before a product is released onto the market the following stages must be completed.

• Firstly, the approved body must undertake initial type-testing of the product and an initial inspection of the factory and production control system which will undergo continuous surveillance, assessment and approval. In addition the approved body has the power to undertake audit-testing of samples. This power may be exercised in respect of products taken from the factory, market or construction site.

- Secondly, the manufacturer should put in place an adequate factory production control system (as explained above) and undertake further testing of samples according to a prescribed test plan (Annex III.2(i)).

On satisfactory completion of these stages, the manufacturer will be issued with a certificate of conformity for either the system of production control or for the product itself. This certificate stands as documentary evidence that the products themselves comply with the essential requirements. However, given that member states have power to impede trade in certain construction products if the latter no longer appear to comply with the essential requirements then it is submitted that the certificate is not conclusive evidence.

The essential requirements

So far it has been demonstrated that the single market programme, the new approach to technical harmonisation, the operation of the CPD, and the means by which construction products can be moved freely across borders all hinge on the employment of and compliance with 'essential requirements' in the construction works. Having explained the specific rights which are available, the exceptions to those rights, and the infrastructure by which those rights are obtained, it is now appropriate to examine these central components of the CPD.

There are six essential requirements set out in brief in the CPD. Article 3 states that one, some or all of the ERs may be relevant to the technical characteristics of a product. If they apply they are to be satisfied during an economically reasonable working life of the product. However, it will be recalled that in actual fact products must comply with technical specifications which give practical effect to the essential requirements in the construction works. Thus, on their own they simply encapsulate the objectives to which those technical specifications must aspire.

Moreover, because of that simplistic role, they do not offer sufficient substance in the complex and variable context of construction products. For this reason it was envisaged in the CPD that it would be necessary to draw up an interpretative document for each of the essential requirements. According to Article 12 CPD, these interpretative documents give concrete form to the essential requirements by indicating classes or levels for each requirement where necessary and where the state of scientific and technical knowledge so permits.

The interpretative documents also act as the method of correlating these classes or levels of requirement with the technical specifications with which a product must comply. Therefore in the technical hierarchy of the CPD one would place the essential requirements on top, the interpretative documents underneath, and the technical specifications (whether approved or harmonised) making up the base. Accordingly a full examination of the essential requirements in isolation would be incomplete, but pressure of space in this book prevents the corresponding interpretative documents from being considered in detail.

The essential requirements are summarised below.

Mechanical resistance and stability

The construction works must be designed and built in such a way that the loadings that are liable to act on them during construction and use will not lead to collapse, major deformations to an inadmissible degree, damage to other parts of the works or to fittings or installed equipment, or damage disproportionate to the original cause.

Safety in case of fire

The construction works must be designed and built in such a way that in the event of an outbreak of fire:

- the load bearing capacity of the construction can be assumed to remain stable for a specific period of time;
- the generation and spread of fire and smoke within the works and to neighbouring works is limited;
- occupants can leave the works or be rescued by other means; and
- the safety of rescue teams is taken into consideration.

Hygiene, health and the environment

The construction works must be designed and built in such a way that they will not be a threat to the hygiene or health of the construction workers, occupants or neighbours, in particular as a result of:

- giving off toxic gas;
- the presence of dangerous particles or gases in the air;
- the emission of dangerous radiation;
- pollution or poisoning of the water or soil;
- faulty elimination of waste water, smoke, or solid or liquid waste; or
- the presence of damp in parts of the works or on surfaces within the works.

Safety in use

The construction works must be designed and built in such a way that they do not present unacceptable risks of accidents in service or in operation such as slipping, falling, collision, burns, electrocution, or injury from explosion.

Protection against noise

The construction works must be designed and built in such a way that noise perceived by the occupants or people nearby is kept down to a level that will not threaten their health and will allow them to sleep, rest and work in satisfactory conditions.

Energy economy and heat retention

The construction works and their heating, cooling and installations must be designed and built in such a way that the amount of energy required in use shall be low, having regard to the climatic conditions of the location and the number of occupants.

The interpretative documents

The legislative basis of the IDs is Article 12 of the CPD. Therefore, whilst the IDs come in the form of a Communication of the Commission, which is of no binding authority whatsoever, they nevertheless have the same legal effect as the CPD itself.

Standing alone, the IDs are not of a great deal of importance. Their language is technical as is their nature and purpose. On the other hand, once placed in the context of the CPD and its objectives, their status is transformed. Whenever a manufacturer encounters difficulties in either getting approval to market his product at all, or simply gaining access to the market of one particular member state, then the IDs are an important point of reference. These are areas where the lawyer should be on hand to assist, therefore a working knowledge of the IDs is desirable.

The IDs should be seen in this context and for this reason an outline is provided below of how each essential requirement is interpreted in its respective ID.

Mechanical resistance and stability

This ER stipulates the need to design and build the construction works to avoid the risk of collapse, deformation and damage.

The ID interprets this as actions and other influences which may cause stress, deformations or degradation in the structure during its construction and use. Inadmissible deformation refers to deformation or cracking which invalidates assumptions about the stability, resistance or serviceability of the structure or otherwise reduces its durability. Disproportionate damage has causes such as explosions, impact overload or human error in mind, and other causes which could have been avoided or limited without unreasonable difficulty.

Testing whether this ER is satisfied, requires examination of the planning and design of the works, the execution of the works and necessary maintenance, and the properties, performance and use of the construction products. It is this ER which probably has the most relevance to issues of liability for defective design and building.

Safety in case of fire

This ER stipulates that the construction works must be designed and built to ensure reasonable stability in the event of fire and that due consideration be given to the position of occupants and rescue teams in such circumstances.

The ID deals with this ER in terms of levels or classes. Such divisions are provided for in the CPD and permissible for any ER, although they have only arisen in relation to safety in case of fire. As a concept using classes is a great deal less straightforward than a simple objective. Classes are used to take account of possible differences in geographical or climatic conditions or in ways of life, as well as the different levels of protection that may prevail at national, regional or local level. Thus, instead of having one all-embracing requirement for all products, requirements are adapted or qualified to match a family of products or a particular area of the EU.

The concept of fire safety needs little further explanation. The ID concentrates on mitigating the various factors affecting the development and growth of fire, including fire load, air supply, thermal properties of the works, fire control systems, reaction to fire, performance of the works, etc. The ID goes into great detail about the testing of any product to this ER which will not be repeated here.

Hygiene, Health and the Environment

This ER protects the hygiene and health of occupants or neighbours from emissions pollution and the effects of damp.

The ID identifies this ER as relevant to the dangers of using substances like asbestos, and in certain cases it might possibly be relevant to instances of 'sick-building syndrome' or legionnaires' disease, insofar as these relate to the installation of equipment.

Safety in Use

This ER stipulates design and building of the construction works to avoid unacceptable risks of accidents in service or in operation.

Protection against noise

This ER stipulates protection from noise for the occupants and people nearby. It is not relevant to complaints made in the course of building on site, rather it requires the works to perform satisfactorily in their completed state.

Energy economy and heat retention

This ER stipulates the design and building of the construction works and their heating, cooling and ventilation installations to keep energy use as low as possible.

Again the ID identifies this as a largely straightforward requirement on the choice of materials used in the construction of a building and its performance.

European technical approvals

The Construction Products Directive (CPD) is the facilitator for free movement of safe and reliable products that are fit for their intended use in the construction process. In order for any product to have unrestricted access onto the European market by right, it must enable the completed works to comply with the six essential requirements enshrined in the CPD. Those requirements set the general objective. However, at a practical level, the system is founded on a set of technical standards.

One of the types of standard provided for by the CPD is the European technical approval (ETA). This concept is designed to fill the gap whenever there is a product for which there are neither European harmonised standards nor national standards in existence. As from January 1994 there are common procedural rules setting out how a manufacturer can obtain an ETA.

These common procedural rules apply throughout the European Union, so it should not matter where approval for a product is obtained. A single act of approval is intended to act as a passport to the entire internal market, avoiding duplication of paperwork and costs, as well as contradictory assessments.

ETA is a highly flexible measure. It can be used as a permanent standard, or as a temporary measure in place of inchoate harmonised standards. It operates on the basis of examination and testing of a product according to the principles of the CPD and guidelines drawn up by the body responsible for overseeing the operation of ETA, the European Organisation for Technical Approval (EOTA) based in Brussels. Day to day testing and the issue of ETAs is to be carried out by 'approval bodies' in the member states.

Under the CPD it is the manufacturer who must ensure that his product meets the essential requirements before he places it on the market. It is the duty of the approval body to assess the fitness for use of new products on the basis of scientific and practical knowledge, to take impartial decisions in relation to the interests of the manufacturers concerned, and to collate the contributions of all interested parties in a balanced assessment.

Applying for ETA

There is a standard application to be completed in the language of the approval body. This asks for the trade mark names of the product, the addresses at which it will be manufactured and whether any previous application has been made to any approval body.

In seeking ETA there are a number of conditions with which the manufacturer must comply. Overall, there is the duty to 'support the approval body in its assessment task'. The approval body is empowered to ask for anything it needs to assess the fitness of the product for its intended use. To this end the manufacturer must supply the approval body with necessary information and documents, such as test results, calculations, specifications, drawings, etc. Furthermore, he must describe his product and explain its intended use in detail. Also, the applicant must agree to other approval bodies and the Commission being notified of the application. Later, following submission of the application, the manufacturer must ensure that the places of manufacture can be visited at any time by the approval body or its representative during working hours. Finally, the manufacturer must agree to pay the costs arising from the approval procedure. Breach of these requirements can result in the application being cancelled.

The granting of ETA in the absence of guidelines

ETA, like any method of assessment in this area, cannot operate without the application of technical criteria. Ordinarily these will come in the form of existing guidelines, in which case the process is straightforward. However, participants ought to be aware of an *ad hoc* (and intrinsically bureaucratic) procedure which will be followed in the absence of any guidelines where the product is an entirely new development.

Applications submitted to an approval body will automatically be referred to the Technical Board of EOTA to decide whether ETA can be granted in principle. The latter does this on the basis of consensus, and subject to confirmation by the Commission. In cases where a product happens to differ only slightly, but significantly, from existing harmonised or recognised national standards, the Commission and EOTA must also agree that the product is significantly different. If a consensus is not reached, then the Executive Commission of EOTA will consider the position before passing it to the Commission for the final decision.

In the happy event of consensus, the approval body formulates a test programme after seeking the comments of other approval bodies around the EU. The finished test programme is subject to scrutiny by EOTA. The product is then tested. If the result is positive, then, because a new standard has been created, all approval bodies are required to give their consent in writing to the issuing of the ETA. Objections will be resolved by the Technical Board, failing which by the Executive Commission, failing which, it is referred to the CPD Standing Committee on Construction via the Commission.

On successful completion of the process the manufacturer will be issued with his ETA in a form corresponding to the general format agreed by the Commission. It will last five years. Applications for renewal or modification must, it seems, be made in the usual way to the same approval body. In the case of renewal, the application must be submitted within six months of expiry.

If the application is refused the approval body must give reasons. The applicant will be free to submit a fresh application to another approval body at any time. In fact, an applicant could submit the same unaltered product elsewhere, but presumably any reasonable manufacturer will endeavour to correct the 'defects' in his product before attempting to obtain approval once again.

Free movement and public works contracts

Invitations to tender for public works contracts are governed by Directive 93/37, covered in Chapter 7. Obviously, the major feature of the contract specifications, other than the design, will be the materials that are required for incorporation into the works. This raises a problem of how much discretion a public authority has to stipulate materials, and whether it has any discretion to exclude materials from other member states.

The Court of Justice has dealt with this issue in a number of cases. It did so firstly in *Commission* v. *Ireland* ((45/87R) [1987] ECR 1369). Here the Court ruled that it was contrary to Article 30 for a public authority to specify materials in a public works contract to be certified according to Irish standards. In this case Dundalk Urban District Council invited tenders for the construction of a water main. It will be recalled that under that directive technical specifications can be defined by reference to European standards (or at least the national versions thereof); but the Dundalk case occurred before the directive was amended with provisions relating to technical specifications. Amongst the specifications stipulated by Dundalk Council, however, was one requiring all asbestos cement pressure pipes to be certified as complying with a purely Irish standard. On its own initiative, the Council therefore refused to consider an Irish company which proposed using pipes manufactured in Spain. These pipes were certified under an equivalent Spanish standard compatible with international technical specifications.

The Commission sought to challenge this under Article 30 and its claim was upheld by the Court. The Court observed that it was both normal and necessary for materials in a public works contract to comply with technical standards – even national standards. It added, however, that 'a technical standard cannot, without creating *prima facie* a barrier to trade, which is contrary to Article 30, have the effect of excluding, without so much as an examination, any tender based on another technical standard recognised in another member state as providing equivalent guarantees of safety, performance and reliability.'

In another case, *Du Pont de Nemours Italiana* v. *United Sanitaria Locale* (C-21/ 88) [1990] ECR I-889), Italian law required public authorities to purchase at least 30% of their supplies from industrial and agricultural undertakings established in southern Italy. This too was condemned by the Court of Justice on the basis of Article 30.

In other cases, the Court has ruled that observance of Article 30 and the non-discriminatory treatment of materials from other member states, applies to the whole procurement procedure from start to finish (*Commission* v. *Denmark* (C-243/89) [1993] ECR I-3353), and that specifications which stipulate particular 'brand-named' materials should include the words 'or equivalent' to enable suppliers or users of other materials to tender – or at least not discourage them from doing so (*Commission* v. *Netherlands* (C-359/93), not yet reported). This last point cannot be left without further comment. Difficulties in compliance with the ruling will arise when a public purchaser considers specific particularisation of certain materials as an essential part of the works; for instance, in matching materials such as stone or brickwork with the works' surroundings or neighbouring buildings. Although aesthetic appearance or quality will weigh heavy in the authority's considerations, it cannot but invite and, if necessary, accept materials of sufficient equivalence.

Chapter 11
The Free Movement of Contractors and Construction Professionals

The principles set out in Chapter 9 can, in relation to the construction industry, be distilled into three simple rules.

Firstly, that in conjunction with the procurement rules contractors and professionals may tender for and execute contracts in other member states, and in so doing transfer their staff and workers to site on a temporary basis.

Secondly, individuals who hold themselves out as having a special skill (whether of a professional or non-vocational nature) which is evidenced by qualifications can, if those qualifications meet certain criteria, rely on them upon to seek work anywhere in the Union either on an employed or independent contractor basis. Where the potential employer or client is a public authority then the principles of European law (as set out below in detail) may be relied upon directly. Otherwise the member state concerned ought to have adapted its national law so that all private enterprises are bound likewise. In this regard, where the legislation of a member state is silent as regards the right of nationals of other member states to become ordinary members of a professional body, then this gives rise to an ambiguous state of affairs and keeps the persons concerned in a state of uncertainty as regards the possibility of relying on the provisions of Articles 52 and 59 of the Treaty which have direct effect. The retention of legislation with such a lacuna therefore amounts to a failure by the state in question to comply with the Treaty, and mere administrative practices (by their nature alterable at will by the authorities and not given the appropriate publicity) cannot be regarded as constituting the proper fulfilment of the state's obligations. A member state cannot plead provisions, practices or circumstances in its internal legal system to justify failure to comply with its obligations under community law, as held in a case regarding the conditions for access to and exercise of the professions of architect, civil engineer, and surveyor (*Commission* v. *Hellenic Republic* (38/87) (1988)).

Thirdly, arising out of this principle of mutual recognition of qualifications, individuals, and by extension companies and firms whose officers are appropriately qualified, may exercise their right under Article 52 TEU to establish themselves in another member state and compete in that market.

However, despite the equalisation of education and training member states can impose certain requirements over and above those met by the individual in his home state if there are substantial differences in the practice of the profession in that state or there are objectives justified by the general good which require additional safeguards.

Notwithstanding this last basic point, one might optimistically observe that there is no-one in the construction industry who would not benefit from this regime. As will be seen architects benefit from a specific directive which gives mutual recognition to the training and education required by each national regime. All other professions which have a degree as the essential entry requirement are beneficiaries of the main piece of legislation, the 1989 Mutual Recognition of Diplomas Directive (89/48/EEC). Other professions which in cultural terms might be regarded as 'trades' are dealt with under a separate directive, the 1992 Mutual Recognition of Diplomas Directive (92/51 EEC). These pieces of legislation apply to both cross-border services and the establishment of businesses and they come under detailed scrutiny in this chapter. In addition the chapter focuses on the main authority for the movement of site staff which arose in a construction context.

Free movement of architects

The directive

Council Directive 85/384/EEC ([1985] OJ L223/15) of 10 June 1985 deals with the mutual recognition of diplomas, certificates and other evidence of formal qualifications acquired under the professional title of architect and enables holders to exercise the right of establishment and freedom to provide services across borders. National professional associations and all authorities are required to recognise all formal qualifications acquired as a result of education and training which meet certain standard requirements as evidence of the ability to practise as an architect regardless of where in the Union such qualifications are conferred. The standard requirements for the schools and colleges offering such education refer to content and duration. However the directive also sets out an exhaustive list of such establishments which do meet the requirements.

Course content and duration

Course content must be balanced between the theoretical and practical aspects of architectural training. These courses must also demonstrate wide ranging knowledge and ability. The directive sets out the requirements as follows:

- Holders must have the ability to create architectural designs that satisfy both aesthetic and technical requirements.
- They should have an adequate knowledge of the history and theories of architecture and the related arts, technologies and human sciences as well as of fine arts as an influence on the quality of architectural design. They

need an adequate knowledge of urban design, planning and the skills
involved in the planning process.

- They should be able to understand the relationship between people and
buildings, and between buildings and their environment; and appreciate
the need to relate buildings and the spaces between them to human needs
and scale.
- On a more technical level, they need to understand structural design and
the constructional and engineering problems associated with building
design; and have an adequate knowledge of physical problems and
technologies and of the function of buildings, so as to provide internal
conditions of comfort and protection against the climate.
- Finally they should have the necessary design skills to meet building
users' requirements within the constraints imposed by cost factors and
building regulations.

As regards duration, the total length must be at least four years full-time
study at a university or comparable educational establishment, or six years
of which at least three must be full-time. Part-time university courses also
qualify so long as the person concerned has been employed in architecture
for not less than seven years under the supervision of an architect or firm of
architects. In all cases (unsurprisingly) the individual must have successfully completed the course with an examination of degree standard. On
successful completion certificates issued by the member state of which the
holders are nationals, or from which they come, shall constitute proof of
their status as architects. In addition the Court of Justice has held that that
education and training which lasts for four years and which includes
practical semesters organised and supervised by the educational establishment must be regarded as four years of full-time studies (*Nationale Raad van
de Orde van Architecten* v. *Egle* (C-310/90) 1992)).

In the rare event that doubts arise about the validity of a specific qualification meeting these requirements it is intended that the matter should be
scrutinised by the Commission itself. This will bring in before it an advisory
committee on education and training in the field of architecture for an
opinion on the basis of which it will reach a binding decision.

Use of titles

Thereafter national authorities of member states ('host states') (and indirectly following implementation all firms and organisations as well) are
required to recognise formal qualifications awarded by other member states
('states of origin') to nationals of the Union. This entails the right of the
qualified architects to use their lawful academic title and any appropriate
abbreviation deriving from their state of origin (or the state from which they
come) in the language of that state. Host states may require this title to be
followed by the name and location of the establishment or examining board
which awarded it. If the academic title used in the state of origin can be

confused in the host state with a title requiring additional education or training, which the person concerned has not undergone, the host state may require that person to use the title employed in the state of origin but in a suitable form to be specified by the host state.

Proof of good character

A host state which requires of its nationals proof of good character or good repute when they take up the profession of architect for the first time shall accept as sufficient evidence, in respect of nationals of other member states, a certificate issued by a competent authority in the state of origin attesting that the requirements of that state as to good character or good repute for taking up the activity in question have been met. In cases where the state of origin does not offer such evidence then the host state may require an extract from the 'judicial record' or, failing this, an equivalent document issued by a competent authority in the state of origin. In exceptional circumstances where no documentary proof is available then there can be substituted a declaration on oath made by the person concerned before a competent judicial or administrative authority usually in the state of origin but if necessary in the host state.

In the event that a host state has detailed knowledge of a serious matter concerning an architect and this is likely to affect the taking up within its territory of the activity concerned, it may inform the architect's national authorities. The authorities in the state of origin must verify the accuracy of the facts and shall inform the host state of any consequential action taken with regard to the certificates or documents issued. Likewise, the state of origin must forward to the host state all necessary information regarding any measures or disciplinary action of a professional or administrative nature taken against the person concerned or any criminal penalties concerning the practice of his profession.

Actually conferring recognition of a person's ability to take up the architectural profession must be completed as soon as possible, and not later than three months after presentation of all the documents relating to that person, unless enquiries are sought from the state of origin.

Local registration

Certain special provisions relate only to the cross-border provision of services. Any requirement to obtain local authorisation from or membership of or registration with a professional organisation or body is exempted so far as nationals of other member states are concerned. Otherwise, the person concerned must provide services with the same rights and obligations as nationals of the host state; in particular he will be subject to the rules of conduct of a professional or administrative nature which apply in that member state. In this regard, some member states require automatic temporary registration or *pro forma* registration with a professional organisation or body or in a register. This is acceptable provided that this registration does not delay or in any way complicate the provision of services or impose any additional costs on the person providing the services. To this end, a migrant architect can be required to supply a declaration on oath and certificates of good standing and compliance with this directive as regards his diploma.

Regardless of whether an architect seeks to establish himself or simply provide cross-border services, he is conferred the professional title of the host state and the abbreviated form thereof once he has fulfilled any conditions as to practical training experience laid down by that state. As with evidence of diplomas, a certificate from the state of origin stating that appropriate practical experience for a corresponding period has been acquired in that country is sufficient to comply with this requirement. Evidence of solvency and insurance can come in the usual form acceptable in the state of origin.

At any time, the person concerned must have access to information on the laws and, where applicable, on the professional ethics of the host state. The directive even includes the facility for setting up information centres from which such persons may obtain the necessary information, although in the event of establishment, the host state may require them to contact these centres. Last but not least, national authorities are to ensure that, where appropriate, the persons concerned acquire, in their own interest and in that of their clients, the linguistic knowledge needed to follow their profession in the host state.

Whenever there is a legitimate doubt over the authenticity of the diplomas, certificates and other evidence of formal qualifications awarded, and of other information the host state may require the competent authorities of another member state to confirm such details.

Free movement of other professionals

Professions

A general as opposed to sectoral approach to integration of the professions was undertaken in order to provide a rapid response to the expectations of nationals of community countries holding higher-education diplomas awarded on completion of professional education and training issued in a member state other than that in which they wish to pursue their profession. Moreover it was envisaged that this would open up to graduates all those professional activities which in a host member state are dependent on the completion of post-secondary education and training, provided they held a diploma preparing them for those activities awarded on completion of a course of studies lasting at least three years and issued in another member state.

The 1989 Mutual Recognition of Diplomas Directive

The Council Directive of 21 December 1988 on a general system for the recognition of higher-education diplomas awarded on completion of professional education and training of at least three years' duration (89/48/EEC) emerged out of the observation that three years was almost universally the duration of a university education. Accordingly, the directive defines a diploma as any certificate or other evidence of formal qualifications which has been awarded by a competent authority after successful completion of a post-secondary course of at least three years' duration, (or of an equivalent duration part-time) at a university or establishment of higher education (or another establishment of similar level) and, where appropriate, successful completion of any professional training required in addition to the post-secondary course. In addition it includes any qualification which shows that the holder has the professional qualifications required for the taking up or pursuit of a regulated profession in that member state. In this regard the education and training attested by the diplomas, certificates or other evidence of formal qualifications ought have been received mainly in the community, or at the very least in a third country whose diploma, certificate or other evidence of formal qualifications are recognised.

'Profession' defined

The emphasis is therefore on the ability to use qualifications meeting minimum criteria in order to gain access to professions throughout the Union. By 'profession' is meant those activities which are regulated by any or all member states and to which access is subject, directly or indirectly, by virtue of laws, regulations or administrative provisions to the possession of a diploma (e.g. surveyor, town planner, etc.). This includes the pursuit of an activity under a professional title, insofar as the use of such a title is reserved to the holders of a diploma governed by laws, regulations or administrative provisions, and the pursuit of a professional activity relating to health, in so far as remuneration and/or reimbursement for such an activity is subject by virtue of national social security arrangements to the possession of a diploma. In general, however, an activity will constitute a profession if it is pursued by the members of an association or organisation:

- the purpose of which is, in particular, to promote and maintain a high standard in the professional field concerned;
- which, to achieve that purpose, is recognised in a special form by a member state and awards a diploma to its members;
- which ensures that its members respect the rules of professional conduct which it prescribes; and
- which confers on them the right to use a title or designatory letters, or to benefit from a status corresponding to that diploma.

Supplemented aptitude tests and requirements for recognition

In order to permit this test to be carried out, the competent authorities shall draw up a list of subjects which, on the basis of a comparison of the education and training required in the member state and that received by the applicant, are not covered by the diploma or other evidence of formal qualifications possessed by the applicant. The aptitude test must take account of the fact that the applicant is a qualified professional in the state of origin or the member state from which he comes. It shall cover subjects to be selected from those on the list, knowledge of which is essential in order to be able to exercise the profession in the host member state. The test may also include knowledge of the professional rules applicable to the activities in question in the host state. The detailed application of the aptitude test shall be determined by the competent authorities of that state with due regard to the rules of community law. The status, in the host state, of applicants who wish to prepare themselves for the aptitude test in that state shall be determined by the competent authorities in that state.

The basic principle is that where, in a host state, the taking up or pursuit of a regulated profession is subject to possession of a diploma, then the competent authority may not, on the grounds of inadequate qualifications, refuse to authorise a national of another member state to take up or pursue that profession on the same conditions as apply to its own nationals. The authority is bound by this if the applicant:

- holds the diploma required in another member state for the taking up or pursuit of the profession in question in its territory, such diploma having been awarded in a member state; or
- if the applicant has pursued the profession in question full-time for two years during the previous ten years in another member state which does not regulate that profession;
- if the applicant simply possesses evidence of one or more formal qualifications.

These qualifications in respect of this last category ought to have been awarded by a competent authority in a member state, designated in accordance with the laws, regulations or administrative provisions of such state, and show that the holder has successfully completed a post-secondary course of at least three years duration as set out above. Moreover 'qualification' includes absolutely any formal recognition of completed training. Therefore it includes qualifications treated as equivalent in the state of origin, although the directive does require notification of such qualifications to other member states.

Authorised additional requirements

Notwithstanding this framework, differences still remain in the training and education of professionals. Consequently, a host state does have certain prerogatives it may exercise to regulate admission.

Firstly it may require the applicant to provide evidence of professional experience where the duration of the education and training adduced in support of his application is at least one year less than that required in the host state. In this event, the period of professional experience required may not exceed twice the shortfall in duration of education and training where the shortfall relates to post-secondary studies and/or to a period of probationary practice carried out under the control of a supervising professional person and ending with an examination, and in any event may not exceed four years.

Alternatively, it may require the applicant to complete of an 'adaptation period' not exceeding three years or to take an aptitude test. Should a host state exercise this possibility then it must give the applicant the right to choose between the two. However it is not obliged to offer a choice if a host state profession requires precise knowledge of national law. In these circumstances it is the member state which may choose the method of testing ability and experience. An adaptation period involves being admitted to the profession in the host member state but under the responsibility of a qualified member of that profession for a period of supervised practice possibly being accompanied by further training. This period of supervised practice will be the subject of an assessment, but all adaptation rules should be clearly set out by the national authority. An adaptation period may be required where the matters covered by the education and training the professional has received in his home state differ substantially from those covered by the diploma required in the host state, or where the host state profession comprises one or more regulated activities which are not in the profession regulated in the home state, which again renders the training and education substantially different. Meanwhile the aptitude test is defined as a test limited to the professional knowledge of the applicant with the aim of assessing the ability of the applicant to pursue a regulated profession in that member state.

On a more constructive note, the directive encourages member states to allow applicants, with a view to improving their possibilities of adapting to the professional environment in the host state, to undergo that part of their professional education and training with the assistance of a qualified member of the profession which they have not undergone in their state of origin.

Formalities for admission and recognition

Admission to a profession is regulated not only in terms equating ability but also has a significant formal dimension. Here, in ensuring that the golden rule of equality of treatment is not undermined, the directive sets out the requirements in the issue and acceptance of documentation.

Where the competent authority of a host state requires applicants to prove that they are of good character or repute, or that they have not been declared bankrupt, or suspended or prohibited from practice for serious professional misconduct or a criminal offence, that state shall accept as sufficient evidence the production of documents issued by home state authorities. Where no such documents are ordinarily issued then this requirement is to be replaced by a statement on oath or a solemn declaration made by the person concerned before a competent judicial or administrative authority or, where appropriate, a notary or qualified professional person. A certificate is to be issued attesting to the authenticity of the declaration as to the matters set out above.

The position is similar in respect to any requirement for a certificate of physical or mental health. The host authorities must accept as sufficient evidence the production of the document as required in the state of origin. Where there is no such requirement in the home state then any certificate which corresponds to those in the host state will be adequate for the holder to exercise the right of free movement and entry to that state's profession.

Once these substantive and formal conditions are met then the authorities of the host state must recognise the right of nationals of other member states to use the professional title of the host state corresponding to that profession in addition to their lawful academic title and, where appropriate, the abbreviation thereof deriving from their state of origin in the language of that state. However, the host state may require this title to be followed by the name and location of the establishment or examining board which awarded it. On the other hand, where a profession is regulated in the host state by an association or organisation then it is not unlawful for the host state to restrict use of this professional title or the designatory letters conferred by that organisation or association on proof of membership. Where the association or organisation makes membership subject to certain qualification requirements, it may apply these to nationals of other member states who are in possession of an appropriate diploma as regulated by the directive.

The procedure for examining an application for admission to a profession is to be completed as soon as possible and the outcome communicated in a reasoned decision of the competent authority in the host state not later than four months after presentation of all the documents relating to the person concerned. A remedy shall be available against this decision, or the absence thereof, before a court or tribunal in accordance with the provisions of national law.

In the United Kingdom, the professions relevant to the construction sector which are considered to come within the scope of the directive are those governed by the Royal Institution of Chartered Surveyors, the Chartered Institute of Building, the Engineering Council, the Institution of Structural Engineers, the Institution of Civil Engineers, the Royal Town Planning Institute, and the Chartered Institution of Building Services Engineers.

Trades

The 1992 Mutual Recognition of Diplomas Directive

The single characteristic that defines the 1989 Directive is the requirement
that any qualifications be granted following a three year degree, whereas of
course there are a considerable number of practical based education and
training diplomas which are granted following courses of lesser duration.
Holders of such diplomas are given rights of free movement under the
Council Directive (92/51).

The regulatory framework envisaged by this directive is similarly
structured to that of the 1989 directive. Here a diploma (awarded by a
competent authority in a member state designated in accordance with the
laws, regulations or administrative provisions of that state) is considered
evidence of education and training, and shows that the holder has
successfully completed either a post-secondary course of at least one year
duration or of equivalent duration on a part-time basis.

Course requirements

However, there is a greater of emphasis on the conditions of admission to the
course. Such diplomas must have as their entry requirements the general
condition of a successfully completed secondary course leading to a diploma
which entitles the holder to entry to a university or higher education. Certain
institutions are presumed to meet this requirement and these are set out in
the directive. However, even these institutions must demonstrate that the
education and training gives the holder the professional qualifications
required for the taking up or pursuit of a regulated profession in that
member state.

Again the education and training must be received mainly in the community, or outside the community at teaching establishments which provide
education and training in accordance with the laws, regulations or administrative provisions of a member state. In exceptional circumstances, the
holder may rely on three years professional experience certified by the
member state which recognised third-country evidence of education and
training. Likewise, certain diplomas which do not immediately meet these
requirements will also qualify. For instance, the directive covers any
diploma awarded on the successful completion of education and training
received in the community and recognised by a competent authority in that
member state as being of an equivalent level which confers the same rights in
respect of the taking up and pursuit of a regulated profession in that member
state. It also covers non-vocational certificates which record the successful
completion of a secondary course plus completion of either other courses of
education or training provided at an educational or training establishment,
or on the job, or in combination at an educational or training establishment
and on the job, and complemented (where appropriate) by the probationary

or professional practice required in addition to this course. It extends also to secondary courses of a technical or vocational nature which show that the holder has the professional qualifications required for the taking up or pursuit of a regulated profession in that member state. In this particular situation two years of recognised professional experience outside the Union will satisfy the requirements.

Attestation of competence

Where recognition of experience or completion of a course comes not in a certificate but by way of attestation of competence even if this attestation does not form part of a formal diploma then so long as it is awarded following an assessment of the personal qualities, aptitudes or knowledge which it is considered essential that the applicant have for the pursuit of a profession by an authority designated in accordance with the laws, regulations or administrative provisions of a member state, without proof of prior education and training being required, then this too can be relied upon in other member states.

Definition of 'profession'

This is the same as under the 1989 directive (see above) save that rather than the award of a diploma the association or organisation awards evidence of education and training to its members, and the duration of the training is shorter. The distinction between 'trade' and 'profession' as understood in British culture is not, therefore, a matter of terminology with the obvious linguistic pitfalls as requirements are applied across the Union.

The primary right

The primary right set out in the directive consists of the prohibition imposed on all trade organisations not, on the grounds of inadequate qualifications, to refuse to authorise a national of a member state to take up or pursue that profession on the same conditions as those which apply to its own nationals if the applicant holds the diploma required in another member state for the taking up or pursuit of the profession in question in its territory, or if the applicant has pursued the profession in question full-time for two years (or for an equivalent period on a part-time basis) during the previous 10 years in another member state which does not regulate that profession. As under the 1989 Directive that person must possess evidence of education and training (rather than a 'diploma') awarded appropriately by a competent authority either showing that the holder has successfully completed a post-secondary course of at least one year's duration (or a part-time equivalent) or attesting to regulated education and training that has prepared the holder for the pursuit of his profession.

'Regulated education and training'

The two years professional experience referred to above may not be required where the evidence of education and training held by the applicant is awarded on completion of 'regulated education and training'. This consists of education and training specifically geared to the pursuit of a given profession comprising a course or courses complemented (where appropriate) by professional training or probationary or professional practice. The structure and level of these elements are determined by the laws, regulations or administrative provisions of that member state or are monitored or approved by the authority designated for that purpose.

Additional requirements

Notwithstanding the primary right the host member state is entitled (as under the 1989 directive) to require the applicant to meet certain formalistic and substantive conditions. The same evidence of professional experience can be required where the duration of the education and training is at least one year less than that specified in the host member state. As above it must not exceed twice the shortfall in the duration of education and training. Professional experience may not, however, be required of an applicant holding a diploma attesting to a post-secondary course set out in the directive.

Alternatively, applicants can again be asked to complete an adaptation period, likewise not exceeding three years, or take an aptitude test where the theoretical and/or practical matters covered by the education and training which they have received differ substantially from those required in the host state, or if there are differences in the specific education and training required in the host state.

Once again should the host state make use of this possibility, it must give the applicant the right to choose between an adaptation period and an aptitude test unless an essential and constant feature of the professional activity is a precise knowledge of national law or unless a condition of entry into the profession is the completion of a post-secondary course of at least three years duration or an equivalent period on a part-time basis. However, the host member state may not apply these alternatives cumulatively.

Free movement of site staff

It is perhaps axiomatic that any contractor bidding for a contract will build labour costs into the price submitted based on current contractual commitments or on the basis of market conditions pertaining in the state in which he operates, and not least the social security and other legislative constraints with which he must comply. Given that standards of living are different between member states, and that collective agreements between the two sides of industry are nationally based, it follows that these labour costs will differ. Therefore, in an embryonic single market in which national market conditions are prevalent contractors in one state may be able to compete legitimately on price on account of lower labour costs. Of course this simple proposition does not overlook the fact that in moving local labour to site involves the additional cost of transport and accommodation. However, the measure of resources employers apply to this quarter is very much a matter for themselves and the workforce.

If under Article 52 TEU a contractor is setting up a branch or agency in another member state then he is entitled to transfer staff from his primary or original establishment if their intended role is managerial or supervisory (Article 54 TEU). This is so regardless of the nationality of the employees and even if they are non-EU nationals. However non-EU nationals will still be subject to the host state's immigration and visa rules, whereas no such restrictions can be imposed on citizens of the Union. Alternatively, whilst employers do not have any direct rights under Article 48 TEU, which confers the right of free movement on workers, they can indirectly benefit in that a business which is established may employ any worker it wishes. Thus the right of a worker to take up offers of employment by businesses established in another member state translates into a right of an employer to offer contracts of employment to workers from other member states. In both these situations, however, the employer is bound to comply with the social security and other conditions of work. This is in contrast to the cross-border service provider for which there is the implied right in Article 59 TEU to undertake and carry out services in the state where the service receiver resides or is based using staff from his state of origin, whatever their nationality, EU or non-EU. These workers do not necessarily have to have supervisory or managerial roles as the decisions of the Court of Justice in *Rush Portuguesa* and *Vander Elst* demonstrate.

In 1990 the Court of Justice handed down its ruling in *Société Rush Portuguesa Lda* v. *Office National d'Immigration* (C-113/89 [1990] ECR 1-1417), a reference in response to a request for a preliminary ruling from the Tribunal Administratif de Versailles, France. In this case it held that Articles 59 and 60 TEU must be interpreted as meaning that an undertaking established in one member state, providing services in the construction and public works sector in another member state, may move with its labour force which it brings for the duration of the works in question. In such a case, the authorities of the member state in whose territory the works are to be carried out may not impose on the supplier of services conditions relating to the recruitment of manpower *in situ* or the obtaining of work permits for the 'migrant' work-force. However, those authorities may check whether an undertaking is not circumventing the provisions of Article 52 TEU (on the right of establishment) under the cloak of a provision of services.

This principle arose in proceedings between Rush Portuguesa Lda, a Portuguese based contractor, and France's Office National d'Immigration. Rush Portuguesa entered into a sub-contract with a French main contractor for the carrying out of works for the construction of a railway line in the west of France. For that purpose it brought in its Portuguese employees from Portugal. However, the law as it stood in France only permitted the Office National d'Immigration to recruit in France nationals of third countries. After establishing that Rush Portuguesa were in breach of this rule, the Office ordered Rush Portuguesa to make a special contribution to the social security regime in accordance with the same French law. Rush Portuguesa therefore sought to annul that decision by submitting that it had freedom to provide services within the Union and that, accordingly, the provisions of Articles 59 and 60 TEU precluded the application of national legislation having the effect of prohibiting its staff from working in France.

The main thrust of the case turned upon Portuguese accession arrangements since it had only joined the Union a few years previously to the occurrence of the facts in the case. Nevertheless, this does not weaken the principles established by the Court. In this connection, the Court observed first of all that the freedom to provide services laid down in Article 59 TEU entails, according to Article 60 TEU, that the person providing a service may, in order to do so, temporarily pursue his activity in the state where the service is provided 'under the same conditions as are imposed by that state on its own nationals'. It concluded, therefore, that Articles 59 and 60 TEU preclude a member state from prohibiting a person providing services established in another member state from moving freely on its territory with all his staff and preclude that member state from making the movement of staff in question subject to restrictions such as a condition as to engagement *in situ* or an obligation to obtain work permits. Imposing such conditions on the person providing services established in another member state discriminated against that person in relation to his competitors established in the host country who are able to use their own staff without restrictions, and moreover affects his ability to provide the service.

It added that this should typically apply in the context of the construction industry where there is a temporary movement of workers who are sent to another member state to carry out a construction project or public works as part of a provision of services by their employer. In this respect it noted that these workers ordinarily return to their country of origin after the completion of their work without at any time gaining access to the labour market of the host state.

Furthermore the Court appears to indicate that identifying what activities this principle applies to is to be taken sector by sector. In this regard, the Court pointed out that since the concept of the provision of services (as defined by Article 60 TEU) covers very different activities, the same conclusions are not necessarily appropriate in all cases. In particular, it has to be acknowledged that an undertaking engaged in making labour available, although a supplier of services, within the meaning of the Treaty, carries on activities which are specifically intended to enable workers to gain access to the labour market of the host state. The indication is, therefore, that this kind activity would not benefit as the construction industry does. The Court added, that this observation in no way affects the right of a person providing services in the building and public works sector to move with his own labour force from one member state to another for the duration of the work undertaken.

Against this, the Court said, member states must be free in each case to ascertain whether the cross-border contractor is seeking to avoid the incidence of social security and other obligations which necessarily arise when a business establishes itself in a member state, by availing itself of the freedom to provide services for another purpose, for example that of bringing in its workers for the purposes of placing them or making them available on the local labour market. However, such checks must observe the limits imposed by community law and in particular those stemming from the freedom to provide services which cannot be rendered illusory and the exercise of which may not be made subject to the discretion of the authorities.

Moreover, the Court conceded that Union law does not preclude member states from extending their legislation, or collective labour agreements entered into by both sides of industry, to any person who is employed, even temporarily, within their territory (no matter in which country the employer is established) nor does community law prohibit member states from enforcing those rules by appropriate means.

In *Vander Elst* v. *OMI* (C-43/93) [1990] ECR I-3803, the Court reached the same conclusion in relation to non-EU nationals who were employed by an EU cross-border service provider. A Belgian specialist demolition contractor carrying out works in France employed Moroccan nationals. These non-EU nationals were legally resident in Belgium. On the grounds that these workers were not seeking access to the local labour market whereas their employer was lawfully exercising his right to provide services under Article 59, the Court ruled that the French immigration authorities could not insist on Vander Elst, as employer, obtaining visas for his employees.

Chapter 12
Liability

The final section of this book focuses on Union laws which harmonise the liability of contractors and professionals in pursuit of their activities. It is not as straightforward an exercise as other areas covered since, with one or two exceptions, the object of most laws coming within the subject matter of this section is not harmonisation. Moreover, in the absence of deliberate and wholesale harmonisation of liability rules which protect parties to a contract or consumers and employees, the incidence of liability, as well as the related standards and burdens of proof, are subject to national rules. All one can categorically point out is that national procedural laws should not make it virtually impossible or more difficult to enforce rights originating in Union law than it is to enforce rights in national law. On the other hand, to some significant extent all laws which regulate commercial activity, either by enabling greater integration of the markets or by imposing minimum standards, involve rationalising standards of liability. Therefore the task in hand is simply to examine these laws from a different perspective.

Accordingly, this chapter deals with product liability, the one area in which the Union has successfully brought about substantial harmonisation of national rules. It also covers services liability but, since this is an area in which the Union's proposals for harmonisation have been been rejected, the study (whilst detailed) is more of a prognosis of what the future may hold. The following chapters deal with duties imposed on operators in order to protect the environment and the health and safety of workers. Outside these areas, and particularly in the contractual domain, liability falls to be considered comparatively between member states. That task is too great for a book of this size but it is appropriate nonetheless to comment initially on the mechanism by which one national law or another is chosen to judge a particular contractual or tortious event. This involves a brief study of the international conventions on jurisdiction.

Jurisdiction and choice of law

Parties to a contract are entitled to choose the law by which their relationship will be regulated and so they may choose that the law of a particular state should apply.

However, a party to a contract may discover that a choice of law clause is not effective. Equally there may not be such a clause. Therefore, it falls to be considered how this is to be determined.

A national court is not precluded from judging a claim simply because the law of another country applies. However a national court may not endeavour to hear and judge a case and thereby enforce rights appropriate to a given situation unless it has *jurisdiction* to hear the claim. Therefore in a single market it follows that any cross-border transaction could theoretically be heard by all states of those nationals who are party to it or of those persons who are resident within its territory. Each member state will have its own 'conflict of laws' rules to deal with this but to ensure consistency in the development and application of Union law there is a formula to determine which state should be seized of the case. That formula is provided by the 1968 Convention on jurisdiction and the enforcement of judgments in civil and commercial matters, known as the Brussels Convention. As the title indicates it deals with jurisdiction and with the enforcement of judgments obtained. This brief study will concentrate only on the former.

The general rule is that persons domiciled in a state (and by extension legal persons with their seat or principal place of business in a state) shall, whatever their nationality, be sued in the courts of that state in respect of all civil and commercial matters whatever the nature of the court or tribunal before which the case should be heard (excluding revenue, customs or administrative matters). However, the courts of a state other than the one where the defendant is domiciled may have concurrent jurisdiction in a number of matters.

Firstly, in matters relating to contract, then the courts for the place of performance of the obligation in question also have jurisdiction. The obligation in question is the one upon which the plaintiff's claim is principally made, and where this is in doubt then the state which has the closest connection with the dispute can be chosen in accordance with the principles set forth in the 1980 (Rome) Convention on the law applicable to contractual obligations (in particular the place of performance of the obligation which characterises the contract). In matters relating to individual contracts of employment, then this place is where the employee habitually carries out his or her work, or if there is more than one such place then the employer may be sued in the courts for the place where the business which engaged the employee was or is now situated. Secondly, in matters relating to tort, then there is alternative jurisdiction in the courts for the place where the harmful event occurred. Thirdly, as regards a dispute arising out of the operations of a branch, agency or other establishment, the courts of the place where that establishment is situated can also deal with the matter. There are other instances of special jurisdiction but these are not relevant here.

In the case of contractual matters, then it is open to the parties to agree that the courts of a particular state should have exclusive jurisdiction. This agreement will be lawful so long as it is in writing, or in a form which accords with the practices which the parties have established between themselves or, in international trade or commerce, in a form which accords with a usage of which the parties are or ought to have been aware. It should be noted that the courts of the place where proceedings have as their object rights *in rem* in immovable property will have exclusive jurisdiction regardless of domicile (but not necessarily agreement).

In the construction context then, construction activities will largely be contractual and centred on the place where the works are sited, to which contractors, sub-contractors, professional consultants, and suppliers direct themselves in order to perform their duties. Therefore, it is likely in a number of ways that it will be the courts of this state which will have jurisdiction.

- In any contractual matter the place of performance will be on site. The only possible exception will be in the case of pre-fabricated products and the supply of raw materials where the supplier is not also responsible for incorporation. In this case then the general rule of defendant's domicile will apply unless 'delivery to site' can be successfully argued to be the place of performance of the obligation in question.
- Disputes regarding the operation of the site which are non-contractual would still be heard in the state where the site is situated since it could constitute an establishment notwithstanding that it would be temporary and accordingly may not be regarded as an establishment under Article 52 TEU.
- Tortious matters taking place on site would also meet the requirement that the relevant courts are those of the place where the harmful event occurred.
- Finally, in disputes relating to rights in the completed property (which are also non-contractual) the courts of the place of site have (exclusive) jurisdiction.

Therefore only in respect of contractual matters where the parties have expressly agreed that the courts of a state other than that where the site is located have jurisdiction could one lead to a different conclusion.

Product liability

Defective products

As will be revealed in the substance of what follows, manufacturers and users of defective construction products will be liable for damage caused by the defect. The industry is therefore subject to the whole EU regime on product liability.

The Product Liability Directive

Harmonisation of product liability laws has been principally achieved by the Product Liability Directive 85/374/EEC ([1985] OJ L210/29). As the Commission observed ahead of its original proposal, legal protection differed under the domestic legal systems of the member states on the availability of damages and the need for proof of fault. This translated into cost differentials which distorted competition, affected the free movement of goods and caused uncertainty for the consumer. The directive defines the circumstances in which liability may arise and the extent of that liability. It does not, however regulate general domestic law governing negligence. The chief principle of the directive is that the producer shall be liable for damage suffered by anyone using his product where that damage is caused by a defect, irrespective of fault or contractual relationship.

'Product'

Product means all moveables (with the exception of primary agricultural products) whether or not incorporated into another moveable or into an immoveable. This definition includes tools and industrial machinery (which may already be covered by other safety legislation) and also includes electricity, water, waste, and gas (and so if a water supply is contaminated then loss occasioned by this may be recoverable).

Whilst product is defined to mean 'moveables' it would appear not to apply to buildings but to building components. This is confirmed by the Commission which explained that liability extends only to moveable property. Special rules, it observes,

> 'exist in all member states to cover defective immoveable property such as buildings. However, where moveable objects are used in the erection of buildings or installed in buildings, the producer is liable in respect of these objects to the extent provided for in the directive.' (Com (76) 372 final).

Clearly, then, the test becomes whether an item is a product incorporated into building or is part of the building itself. Two problems could be met with here. Only if the defective product is incorporated can the finished product itself be considered as defective. Secondly, the owner of the final product of which the defective component is part cannot claim damages in respect of the defective product. In terms of liability the test could become: would the finished product have been defective without the defective component?

'Defective'

A product is defective when it does not provide the safety which a person is entitled to expect. An expectation of safety will be ascertained by having regard to:

- the presentation of the product;
- the use to which it could reasonably be expected to be put; and
- the time when the product was put into circulation.

A product is not to be considered defective for the sole reason that a better product is available. According to the Commission, a product may be defective even though it fulfils its design function if hazards associated with its use are not sufficiently brought to the consumers' attention by means of instructions or labelling. Moreover, these hazards may only arise in relation to particular classes of person (e.g. children) in which case more pointed preventative action is needed. However, liability will be limited to injury occasioned by use which was reasonably expected, although if certain misuse was reasonably expected then this requirement would be met. On the other hand, a producer is not liable for a product which becomes defective beyond its useful life or because safety regulations are tightened up after it was placed into the market.

'Producer'

The person liable for a defective product is the producer. This means:

- the manufacturer of a finished product;
- the producer of any raw material or the manufacturer of a component part; and
- any person who, by putting his name, trade-mark or other distinguishing feature on the product presents himself as its producer.

It will also include any person who imports into the Union a product for sale, hire, leasing or any form of distribution in the course of his business. Moreover, where the actual producer cannot be identified, each supplier of the product shall be treated as its producer unless he informs the injured person within a reasonable time of the identity of the producer or of the person who supplied him with the product. Where two or more persons are liable for the same damage then they shall be jointly and severally liable for the loss occasioned. This is without prejudice to national rules concerning the rights of contribution or recourse, but these national rules may not be relied on if they reduce liability of the producer because of the joint act or omission of a third party. On the other hand rules allowing contributory negligence are not prohibited.

'Damage'

'Damage' means that caused by death or by personal injury, and, although the recovery of damages for non-material loss is to be regulated by national law, a person or (in case of death) his dependants should be able to recover financial loss. In this regard the liability of a producer may not be limited or excluded. Damage also covers damage to, or destruction of, any item of property other than the defective product itself, so long as the product is of a type ordinarily intended for private use or consumption and was used by the injured person mainly for his own private use or consumption. This

excludes property used by the injured person as part of his work or profession and therefore also excludes damage to economic interests. However
the Commission is maintaining a watching brief on whether these excluded
areas should themselves be the subject of further harmonisation, and it can
be observed that the property need not be solely for private use. In any event,
damage which consists of the defective product itself is excluded.

There are financial limits to the right to claim compensation. The first ECU
500 is irrecoverable irrespective or the size of the claim. There is no limit to
the producer's liability for damage to property, but member states have the
discretion to limit the producer's total liability resulting from death or
personal injury and caused by identical items with the same defect to not less
that ECU 70 million. Nowhere is there any requirement to guarantee the
ability to meet claims of damages for defective products.

Defences

There are six potential defences under the directive.

- Firstly, that the product had not been put into circulation with the
  producer's consent (and giving of consent need not be evidenced by
  contract or payment).
- Secondly, that the defect did not exist at the time the product was put into
  circulation. That is, the defect was either caused independently by a third
  party or the product was misused in a way that was not to be reasonably
  expected.
- Thirdly, that the product was not manufactured for an economic purpose
  or not manufactured or distributed by the producer/supplier in the
  course of a business.
- Fourthly, that the defect was due to compliance with mandatory regulations issued by the public authorities. That is, the defect was the unavoidable result of compliance with a regulation imposed by law (although
  one might question the applicability of a national regulation which is
  clearly in contravention of a European standard).
- Fifthly, that the state of scientific and technical knowledge at the time
  when he put the product into circulation was not such as to enable the
  existence of the defect to be discovered. This 'state-of-the-art' defence is
  open to review and repeal by the Commission given that it condones
  inadequate research and development.
- Finally, that in the case of a manufacturer of a component the defect is
  attributable to the design of the product in which the component has been
  fitted or to the instructions given by the manufacturer of the product.

To these one can add the defence that the plaintiff, notwithstanding the
absence of a need to show fault, has unreasonably misused the product or
has not shown the product to be defective, as well as the limitation defence
in that proceedings were not initiated within three years from the day on

which the plaintiff became aware or reasonably ought to have become aware of the damage, the defect and the identity of the producer.

Product safety

If the Product Liability Directive was not sufficient, the EU has the parallel Product Safety Directive 92/59/EEC ([1992] OJ L228/24) which requires producers to place only 'safe' products on the market and to require distributors not to supply products which do not comply with the general safety requirement. Whilst this places a civil duty on such persons it is also backed up with criminal sanctions (which member states are required to impose) to achieve, in conjunction with the Product Liability Directive, criminal and civil measures to ensure the health and safety of consumers.

The directive is, however, of qualified relevance to the construction industry. It applies to any product intended for consumers (or likely to be used by consumers) supplied (whether for consideration or not) in the course of a commercial activity and whether new, used or reconditioned. It does not apply to products which are subject to specific Union safety legislation save insofar as those provisions do not make specific provision governing an aspect of that product's safety. On the one hand, the Construction Products Directive is specific health and safety legislation in respect of which criminal sanctions are envisaged. Moreover, a great many construction products are arguably not intended for consumers, not least because the Safety Directive does not place any direct emphasis on incorporation of products into others. On the other hand, the Product Safety Directive is there to catch the few (perhaps theoretical) situations in which the CPD does not apply.

In this regard it is to be noted that a 'safe' product is one which under normal or reasonably foreseeable conditions of use (including duration) does not present any risk, or only the minimum risks compatible with the producer's use considered as acceptable and consistent with a high level of protection for the health and safety of persons. There is to be taken into account in determining this the characteristics of the product including:

- its composition, packaging, instructions for assembly and maintenance;
- the effect on other products where it is reasonably foreseeable that it will be used with other products;
- the presentation of the product;
- the labelling, any instructions for its use and disposal and any other indication or information provided by the producer; and
- the categories of consumers at serious risk when using the product.

Any product which does not adequately meet these requirements and considerations is defined as 'dangerous'.

The duty applies to the producer, i.e. the manufacturer of the product when he established in the Union or any person presenting himself as or acting on behalf of such. Suppliers and importers will also incur liability in the absence of a Union-based manufacturer, but in any event distributors of a product are under the slightly less onerous duty to act with due care in order to help ensure compliance with the general safety requirements, in particular by not supplying products which they know or should have presumed, on the basis of the information in their possession and as professionals, do not comply with that requirement. The available defences include that the product was not intended for consumers or that the product only became dangerous after it was put onto the market. However, the wording of the directive implies a duty incurring strict liability which would seem to exclude any reliance of the principle of 'due diligence'.

The Construction Products Directive

The analysis of the Products Liability Directive revealed that the producer is liable for any damage caused by his product and that this includes products intended for incorporation into another. Whether a product is defective will turn on whether it was fit for the purpose or use for which it was intended or to which it was reasonably expected to be subjected. In turn this depends upon products, including those in the construction field, meeting the appropriate technical requirements since compliance with a standard is a defence to the incidence of otherwise strict liability. Likewise, the Product Safety Directive established the duty of producers to place only safe products onto the market, but this directive is without prejudice to more specific provisions, such as the Construction Products Directive (CPD).

The CPD is analysed in depth in Chapter 10 from the point of view of its free movement provisions. As was observed there, technical requirements are, when regulated at a national level, regarded as barriers to trade and it is only by harmonising these measures that one begins to achieve a single market in construction products. To harmonise technical standards one has to have regard to the purpose of standards, chiefly being the protection of those who come into connection with the products, i.e. the health and safety of the end user. This the CPD does by setting down essential requirements for the construction works to ensure all products are fit for the purpose intended, there being:

- mechanical resistance and stability;
- safety in case of fire;
- hygiene, health and the environment;
- safety in use;
- protection against noise; and
- energy economy and heat retention

As its name indicates the CPD applies to all products and materials which are produced for incorporation in a permanent manner in construction works, including both building and civil engineering works. In fact the CPD and the Interpretative Documents explain explicitly that the essential requirements apply to products although they are defined by reference to the works into which they are incorporated. However, this necessitates an unnatural premise that the works and the products are two distinct properties. It will be observed that the fitness of purpose element relates to the works and not the specific product itself. The directive states that a construction product is fit for its intended use when it permits the works in which it is to be incorporated to satisfy the applicable essential requirements. Furthermore, the IDs constantly refer to the need for the 'construction works to be designed and built in such a way so as to' achieve some objective or other.

That is not to say the essential requirements are immaterial to the placing of a construction product on the market. On the contrary, they have every-thing to do with construction products. Rather the purpose of focusing on the construction works is to put the CPD into a realistic context. This is something of a novel technique by which one can say that the CPD does apply to buildings indirectly.

Although it applies to products and not buildings, products which are intended for use in construction works may only be placed on the market (i.e. be bought and sold) if they are fit for this intended use. In order for products to be fit for their intended use, then they must have such char-acteristics that the works in which they are incorporated will, if properly designed and built, satisfy the essential requirements contained in the CPD.

Thus the safety element is manifested when the construction products are incorporated into building and civil engineering works.

One can therefore conclude that the construction of a building is subject to two requirements:

- it must be properly designed and built; and
- it must be made of products which are fit for their intended use and which comply with the essential requirements.

The health and safety element is to be found in the reference to the essential requirements. Hence, the directive imposes a duty on manufacturers to ensure these requirements are met. It also places a duty on designers to specify only those products which comply with the essential requirements and are fit for the purpose intended by the manufacturer, since any product which does not comply can be presumed to be dangerous. Finally, there is a duty on the contractor to incorporate those products correctly into the work in accordance with the designer's and manufacturer's instructions so that the works themselves satisfy the essential requirements.

In this way, the CPD can be seen to have a very prominent involvement in determining the question of liability in the event, say, that the foundations suffer structural damage. In these circumstances, the CPD – or at least the UK transposition thereof – would be relevant, but not if the issue was an error in mixing or application or design.

Services liability

The logical corollary on product liability is a common regime for the liability of service providers. However in the years between the adoption of the Products Liability Directive and the creation of a single market there was something of a 'wind of change' blowing over the attitude of member states, prompted by their constituencies, to temper the progress of harmonisation, especially in areas of the law in which they felt it should be left to the member states to decide whether action should be taken. Hence, the planned directive on services liability failed to materialise after work on the proposed text was abandoned on the express wishes of the European Council. Had the proposal been adopted then, unlike under the Products Liability Directive, the construction sector would have been excluded from the scope of the services liability directive. Instead, it would have been made subject to a separate piece of legislation amending national laws on liability and warranties in the construction sector.

Whilst demand for such a text is officially non-existent, a considerable amount of work has been put into deciding what the ultimate text might look at. A definitive statement of the Commission's view on the matter is contained in a Commission Staff Discussion Paper *Concerning Possible Community Action With Regard To Liabilities and Guarantees in the Construction Sector* (1993). This Discussion Paper was the responsibility of the Construction Unit of the Directorate General for Industry (formerly responsible for the Internal Market). It was in fact the fourth paper to examine this issue since the White Paper on the completion of the Internal Market envisaged a directive on the reliability and durability of buildings. The previous three were prepared by individuals commissioned by the EC; it is not proposed to examine them here. The Commission Staff Paper offers all professionals involved in the construction industry the glimpse of what these intentions are.

The Discussion Paper runs to nearly 100 pages and is divided into five sections. These cover:

- (I) background;
- (II) principles;
- (III) form of action;
- (IV) suggested legislative text; and
- *inter alia*, (V) a comparison of the laws of the Member States.

The suggested text (IV) is in fact the one submitted by the Groupe des Associations Interprofessionnelles Européennes de la Construction (GAIPEC) in September 1992. The focus of the Discussion Paper expands on four aspects of the construction process that were previously examined by GAIPEC and have their origins in the Groupe Réflexion, Information, Management (GRIM), convened by the Commission in 1990 to draw up a list of priority topics. These were:

- acceptance of the construction works by the client;
- the liability of designers and contractors;

- the use of the warranty; and
- financial compensation for defects.

In addition the Discussion Paper examined the justification for action *per se* and looks at the political and structural considerations.

The paper does not offer any concrete conclusions either in fact or, more importantly, opinion. As its title suggests, it is a *discussion* about a *possibility*. The Commission is cautious to the extreme in considering as much as possible, yet being careful not to 'show its hand'. However, it makes clear what it seeks overall, i.,e.:

- achieving freedom of movement;
- eliminating distortions of competition;
- increasing consumer protection; and
- higher quality control ('the ultimate aim').

These, of course, are the cardinal aspirations of the Common Market and should be taken as read, requiring no further explanation.

However the Discussion Paper identifies three factors which the Commission believes have a direct bearing on whether action should, can or will be taken at all. Two of these are the stuff of political control and the third deals with the need for rationalisation in principle.

Firstly, it believes that the life of any specific legislation on construction liability largely depends upon exclusion of the industry from the aegis of the proposed Services Liability Directive which is designed for general application. This proposal was nearing its final stages before the European Parliament when it was withdrawn by the Commission for reconsideration. This course was taken because of the guidelines on subsidiarity agreed at the Edinburgh European Council Summit in December 1992. The Commission is examining whether the proposed directive comes within the jurisdiction or 'competence' of the Commission.

Secondly, the principle of subsidiarity affects the entire spectrum of Union policy and law, yet its parameters and the distinction between Union and national competence have yet to be practically defined. Accordingly there is little guidance to be found in the Discussion Paper. In essence, though, the issues to resolve are whether liability/warranty legislation can or should be used in furtherance of removing barriers to the freedom of movement of goods, persons, services and capital; and, whether Union action is necessary to achieve this free movement or it can be achieved by the Member States. No arguments are offered, although the Discussion Paper cites the following good reasons for action at the Union level:

- The existence of 15 different liability systems is a hindrance to the freedom of movement of professionals.
- These 'considerable differences' cause distortions of competition between participants in terms of economic cost.
- The cost of construction works/buildings is too great – particularly

when it is borne by private individuals – to be subject to general legislation.

- Quite apart from the different systems, the construction process is over-complicated – especially in respect of sub-contracting – and rationalisation would 'mitigate' the problems which arise
- A directive would co-ordinate, supplement and make fully effective Union legislation on public procurement, construction products, the right of establishment of architects, and health and safety.

The Paper goes so far as to say that legislation is essential to the proper working of the Public Works Contracts Directive and the Construction Products Directive. Partial measures are not ruled out, but there is no indication as to what the minimum level of competence belonging to the Union will be.

Finally, the Discussion Paper recognises that the characteristics of construction activity are not apposite to harmonisation. That is to say, construction activity is usually centred on a single geographical site and as such then there is little scope for cross-border movement of services in the sense that other industries manufacture a product and *export* it. The Commission recognises that once a foreign competitor has entered an overseas market it competes on the same local conditions as its resident counterparts. To this end it admits that 'the present system does not constitute a direct barrier to the movement of construction sector professionals'.

It is not just infrastructural incompatibility that is a problem. The Commission also anticipates confronting resolute national system loyalty. However, the most disturbing revelation is the belief by the Commission that alignment of the various national systems could cause an inestimable upset in the internal balance of national laws, of which they recognise construction law as a deep-rooted component.

The industrial viewpoint as revealed above illustrates the vastness of the issue and the hesitation of the Commission, for the Discussion Paper recommends studies into determining whether Union action is necessary and desirable, and what differences exist in the various systems of consumer protection.

The possible forms of action

The Discussion Paper presents three options. These are, for the most part, mutually exclusive and, unless a better idea is proposed, exhaustive.

Mutual recognition of national legislation

This involves minimum amendment to national laws and is highly flexible. It operates as a system of equating the different Member State systems so that they can be applied across the Union (i.e. a form of extraterritorial jurisdiction). It can operate in two ways; either

- by one Member State simply applying the law of another Member State (called 'reciprocal' mutual recognition); or
- by one Member State applying its own law that has been amended to take account of the law of another Member State ('conditional' mutual recognition).

By this, the Commission envisages that, since all legislation will be equivalent, then all participants can continue to be subject to their own national liability rules even if they carry out their activities in another country.

Standard Union contract

Action in this form would be highly flexible and is the least burdensome on national law and systems. The Discussion Paper envisages an arrangement wherein the 'parties would be free to choose a standard Union contract'. This suggestion is dealt with very briefly, and there is no indication whether the parties would be obliged to choose such a contract or whether it is intended that they be voluntary.

A directive

This, as mentioned earlier, is the form as originally conceived. It would, of course, greatly affect legislation and require confirmation that the Union is the more appropriate forum for action. For this reason, perhaps, very little detail is given other than to invite comment on a variety of issues which form the substance to wider questions on whether action can be justified *per se*.

The GAIPEC study

As mentioned earlier, the Commission has been extremely cautious not to give any concrete indications on the most likely form of action. That prudence is illustrated by the treatment of the GAIPEC suggested text which, on the one hand, is not even referred to as a potential draft directive under the last heading, but, on the other, has a whole section devoted to it.

The GAIPEC text was drafted by industry representatives, and so could be seen to be the absolute benchmark for any future directive so far as the industry is concerned. GAIPEC consisted of experts from across the whole spectrum of construction activity, from architects and surveyors to construction economists and developers via insurers and inspectors. The European Construction Industry Federation co-ordinated the work. It examined three aspects being acceptance, liability and warranties.

Acceptance

The Commission wants to see a common form of acceptance, because it sees the moment of acceptance as fundamentally important. The Discussion Paper is completely open to the form, meaning, and process of acceptance. Its options range from making acceptance a single act to introducing an automatic acceptance mechanism. In coming to a decision it will be necessary to assess:

- what the conditions governing validity of acceptance should be;
- at what point it should take place; and
- what the consequences should be.

However, despite detailed discussion there is little indication of the Commission's plans.

Liability

On liability, the Commission sets out three options for perusal. It is a simple choice. Either the action adopts a fault based approach, or it introduces a presumption of liability, or it concocts a hybrid of the two. The Discussion Paper reports that the first is more popular across the Union but recognises that a presumption of liability will offer significant consumer protection. With the first, the Commission envisages proof as a precondition to liability with the six essential requirements of the Construction Products Directive playing a central role in the exercise. In addition vicarious liability, and joint and several liability are not ruled out. The second option, the Commission envisages, would require showing a causal link between defect and activity. The third option could operate by applying the first option to commercial agreements and the second to private residential works.

   The limitation period is proving to be the most controversial issue in the matter. A choice has been set at either five or ten years and the Commission sets out the merits for both. A ten year period is in greater use across the Union. Five years is the unsurprising choice of the industry according to GAIPEC. The proposed Services Liability Directive suggested 20 years but this has been virtually discounted. Among the facts considered, the Commission cites that 75–80% of defects appear within five years and after ten years that figure has increased to 90%. The longer period is likely to increase insurance costs, although the Commission believes that the difference will be small. System loyalty and difficulties in the introduction of change are cited as the major issues to address.

Warranties

On the subject of warranties, the Commission is keen to establish a system of rapid and effective compensation and says that it has wide support from various industrial sources. However, it notes that only France has a compulsory form of financial guarantee, and thus the potential effect on existing systems is likely to be significant. The decisive factor appears to be how much consumer protection the industry can afford.

Other than that the paper does not set out any concrete rules for its inception and operation, which, bearing in mind that it forms an essential part of the framework for harmonisation, once again shows the cursory treatment that the Discussion Paper gives the whole issue.

The GAIPEC suggested legislative text

The text is divided into five sections and runs to twenty-six Articles. Readers will recognise those parts of the text which do no more than reflect British law and the author apologises for being a messenger of duplication.

The text is applicable to all construction works, both new and existing, and to all persons involved in the construction process (the 'Participants'), but only insofar as their contractual relationships are concerned (but note comments below on the duty owed). Many of the sixteen definitions included are simple enough and thus do not strictly require explication. Two are of interest though. Firstly, there is an express reference to compliance with 'Essential Requirements' of the Construction Products Directive; and, secondly, 'Material Damage' – which is the minimum level for a complaint – consists of a defect which either causes direct physical damage, or which presents an imminent risk of doing so, or has a significant and adverse effect on the health and safety of the occupants of the building. These definitions are, as is the rest of the text, given in English, French and German.

The *de facto* starting point is the date of acceptance by the Client of the Construction Works. This 'Commencement Date' (which is binding on all Participants) is determined by a point akin to substantial completion and triggers a number of events; for instance, the ownership and risk of the building pass from Contractor to Client, the Contractor's liability for liquidated damages for delay ceases, and liability and warranty periods begin.

Acceptance is required to be a single act. It is to be declared in and effected by a certificate bearing the Client's signature and which must specify certain information about the contractual works. Notwithstanding the requirement for singularity, the Acceptance Certificate may apply to part of the works (in which case a series of certificates may be given), or may, alternatively, include reservations to take account of incomplete or sub-standard work. For more substantial deviations the Client has the right to refuse acceptance by doing so in writing with reasons. If the Contractor considers this refusal to be unreasonable or frivolous he can obtain 'tacit acceptance' by serving formal notice to proceed to acceptance within at least one month. In default and on expiry of this notice period, acceptance will be deemed to take place. Tacit acceptance is conditional on expiry of the contract period and completion of the works, and must have followed an initial (informal) notice to accept. Alternatively the Contractor can seek an order and declaration from the court.

On the question of liability, the duty owed by each individual Participant is one of due skill, care and diligence, and it is in respect of acts, omissions and decisions in the performance of all *legal and contractual obligations*. It is owed to the Client and will be automatically transferred – without the need for express assignment – to any subsequent owner of the building. Liability also extends to those acts etc. of the Participant's employees and of the sub-contractors which are 'freely chosen or accepted by him, even if they have been approved by the Client or by other Participants'. Similarly, the Participant will be proportionally liable for the work of others which he had the 'right, obligation, and opportunity' to check for apparent or immediately verifiable defects before accepting it. In this regard, a duty is placed on any person discovering a defect to mitigate the damage as soon as possible.

The Participant responsible for a defect is, upon receiving notification of such, obliged to repair it within reasonable time or pay damages, *as well as* paying compensation for 'all costs directly and necessarily incurred' (e.g. loss of rent). Liability can be excluded on several grounds, including state-of-the-art design and construction techniques when the resultant damage is the outcome of facts exceeding the probabilities on which the technical standards were based.

The major duty on the Client is to obtain a warranty for the benefit of the owner for the time being. An obligation arises when the contract sum exceeds ECU 20 000 (£25 000). Except in the case of dwellings, the Client can elect not to obtain a warranty, but he is under a continuing duty to declare in writing the existence or otherwise of any warranty in any dealings in respect of the legal title to the building. This duty runs for five years, although note the Warranty Period itself can be for a longer period if extended by agreement. Breach of either of these duties will render the Client/Vendor liable to subsequent owners to the same extent as the original Participant.

The Warrantor shall compensate the Beneficiary (i.e. Client/Owner) for all financial loss caused by material damage arising within a period of five years (or for such longer period which is agreed) from the Commencement Date (i.e. date of acceptance). Only *prima facie* proof of material damage/personal injury is required to put the Warrantor on proof of the claim, irrespective of any fault on the part of any Participant. Financial loss means cost of repair, all direct economic loss, and damages for personal injury. In the case of the cost of repair, if this is 'seriously disproportionate' to the loss in value to the building then the Warrantor will be entitled to pay a sum equal to the diminution in value. Compensation will be unrecoverable if certain conditions apply, e.g. abnormal or material alteration in use, failure to maintain, failure to notify as soon as possible, etc. A Warrantor's liability will be limited to the value of the construction works at the time of the claim. The Warrantor will have a right to recover compensation *paid* from the Participant responsible for defects on proof of fault or breach of contract to the normal civil standard. In order to do so, he must have given that Participant the opportunity to repair the damage.

The Warranty is designed to avoid litigation, but if that course is unavoidable, then all actions must be brought either within *one* year from the time a defect was or ought to have been notified, *and* within *five* years of the Commencement Date. Proof of fault is a precondition to liability. However, the parties will be free to reverse this burden of proof by agreement.

Comment

It is not the custom of the Commission to produce inconsequential discussion papers which fail to give direction or offer conclusions on such an important issue as this. The document is plagued by chronic indecision that sweeps through the text rendering any action many months, if not years away. The fact that the document does not even bear a reference number and is obliquely titled is further evidence of its lowly status.

On the other hand, the fact that the proposal has not been buried by its opponents, even after eight years, is a testament to the Commission's stamina (or more accurately that of its staff). It appears that the issue is not going to go away just yet. Apart from the Commission, it is clear the major influential force at work is the industry itself. On the one hand the industry is setting the agenda, and appears to be the driving force for change; on the other hand, it is the industry which is threatening the proposal's life with an intense lobbying campaign that, for example, has resulted in action still being loosely talked about as a mere possibility.

Of the issues the Discussion Paper raises, and ignoring the pre-empting arguments on subsidiarity for a moment, there are many which deserve to met head on. For instance, it would be logical for a legislating authority to tie up the public procurement directives with the Construction Products Directive. In doing so, it is not surprising that the legislator should want to raise or maintain standards accordingly. The question of liability is a sensitive one because all industrial participants know that they are prone to making mistakes no matter how diligent they are in trying to avoid them. Harmonised legislation will not make them more likely to make mistakes, but it may shift the balance in bargaining power towards the consumer. It is in that domain where the conflict of interests is so apparent, for the Commission is likely to address those areas where consumer protection/bargaining power is weakest. As to the specific forms of action, there is little difference in the effect of mutual recognition compared to a directive. It is difficult, however, to predict how easily specific liability legislation would fit into the wider ambit of the English law of negligence, whether the duties arise in contract or in tort. However, the third option, a standard Union contract, is highly imaginative and could offer a realistic compromise in the event of a deadlock between the Commission and the industry.

It is difficult to advise on the ramifications of conjecture and thus the Commission's comments are simply there for reflection. However, assuming that the ideas promulgated in the Discussion Paper succeed in equal measure to the GAIPEC report, then the GAIPEC suggested text does give something to ruminate on.

In spite of a text having been prepared by the industry, some allowance has been given to consumers. The obvious example is the warranty which, by building alternative dispute resolution into the contract, is as close to a duty to act in one's own interest as one will get. It should encourage the avoidance of litigation by giving redress to beneficiaries for defects discovered only on *prima facie* proof of damage. As well as providing a means for redress, the existence or otherwise of the warranty should have a material effect on the value of the development. The relatively low threshold of £25 000 will surely cover most construction projects in the residential sphere. However, other works, particularly extensions and repairs, are more likely to fall short of this figure yet still amount to a massive part of private resources. The concept of a warranty is most closely aligned to the system operating in France. Since the Spinetta Law of 1978 all participants (i.e. contractors) are obliged to have insurance cover to guarantee perfect achievement for one year, satisfactory functioning over two years, and 'décennale' responsibility (a contractual/common law duty) over ten years. However the text envisages introducing a duty to obtain a warranty, rather than to give one as in France.

The warranty could affect professions in two ways. Firstly, a professional may or may not have to offer the warranty to his client. Additionally, although the duty to obtain a warranty is on the clients, a client could enter into a contractual arrangement with his architect or surveyor to advise him on the need and extent of the warranty, as well looking upon him to administer it. If the professional is acting as the client's agent then he will have to look after his interests. This could include:

- ensuring that the client complies with his continuing duty to declare in writing the existence or otherwise of any warranty in any dealing with the building;
- ensuring that notice of technical defects is given to the warrantor (for the client may be relying on the surveyor to alert him of defects which have no cosmetic symptoms); and
- ensuring that the participant concerned is given the opportunity to rectify the defect and does so correctly.

Also he will have to ensure that the building is not put to any abnormal use during the warranty period, for if any damage arises out of such misuse then the warranty will become inapplicable.

There is, perhaps more scope for redesign of the acceptance procedures which already exist in the national systems than one would imagine. Contractual arrangements differ across the Union, sometimes vastly, and represent a significant restriction to increasing mobility. In some systems the changes will be no more than cosmetic ones to the certificate – probably by standardisation – in others rationalisation could be welcomed. Generally, though, the inclusion of acceptance is more of a prelude to the rest of the scheme, rather than due to a need to raise standards *per se*.

There is unlikely to be much practical change to the respective duties owed by the participants. There is nothing new in ensuring that the development agrees with specification, nor that the materials are adequate for use, or that the building is fit for the purpose intended. As with many sectors where national systems are well established, Union legislation only serves to be a re-interpretation of various common sense rules. That said, to act properly, the professional is going to need to know the rules relating to procurement – and as and when necessary apply them – and also possess a sound insight into the ways and dealings of the essential requirements aspects of the Construction Products Directive, as well as the interpretative documents and guidance papers which have been published to put the directive into effect. Moreover, as the participants who perform the role of monitoring – a term which is extensively defined in the text – then their duty is enlarged to cover the work of others. In this respect if they check and accept the work of others then they are deemed to be proportionately responsible and thus liable for it. Alternatively, if they reject that work then they are obliged to mitigate any damage as soon as possible.

With regard to general liability, the emphasis attached to the general application of the text to contractual relationships will have been noticed, and the distinction made in respect of the duty of care which applies to all legal and contractual obligations. Legal duties could, of course, connote all duties including tortious ones. Following the ramifications through, then, if a participant is in breach of a legal duty his liability could extend beyond the client to a fellow participant, with whom he has no contractual arrangement.

As regards the limitation period, then all participants have the same interest at heart. The shorter the limitation period, then the less their costs and charges will be, as well as those of the client/consumer. The costs involved include insurance premiums and a greater need for double-checking – not that with a short period the professions become slack or incompetent, but if one is facing a considerable limitation period (10 or 20 years), then there could be correspondingly more cautiousness and less innovation. (Note, however, that the contractual limitation period in Spain is fifteen years.) Complex multi-national cases will also increase the cost of litigation.

Finally, it is the author's belief that surveyors could stand to gain from harmonisation. Theirs is a discipline without equal in the Union. There is simply no counterpart which possesses the depth and breadth of knowledge of the chartered surveyor. Indications from the Commission are that there is no solution for creating a truly transparent market, where the professions are equated *inter se*. However, a harmonised system could bring a greater identity through recognition of the role chartered surveyors play. Of the suggested forms of action, it is perhaps the standard Union contract which could offer the profession the greatest exposure. This, presumably, would be published in the eleven working languages, thus it offers surveyors, or any other profession who regard their uniqueness as a disadvantage to increased mobility, official recognition as to their abilities and a chance to educate the construction industry across the Union; and gives them equal standing in the consideration of tenders.

It is ideas like this that the Commission sought during the consultation period that followed the discussion paper. The results were assessed in January 1994 at a meeting of the GAIPEC group. This appraisal revealed a conspicuous lack of consensus on the need for action at the Union level between national and European representative bodies and departments. Whilst it was agreed that the Commission should again 're-invent the wheel' of change and delve deeper into the justification for harmonisation, one cannot help but feel that this, like the discussion paper and the consultation period, is no more than a token gesture – tactics in a waiting game.

It is said that this initiative is a victim of subsidiarity. Certainly, it is wounded. However, one should not be led into a false sense of security. The principle of subsidiarity is a weapon of political origin which is wielded in all manner of circumstances. On the other hand, the desire to trade and the pursuit of profit are more hardy fellows. The author believes that the crucial element is the attitude of the industry. The industry is far more concerned with economic advancement than political rhetoric. For the moment, certain sectors of the industry are uncomfortable with the effect of harmonisation. However, when the industry is unable to resist the beckoning of a single market then one is bound to see a surfeit of justification for a common system of liabilities and warranties. And subsidiarity will just be a quaint idea.

Chapter 13
Environmental Protection

Introduction

Much is made of the 'built environment' but until recently there was little concern about its significance beyond its aesthetic and functional properties. The same goes for any industrial sector. However, environmental protection has now emerged from obscurity to become an essential factor in the make up of policies ranging from energy and waste to economics and competition.

European law has reflected this trend. The environment simply did not feature in the European Community Treaty when it was signed and ratified in the mid-1950s. However through the years the policy orientations of the Community have shifted towards ever more complex and broad environmental regulation with increased practical implications on cost. The trend culminated in the mid-1980s when, firstly, the Court of Justice recognised the environment as an essential objective (Case 240/93 *Procurer de la République* v. *Abdhu* [1985] ECR 531); secondly, the environment was adopted as a policy in its own right by the Single European Act of 1986; and finally, the Court again held that the environment could displace one of the central pillars of the single market and the Community legal order, the free movement of goods (Case 302/86 *Commission* v. *Denmark* [1988] ECR 4607).

Community policy in this field is presently focused on 'sustainability'. In 1993 the Commission published details of its Fifth Environmental Action Programme which targets six key areas

- the sustainable management of natural resources;
- integrated pollution control and prevention of waste;
- reduction in consumption of non-renewable energy;
- sustainable transport policies;
- improved environmental quality in urban areas; and,
- improvements in public health and safety (especially risk assessment and management, nuclear safety and radiation procedures).

Each of the foregoing has an impact on the construction sector ranging from the need to rehabilitate existing sources of quarrying material and finding new ones to better town planning and sewerage and waste treatment.

Against the positive imagery that the Community paints with its environmental policies it should not be forgotten that the Community, too, is encouraging and funding projects which will have a considerable impact on the environment. The Trans-European Network programme is a case in point. The TEN programme aims to connect the peripheral, less accessible parts of the Community with the geographically central urban and industrial heartlands through the development of road and rail networks, invariably through green-field locations.

There is however a tendency for the positive role to be overwhelmed by the negative points. This cannot be demonstrated more poignantly by the sobering 'polluter pays' principle which underpins all environmental legislation adopted under the Treaty.

The construction industry's perspective on environmental protection

It is in this context, therefore, that the construction industry (technically instrumental for nearly all intrusions into the environment) must be conscious of both the need for its involvement and the impact its actions and omissions have on its surroundings.

It is submitted that environmental protection impacts on the construction industry from three different perspectives which are complementary to the generality of more dedicated environmental legislation. These are the manufacture of construction products, the construction process, and the duty to have regard to health and safety in the management of construction sites.

Construction products

Under the Construction Products Directive (89/106/EEC) products produced for incorporation into construction works must have such characteristics that, when they are incorporated, the building, if properly designed and built, satisfies the 'essential requirements'. (For a fuller analysis of the directive see Chapters 10 and 14.)

The third essential requirement is 'hygiene, health and the environment'. This requires that the construction works must be designed and built in such a way that there is no threat to the hygiene or health of the occupants or neighbours, in particular as a result of:

- the giving-off of toxic gas;
- the presence of dangerous particles or gases;
- the emission of dangerous radiation;
- pollution or poisoning of the water or soil;
- faulty elimination of waste, water, smoke, solid or liquid wastes; or
- the presence of damp in parts of the works or on the surfaces within the works.

Whilst the emphasis is on design and construction (and accordingly designers and contractors should take note), manufacturers cannot but accept the contractual and tortious duties they will have to assume if their product is to be incorporated into such works, since the 'essential requirements' are there for the purpose of establishing the suitability of incorporated construction products.

According to the Interpretative Documents, by which the Commission offers elucidation to the essential requirements, the nature of threats to the environment will vary according to the type of the works. Nevertheless, manufacturers should focus on the control of pollutants and dampness, the water supply, and the protection of the outdoor environment.

Construction products should not release pollutants and a waste stream which can be dispersed into the environment and cause changes in environmental quality, resulting in risks for the health of human beings, animals and plants and endangering the balance of the eco-system. The impact on the environment should be considered in every phase of life cycle of the construction including:

- winning the contract;
- production and the building process;
- the works in use; and
- demolition, waste-disposal, incineration or reuse.

Manufacturers are directed to focus on limiting the dispersion and emission of pollutants, or preferably limiting the use of such materials at all. They should endeavour not only to improve technological developments of the product itself but also to have regard to improvements in the design of the works.

In addition to the essential requirement in respect of the environment, there is also one for noise. Noise generally is dealt with under a specific environmental directive, whereas the emphasis within the Construction Products Directive is the health, safety and well-being of occupants of the works and people living nearby once the project is completed.

Procurement

The EU's procurement regime regulates trade and competition in the public purchasing sector by laying down rules for the invitation of tenders, the selection of candidates and the award of contracts on the basis of either the lowest price or the most economically advantageous tender. (See Chapters 6 to 9 for a fuller analysis.)

Nowhere in the text of any of the procurement directives is there an express reference to environmental protection. However, Article 130R(2) of the EU Treaty provides that environmental protection requirements shall be a component of the Union's other policies. Therefore, it is arguable that the procurement rules must be read in conjunction with the environmental objectives of the Treaty, in particular, to preserve, protect and improve the quality of the environment and to ensure a prudent and rational utilisation of natural resources (Article 130R(1)).

This has very real and practical ramifications on the building specifications which contracting authorities issue, the criteria by which they select tenders under restricted and negotiated procedures, and, most importantly, how they assess the most advantageous tender. The question is, do the Treaty provisions translate into the right of contracting authorities to insist on the most environmentally friendly products or processes? – to put it conversely, the right of a tenderer, whose products and processes are more environmentally friendly but possibly cost more, to be considered on an equal basis as his less environmental competitors? Either way can or should a contracting authority consider environmental processes and experience as evidence of technical capability and environmental damage as a quantifiable cost?

These questions illustrate the conflicting notions of trade and the environment.

In fact the directive reminds one that it is important to respect the general principle that measures taken in one member state to protect the environment should not affect the ability of other member states to achieve these objectives. It will be recalled that contracting authorities may not specify construction products which only domestic or local tenderers can supply when imported goods from other member states are equally adequate. It will also be recalled that the protection of the environment is a mandatory requirement, thus enabling national authorities to maintain trading rules relating to the characteristics of goods which are indistinctly applicable but nevertheless hinder trade.

Construction sites

The third focal point for the construction industry with regard to its environmental duties lies within the health and safety provisions of the Construction Design and Management (CDM) rules (92/57 EEC, [1992] OJ L245/8). Here once again we must make the somewhat artificial distinction between health and safety legislation and environmental legislation.

The CDM rules (see Chapter 14) introduce minimum requirements for the management of construction projects and sites. When the work is being carried out, it is the duty – at various stages – of clients, employers, contractors and designers to have regard to health and safety. By Article 8 of the CDM Directive the matters with which they are to have regard include:

- the conditions under which various materials are handled;
- the demarcation and laying-out of areas for the storage of dangerous materials and substances;
- the conditions under which dangerous materials are removed; and
- the storage, disposal and removal of waste and debris.

This entails duties which, although they appear to be very specific, also involve a wide number of provisions concerning waste and pollution.

Designers, supervisors and contractors of construction projects have to manage environmental factors such as waste, pollution, toxic materials, dust and noise just as efficiently as the health and safety of their workers.

Although in many areas such as the CPD, the procurement directives and CDM the construction industry has had little choice but to adapt, it has equally and in keeping with other industries responded to the new challenge. Generally the industry has recognised the direct impact it has on the environment through its participation in building, civil, and engineering projects, in its consumption of raw materials, and in the waste it leaves behind. This has led to new technologies, designs and processes which are themselves environmentally friendly, but which also ensure that the completed projects (the buildings, industrial plants and civil structures) have a minimal impact on local eco-systems through facilities for energy conservation, waste recycling, and the avoidance of pollution. Indeed it is tenders which focus on the need to protect the environment which in an increasing number of cases will have the edge on other bids.

Placing aside the technique of turning every problem into an opportunity the purpose of this chapter is to encapsulate the considerable array of environmental legislation into but a few pages and in doing so pinpoint the impact that each piece has on the construction industry. It is also intended to highlight the environmental dimensions of each of the other subject areas featured in this book. In this regard, it is the modest ambition of the author to present the environmental dimension from the design stage to practical completion and use.

Project development

Planning, land use and conservation

Planning control, so much a part of land use, is and remains the preserve of national (that is to say local) authorities, subject to general policy guidelines. Thus, there are no EU provisions relating to listed buildings or building conservation generally, although there are funds available for the preservation and restoration of historic structures. Under Article 222 the ownership of land is excluded from the scope of the Treaty. The only conceivable exceptions to this are commercial transactions, activities and dealings connected with the use (as opposed to the sale) of land or buildings. In which case European law could be argued to apply, insofar as it does not regulate the ownership of land.

For example, automatic refusal of planning consent or land use on grounds of nationality would be in direct contravention with Article 6 and, as the case may be, Articles 30, 52 or 59. On the other hand, each of these provisions offer exceptions to the primary rights they confer. So for example, if Scottish castles were being dismantled brick by brick for export and reconstruction in another member state, then a ban on exports or, more effectively, listing the buildings to prevent their demolition or removal would be justified under Article 36 TEU which provides for an exception to the right of free movement of goods on the grounds that it is intended to protect national treasures possessing artistic, historic or archaeological value and does not constitute a means of arbitrary discrimination or a disguised restriction on trade between member states. One might observe that it is on this single exception, therefore, that the restrictions conservation puts on commercial activities could be justified under EU law.

Important as these issues are to the built environment, they do not fall squarely within the scope of European environmental law where the emphasis is on protecting green-field sites, animals and their habitat, air, water and mineral quality, etc. This is no better and no more appropriately demonstrated than by reference to the Environmental Impact Assessment Directive (85/337/EEC, [1985] OJ L175/40).

Environmental Impact Assessments

If one assumes that any development will by definition affect the environment then it is clearly a question of the degree to which the environment is harmed. Invariably, however, the extent of environmental damage is uncertain. Therefore, the Union's philosophy is to prevent the creation of pollution or nuisance at source rather than trying subsequently to counteract their effects. It is in this context that the Union adopted Council Directive 85/337/EEC on the assessment of the effects of certain public and private projects on the environment.

This harmonising directive introduced procedures to evaluate the environmental effects of development projects since it was believed that disparities in the various national laws in force would create unfavourable competitive conditions. Its central requirement is that a project which is likely to have a significant effect on the environment should not be granted planning consent unless and until those effects have been assessed. However, whilst its scope is broad, its application is more selective, although where it does apply, it will subject the development project to a wide and most exacting scrutiny.

As the description indicates, the directive includes both public and private development projects – although it is to be noted that, as a directive, it is subject to implementation save as against the state and organs of the state. A project will in principle be covered by its provisions if it involves the execution of construction works or of other installations or schemes, as well as 'other interventions in the natural surroundings and landscape including those involving the extraction of mineral resources' (Article 1(2)).

Thereafter, assessments will be either compulsory or optional – the discretion lying with the local planning authority. An assessment will be mandatory for projects to develop energy, chemical and nuclear installations, heavy industry (iron and steel), or waste disposal installations, trading ports, motorways, express roads, long-distance railway traffic and certain airports.

Meanwhile, all other projects may be assessed so long as they come within one of the following categories (for a full list see Annex II): agriculture, extractive and energy industries, metal processing, glass, chemicals, food, textiles and paper, rubber, infrastructure and other miscellaneous projects (from holiday villages to knackers' yards) insofar as, where appropriate, they are not subject to a compulsory assessment.

The assessment will identify, describe and assess the direct, indirect and interactive effects of a project on the following factors: human beings, fauna and flora, soil, water, air, climate and the landscape, material assets, and the cultural heritage.

The assessment cannot be undertaken without the relevant plans, proposals, and other information. Accordingly member states are required to adopt the necessary procedures to ensure that the developer makes the appropriate information available. This should include information that is ordinarily required by the planning laws, and also information that the developer may reasonably be required to compile having regard to current information and methods of assessment. This second limb may cause concern. If correctly implemented and enforced then a developer would have to make a full disclosure of all studies that he himself has carried out or commissioned. This view is reinforced by the scope and detail of the information required which is set out in the Annex to the Directive. These main requirements are:

- a description of the project and in particular its physical characteristics, the land-use requirements during construction and operation, the nature and quantity of materials used, and an estimate of the type and quantity of expected residues and emissions resulting from operation;
- an outline of the main alternatives studied by the developer and the environmental reasons for his choice;
- a description of the significant effects of the project on the environment including the use of natural resources and extent of emissions and nuisances – this needs to be done from more perspectives than one might think conceivable (direct, indirect, secondary, cumulative, short, medium and long term, permanent, temporary, positive and negative);
- proposals to prevent, reduce or offset any significant adverse effects.

Finally, the developer has to provide a non-technical summary or all the foregoing but may indicate any difficulties encountered in compiling the required information. In return he is entitled to see all relevant information in the possession of the planning and other authorities.

What though is all this disclosure designed to achieve apart from transparency? All relevant authorities, as well as the general public, must be given an opportunity to express an opinion on the project before it is initiated. Other than this there are no standards provided in the directive to measure how much a project affects the environment or, even if it does, whether the effects should be regarded as good or bad. This is left to the politics of the planning process which in recent times have become both contentious and unpredictable, aided somewhat by greater general access to information on the environment.

Council Directive 90/313/EEC ([1990] OJ L158/58) on the freedom of access to information on the environment directs member states to ensure that all public authorities are required to make available information relating to the environment to any natural or legal person at his request and without his having to prove an interest (Article 3). Excluded from the generality of the right is information which is confidential, but this must be read in conjunction with the specific provisions of the Environmental Impact Assessment Directive. An individual who is refused access to specific information may seek judicial review of the decision in the courts.

Environmental impact assessments in context

Where there are duties on national authorities to obtain information, then whilst a failure to do so may not in principle concern the developer, his 'good fortune' (if this is how he views it) will be short lived. Environmental organisations have in the past succeeded to exercising their legal option to force a public enquiry and assessment. Furthermore, a failure to carry out an environmental assessment may not absolve the developer of liability much later on.

In the opinion of an Advocate General in one case, the duties of member states to carry out environmental impact assessments in public and private construction works can be enforced in national courts by individuals. That is to say they have direct effect and are enforceable in the courts against the state and agencies thereof (including local authorities and the Environmental Agency).

A confirmed ruling will not affect developers directly. However, they will no doubt be concerned that their objectors may be able to employ extra leverage on environment inspectors. In the wake of an ECJ ruling making states financially liable to individuals for their breaches of Union law, they may well be increasingly conscientious and firm in their environmental assessments, with pressure groups, competitors and other interested parties pressing them for action (*Aannemersbedrijf P.K. Kraaijeveld* v. *Gedeputeerde Staten van Zuid-Holland* C-72/95).

On the other hand, insofar as economic decisions are taken outside the planning process (but without prejudice to it) then there is one authority to show that there is no right of challenge. In *Greenpeace International and Others* v. *Commission,* three environmental associations sought to annul a Commission decision by which it agreed to finance the construction of two electric power stations because of the effect these would have on the environment. An application lodged before the EU's Court of First Instance was rejected as inadmissible because the applicants were not directly and individually concerned by the decision as required by Article 173. The result is that whereas economic measures can sometimes affect persons individually it stands to reason that, on account of the nature of the environment, individuals will never be able to challenge decisions relating to it.

However, a distinction has to be made between the objective of greater transparency in the planning process – as intended by the EIA Directive – and other directives which seek to put in place a more controlled regime. For instance the Birds Directive (79/409/EEC [1979] OJ L103/1) is designed to ensure that the natural habitats of certain species of bird are protected from development – even that which might be justified on urgent economic grounds. In (*R v. SS for the Environment, ex parte RSPB*, (11/7/95 C-44/95) the Court of Justice ruled in favour of environmentalists who opposed plans to enlarge a British port on the grounds that this put economic interests before environmental concerns.

The Royal Society for the Protection of Birds objected to plans by the British government to expand the port of Sheerness. This was recognised as a region of high unemployment and the investment in the port was designed to increase job prospects in the area. In order to facilitate the development the government kept a certain amount of land outside the scope of a special protection zone order made under the Birds Directive because it was considered vital not to compromise the viability of the port in view of the national and local economic importance of the project. The RSPB sought judicial review of this decision in a case which went to the House of Lords and then to the ECJ on a reference. The ECJ found that a member state is not entitled to take account of economic requirements when choosing and determining protection zones. Economic interests, it added, should not in any event correspond to a general interest higher than the one which meets the ecological objective referred to in the directive.

This case demonstrates the frequent head-on conflict between commerce or trade and the environment, a theme which is focused on briefly below.

Design and construction

The process linking project conception to its final long-term operation – design and construction – is characterised by a double-edged sword of compliance and liability. On one side, compliance with the environmental conditions upon which the proposed development was granted planning approval, and, on the other, the risk of incurring liability for foreseeable environmental damage during construction and operation. The extent to which detailed plans and specifications (relied upon when the planning decision is made) are binding on the developer, and therefore to some extent the design team and contractors, will be a matter of national law. Likewise, liability for environmental damage will be subject to national regimes for the protection of the environment. However, it should be noted that the Union is working towards common rules in this area.

Waste

All waste is treated on one of three levels: prevention, recycling, or safe disposal. The construction industry is a major producer of waste. The UK, however, claims to be a creditable recycler, reusing more than 60% of demolition and construction waste and using far less aggregate per head of population than many other European countries (*Construction Monitor*, June 1995).

EU law contains general legislation on the use and treatment of waste, plus specific legislation on a whole range of related if different matters (including hazardous waste, toxic waste, packaging waste, chemicals, waste landfills, incineration), some of which in turn reflect international treaties and conventions. Beyond this there are health and safety measures, including the CDM rules, which could also be regarded as placing a duty on contractors and supervisors to dispose of and minimise waste. Finally, as yet another provision, the Commission is examining the possibility of adopting a specific measure on the limitation of demolition and construction site waste.

General legislation comes in the form of the Waste Framework Directive (75/442/EEC [1975] OJ L103/1). This attempts to harmonise national legislation on the disposal of waste in order to avoid distortions of trade and to contribute to protecting the environment. Its main provisions do not, however, give rise to directly effective rights for individuals exercisable before national courts (*Enichem* v. *Cinisello Balsamo* Case 380/87 [1989] ECR 2491).

Waste is defined (according to amendment by Directive 91/156) as all substances or objects which are listed in Annex I of the amending directive and which their owner disposes of or intends to dispose of. It is not limited to something having a negative economic value or which is of limited use, a consideration which causes difficulty in distinguishing between 'wastes' and 'products'.

Pollution

If waste is difficult to distinguish from a 'product' then the situation is similar when it comes to pollution. At best this is a relative concept. Having regard to the foregoing, pollution can only be caused by waste which is not properly disposed of – either at all, or it is initially disposed of correctly but later the vessel or means of disposal is corrupted and the waste 'escapes'. The term pollution also indicates evident damage in consequence of a failure to protect or take care and which manifests itself in some form of interference with the environment. Thus, designers and contractors should consider provisions on waste to be the means to adopt best practice, and the spectre of pollution as the consequences of, or liability for, failing to reach or maintain this.

The scope and incidence of liability is a matter to be dealt with under national law. There is, however, another dimension to pollution and that is its control. The Union has taken pollution seriously from the early 1970s and has adopted a number of directives containing emission standards or imposing quality objectives. Union measures generally amount to a form of integrated pollution control. These include measures on:

- the prevention of major accident hazards (Directives 85/501, 88/610 [1986] OJ L221/37);
- emissions from large combustion installations (88/609);
- pollution from industrial plants (84/360 [1984] OJ L188/20);
- municipal waste incineration plants;
- groundwater (80/68 [1980] OJ L220/43); and
- several Water Directives.

These measures are designed to reduce pollution from various industrial sources and so their requirements need to be heeded in the design phase of any project. Likewise, particular measures on the use of certain materials need to be considered. Of most importance to the construction industry is the Asbestos Directive (83/477 EEC [1983] OJ L203/25). This requires national authorities to ensure that asbestos emissions into the air, asbestos discharges into the aquatic environment, and solid asbestos waste are, as far as reasonably practicable, reduced at source and prevented. In the case of the use of asbestos, these measures mean using the best available technology (not entailing excessive cost) including where appropriate recycling or treatment.

Noise

Construction activity creates noise and no matter whether the site is a green-field or brown-field location the local environment will suffer. The emphasis of Union regulation in this area is not on the contractor but on the manufacturer of machinery used in the process. The view taken by the Union in this regard is that there is a need to deal with the problem of noise nuisance not simply on grounds of the environment, but also because disparity between the measures already applicable or in preparation in the various member states limiting the sound emission levels of machinery directly affects the functioning of the common market. A number of directives regulating the manufacture of construction machinery provide for approved national bodies to issue an EEC type examination certificate for each type of appliance certifying that the sound power level is in accordance with European rules. There are directives on:

- powered hand-held concrete-breakers (84/537/EEC [1984] OJ L300/156);
- construction plant and equipment (i.e. all machinery, appliances, plant and installations or components thereof, used, according to their type, to perform work on civil engineering and building sites but which are not primarily intended for the transport of goods or persons (79/113/EEC, 84/532/EEC [1984] OJ L300/111);
- tower cranes (84/534/EEC [1984] OJ L300/130); and
- hydraulic excavators, rope-operated excavators, dozers, loaders, excavator-loaders and other earth-moving machines (88/662 EEC [1988] OJ L382/39).

Operation (the question of environmental liability)

It is impossible to say what legal form any future EU text on liability for environmental damage will take, since the initiative is still a long way from even a formal proposal. However a Commission Communication on harmonising liability for damage to the environment is expected to make the polluter strictly liable in economic terms for any damage caused.

The enforced reluctance to move confidently ahead comes not just from a wide divergence of views between member states (running more or less north-south in terms of decreasing support) but also from the Commissioners within the Commission – a majority are against a binding text on this highly controversial subject.

The Commission held public hearings in 1993, on the basis of which it produced a Green Paper for general discussion. Following that wider consultative exercise it has produced a Communication. This was expected to contain a draft directive. However, it failed to do so, evidence of the Commission's preference for a cautious approach on all pieces of major legislation. Nevertheless, the Commission does appear to be establishing certain fundamental points. These include a principle that only future pollution will be covered by any harmonised rules – thus excluding the estimated 47 000 to 95 000 km^2 of existing registered polluted sites.

It seems to be well established that liability, whether civil or public, should be on a no-fault basis, and should be incurred by the generator of the environmental damage, whether this is purely ecological, or established on a more traditional basis (i.e. damage to property or personal injury). Either way, the Commission appears to have accepted a relatively new idea that an economic value should be placed on damage to natural resources (a process it describes as 'internalising external costs'). In this regard it realises that criteria will be necessary for assessing damage to the eco-system. This said, the Commission is unsure how liability should be established: whether on the basis of *de facto* proof of damage, or based on a list of harmful activities which are identified as causes of damage. As regards the latter option, the list could be either indicative or exhaustive.

Whilst there is no difficulty in enabling private individuals to obtain compensation for direct loss, the Commission is unsure how to impose penalties or who should be able to sue for environmental damage. The Commission's preference is for the freedom of anyone to take legal action. Finally, the Commission is expected to propose that a guarantee fund should be established to fund reparation of damage in the event that the polluter does not have the means to pay. There is no mention of compulsory insurance. A Government White Paper is expected for the end of 1997 or early in 1998.

Chapter 14
Health and Safety

Introduction

Every occupation, activity or task will possess aspects which pose a potential danger to the health and safety of the person carrying it out. Whether the job is sedentary or precarious, no matter how robust the spirit, it is a fact of life that the flesh is weak and physical resources finite. There will therefore come a point when individuals lose control of, or cannot react to, conditions or events around them. When the activities are carried out by one person under the direction of and in return for remuneration from another, then this is the basis upon which the duty of care owed by employer to employee is established.

There is nothing new in this premise. In fact many would be justified in asking what purpose there would be in having common European rules issued forth from the Union; presumably, the necessary protection would seem to be satisfactorily dealt with under national law. The presumption is a fair one, but nevertheless common Union rules do exist. For the reasons why, the reader is respectfully referred to Chapters 2 and 3 and comments on national and Union law, harmonisation, direct effect and supremacy.

Contributing to the attainment of a high level of health protection is set out as a express activity of the EU (Article 3(o)). This gives the EU institutions competence to adopt legislation in this field. Worker protection does not feature as an express activity, but comes under the slightly misleading title of 'Social Policy'. The health and safety of the worker became a specific task and objective of the Union by virtue of the Single European Act 1986. This inserted Article 118a of the Treaty which enables the Council to adopt by means of directives minimum requirements for encouraging improvements, especially in the working environment, to guarantee a better level of protection for the health and safety of workers. The dimension has been reinforced by the Protocol on Social Policy which, as part of the Treaty of Maastricht, was agreed between eleven of the then twelve member states (subject to resistance on the part of the UK to accede to it). The so-called Social Chapter also covered health and safety of workers in addition to giving the Union legislative competence (except over the UK) in the field of employment (i.e. contractual conditions). However, the distinction both geographically and legally is now of much less significance in light of recent acceptance by the UK of the Social Chapter and the ruling of the Court of Justice that measures which relate to the health and safety of workers may validly be adopted under Article 118a (*UK* v. *The Council*, Case C-84/94).

This it is has done on an elaborate scale targeting occupational risks and general conditions of work. In 1989 the Council adopted a general framework directive on the health and safety of workers and work. This contained a general duty of care, but also set in train the adoption of individual directives in a variety of areas. These include the all-important – in construction terms – Construction Sites Directive, but also include a number of other directives of either general or specific application. To date thirteen individual directives have been adopted. In addition, there are a number of one-off, 'single issue' directives adopted before the approach taken by the framework directive. In this chapter it is intended that the coverage of this body of legislation be selective, concentrating on those matters which specifically affect the construction industry.

The general duty of care to workers

The general duty of care is set out in Article 5 of Directive 89/391/EEC ([1989] OJ L183/1), (the framework directive) as follows:

> 'The employer shall have a duty to ensure the safety and health of workers in every aspect related to the work.'

As the directive makes clear, it is not intended that independent contractors should be affected by the principle of responsibility of the employer to the worker. To this end 'worker' is defined as any person employed, by an employer, including trainees and apprentices; whereas 'employer' is any natural or legal person who has an employment relationship with the worker *and* has responsibility for the undertaking and/or establishment (possibly a conjunctive test) (Article 3).

The general duty of care is reinforced by a series of general obligations. These include the requirement to take measures necessary for the safety and health protection of workers, including the prevention of occupational risks and provision of information and training. The obligation is a continuing one since employers are required to be alert to the need to adjust these measures to changing circumstances.

The kind of measures which should be taken are not set out *in extensio* However, there are a number of general principles of prevention which should be followed. These are:

- avoiding risks;
- evaluating the risks which cannot be avoided;
- combating risks at source;
- adapting the work to the individual (especially as regards the design of the work place;
- the choice of work equipment;
- the choice of working and production methods (with a view to alleviating monotonous work and work at a predetermined work rate);

- adapting to technical progress (replacing the dangerous by the safe or less dangerous);
- developing a coherent overall prevention policy which covers technology, organisation of work, working conditions, social relationships and the influence of factors related to the working environment;
- giving collective protective measures priority over individual protective measures; and
- giving appropriate instructions to workers.

Further details are also provided with regard to specific issues such as first aid, fire-fighting, dangerous situations, and worker information, consultation, participation and training.

The enormous significance of this list should not be underestimated. They appear as general – even bland and often repeated – statements, but unfortunately each is a potential Pandora's Box for any employer who neglects or cares not for his duties, or, being conscientious, even just makes a mistake. Particular note is urged of the duty to adapt the work to the worker which would appear to caution employers against making assumptions about the ability, strength, intelligence, faculties, etc. of any worker employed.

The duties though are not one sided. Workers are required to take care as far as possible of their own safety and health and that of other persons affected by their acts or ommissions at work, in accordance with their training and the instructions given by their employer. To this end workers must:

- use machinery and equipment correctly;
- keep the employer informed of situations which represent a serious and immediate danger to safety and health; and
- co-operate with the employer in the interests of safety and health.

The above rules are unlikely to affect laws and precedents in force in the UK. However, they do enable the employer to have an insight into the conditions he may expect to encounter if working in another member state. More importantly, it means that terms and concepts defined may be given a common Union definition rather than the one English law is accustomed to. This will be most likely with regard to any economic concept giving rise to legal rights, such as the right to free movement of workers. Thus, the definition of employer, worker, the tasks assigned and the scope of the duty could all be given a Union definition.

The duty of care in respect of occupational risks

Of the thirteen 'daughter' directives adopted pursuant to the framework instrument, those which can be singled out for their particular relevance to the construction process are directives on:

- work equipment (89/655/EEC);
- personal protective equipment (89/656/EEC);
- manual loads (90/269/EEC [1990] OJ L156/9);
- construction sites (92/57/EEC); and
- safety and health signs (92/58/EEC [1992] OJ L245/23).

For the sake of completeness or interest, others which may affect employers in the general sense are the directives on:

- the workplace (89/654/EEC);
- display screen equipment (87/391/EEC);
- carcinogens (90/394/EEC [1990] OJ L196/1);
- biological agents (90/679/EEC [1990] OJ L334/1); and
- pregnant workers (92/85/EEC [1992] OJ L348/1).

The other three are narrowly concerned with mineral extraction and fishing.

It should be noted that the workplace directive specifically excludes construction sites from its scope. The same concerns are specifically dealt with in the Construction Sites Directive which will be covered separately below. This leaves, therefore, four to discuss.

Work equipment

Construction work involves a considerable amount of equipment and heavy machinery. This is becoming more and more so with technical advancement. The industry has come a long way from using the implements unchanged since medieval times which were still common place five decades ago. This is especially so in the use of electrical circuitry and computer-driven equipment to replace manual labour or fuel-consuming devices. Any piece of equipment or machinery that one might conceivably see in use on site is likely to be considered as work equipment within the meaning of Directive 89/655/EEC.

The directive sets out a number of duties that employers need to bear in mind. First of all is *the general obligation* to ensure that all equipment is suitable for the work to be carried out, or at least properly adapted for that purpose, so that it may be used by workers without impairment to their safety or health. To this end, it will be necessary to ensure that, throughout its working life, the equipment is kept adequately maintained.

Secondly, where equipment involves specific risks then it will be necessary to restrict the use and the repair of such equipment to persons trained for such work. To this end, the employer must ensure that workers have made available to them adequate information and, where appropriate, written instructions on the equipment used. The information should contain details concerning the conditions of use, foreseeable abnormal situations, and conclusions to be drawn from experience though previous use.

Personal protective equipment

One of the most familiar signs and symbols on a construction site is the hard hat, and it is no coincidence that an increase in sightings of both hats and signs comes in the wake of increased regulation in this area in the interests of health and safety.

Personal protective equipment (PPE) can be so identified if it is designed to be worn or held by a worker to protect him against one or more hazards likely to endanger his safety and health. It also includes any addition or accessory designed to meet this objective. On the other hand, it excludes ordinary clothes and uniforms.

The general rule is the PPE should be used when risks associated with work cannot be avoided or sufficiently limited by other means or procedures. To this end, the employer must obtain PPE which itself complies with the relevant EU provisions on design and manufacture, Directive 89/286 EEC, [1989] OJ 399/18.

Manual loads

The Manual Loads Directive regulates the transport or support of a load by one or more workers and includes the lifting, putting down, pushing, pulling, carrying or moving of a load which, by reason of its characteristics or of unfavourable ergonomic conditions, involves a risk of back injury. The employer's obligations in this regard are to take appropriate organisational measures or use such equipment as may be available in order to avoid the need to handle loads manually. However, where manual handling is truly unavoidable then the objective should be to reduce the incidence of risk. This will necessitate taking into account a series of reference factors. For instance:

- the characteristics of the load;
- the physical effort required and the strain on the worker's back and trunk;
- the environment in which the loads have to be handled; and
- the requirements of the activity.

Equally, the employer must have regard to the suitability of the individual employee to the work, including his clothing and training. In this respect the employer must ensure that workers receive general indications and where necessary precise information on the weight of the load and the centre of gravity of the heaviest side. All in all, the employer could be liable if at any time, within the appropriate limitation period, the employee's back gives way and this is attributable to an oversight in relation to one of these reference factors. The directive does not set out any corresponding duties on the worker, for instance to seek guidance or alert the employer to physical inability, but it could be argued that such a duty is implicit in the express duty, derived from the framework directive referred to above, to take care of his own health and safety.

Safety and health signs

Wide linguistic and cultural differences between workers, as well as differences in the signs currently used, is the reason behind this measure, the object being to minimise accidents involving migrant workers. Not without an element of paternalism the directive sets out specific signs which ought to be used in given situations, and further gives the criteria for adopting signs by national authorities, and indirectly and subject to implementation by member states, construction operators themselves. In the latter respect, the duty of employers is to provide safety and/or health signs as laid down in the directive whenever a hazard cannot be avoided or adequately reduced by 'techniques for collective protection or measures, methods or procedures used in the organisation of work'.

All signs have to conform to specific requirements. Signboards for instance have to be of a shape and colour which clearly indicate the specific object of the message they are intended to convey. For example, pictograms must be as simple as possible and should only contain essentials details. They should also be shock and weather resistant, installed at a suitable height and position, and suitable to the local environment such as a construction site. There are also specific instructions for the use of signs in relation to containers and pipes, fire-fighting equipment, obstacles and dangerous locations. These instructions either give greater particularity on the use of and make-up of signs or stipulate colour (red for fire-fighting equipment, yellow and black or red and white for dangerous locations). Any proprietor of a workplace is bound to carry out these instructions, although no mention is made as to whether the workplace should be temporary or permanent. 'Permanence' is used in relation to signs that are permanent, to be contrasted with the use of occasional signs (illuminated, acoustic, verbal and hand signals) as and when required. Accordingly, the directive would in principle, but subject to implementation, impact on all workplaces whether permanent or temporary; and include construction sites, notwithstanding the separate directive that exists and which is considered below.

Working time

It is a characteristic of European social policy that the law is developed not just to deal with health hazards causing disease or infirmity but also the complete psychic, mental and social well-being of the worker. It is for this reason that the Court of Justice was able to rule that the Working Time Directive was a genuine health and safety measure when it rejected a claim by the UK that the legal basis of the directive (Article 118a, see above) was wrong (See Case C-84/94). It did not, the Court observed, relate purely to employment conditions. Whilst the directive has passed its effective date, it nevertheless allows member states to delay implementation for several years. Moreover, it is envisaged that the directive will be implemented in large measure by collective agreement between the 'two sides of industry,' management and labour. As is increasingly the case, therefore, one must have regard to the national position to determine the state of implementation.

The directive provides that a worker's contractual employment conditions should include daily and weekly rest entitlements, annual leave and a maximum working week of 48 hours. Underscoring these is the general principle of humanisation. This is reflected elsewhere in health and safety law and requires the employer who intends to organise work to a certain pattern to take account of the general principle of adapting the work to the worker with a view to alleviating monotonous work and work at a pre-determined work rate (depending on the type of activity) and of safety and health requirements (especially as regards breaks during working time).

Working time is defined as any period during which the worker is working at the employer's disposal and carrying out his activities or duties. It is contrasted with a 'rest period' which is any period which is not working time. It is unclear whether certain activities like trade union activities or public duties can be regarded as working time. In any event the maximum working week is put at 48 hours averaged out over a reference period of four months. However, member states have the option not apply this ceiling for up to seven years or for as long as the option has not been withdrawn. More particularly, an employer can organise his employees' work to exceed 48 hours if he has first obtained each worker's agreement. However this is without prejudice to the requirement that each employee has one full day's rest a week (again averaged out over four months). Moreover, the employer who needs to operate with these arrangements has to keep up-to-date records of all workers carrying out such work and make them available to the national authorities. It is thought that this bureaucratic burden will make the option less attractive.

Otherwise, each worker is entitled to a break every six hours of a duration which will really enable the worker to rest. Each day the worker should receive at least 11 consecutive hours rest per 24 hour period. Each week, the worker should take 24 consecutive hours in addition to his daily entitlement. And every year a worker should be able to take four weeks paid leave. However, whilst these are EU minimum standards, the employer may not abide to them slavishly in all cases but must also have regard to general health and safety requirements. Accordingly, workers engaged in hazardous or mentally tiring work, especially those working through shifts or through the night, are given protection appropriate to the nature of their work. Once again, employers will be held liable for injury caused to workers as a result of excessive work regimes – even, it could be argued, when the employee has consented to the regime.

The duty of care in respect of construction sites

The Construction Sites Directive

Site safety is not an area in which the construction industry excels. This is a state of affairs which repeats itself across the Union, which suggests that the problem is endemic to construction activity rather than inherent in any national system. According to the Secteur Report:

'Health and safety measures are seen by many, both in construction firms and materials producers as irksome and costly. The industry ought, however, to take an active role in promoting health and safety measures, both to reduce costs of time lost through sickness, disability and accident and to improve the image of the industry' (paragraph 8.12).

Rather than the industry being invited to take the initiative in promoting health and safety measures, the Union has stepped in and tackled the problem head on. In 1992 the Council adopted Directive 92/57/EEC on the implementation of minimum safety and health requirements on temporary or mobile construction sites.

Construction (Design and Management) Regulations 1994

It created considerable interest and concern when the UK implemented the Directive by means of the Construction (Design and Management) Regulations 1994. These came into force on 31 March 1995. They have triggered a flurry of activity in their wake as professional associations and non-governmental organisations within the sector attempt to reassure members of their duties in what is generally considered to be a climate of uncertainty.

The Directive gave rise to criminal offences to reinforce the seriousness with which the European Union takes death and injury in the construction sector. A number of prosecutions have been brought and press reports indicate that CDM is beginning to bite with fines in one infringement case amounting to £13 000.

In the UK, notification of the construction activity to the Health and Safety Executive and the early completion (with attention to detail) of the health and safety plan in relation to high risk activities such as demolition work should be regarded as sufficient to discharge the duties of the respective parties in the construction process. Failure to notify at all or to draw up a plan in particular circumstances can and will probably lead to prosecution. In some cases, local firms with previous good reputations for competence can be tarnished with the stigma of a conviction which receives local publicity. This, plus the fines that are imposed, could have serious consequences.

Indeed, the level of fines is unpredictable, as Magistrates' Courts have chief responsibility for hearing CDM prosecutions, and these courts have considerable latitude in fixing a fine, coupled with little national coordination. For instance a sole practising architect and family construction firm received fines in one case in the region of £3,000 each for failing to comply with their respective duties in respect of demolition work at a site upon which a few houses were to be built. This compared with a similar level of fine which a major hospital received under different health and safety legislation, for a large number of infringements over a significant period of time which potentially exposed a considerable number of patients to risk. Therefore there is a need to keep site supervision and contract management under constant review, and to ensure that all parties along the line are aware of their responsibilities.

Installing and managing a construction site

The spirit of the Construction Sites Directive is manifested in the recognition that temporary and mobile construction sites constitute an area of activity that exposes workers to particularly high levels of risk. Moreover, unsatisfactory architectural and/or organisational options or poor planning of the works at the project preparation stage play a role in more than half of the occupational accidents occurring on construction sites in the EC. Many others still are caused by inadequate co-ordination on site, particularly where various undertakings work simultaneously. More generally, it is appropriate to note that most accidents involve young or temporary workers or foreign workers. Clearly then it is these three categories that require most supervision.

These factors have brought about the following two central features of the directive which are:

- the appointment of a project preparation co-ordinator and a project execution co-ordinator; and
- the sharing of responsibility for health and safety by all parties involved – the directive establishes a chain of responsibility so that the succession of decision making processes has a major bearing on the working conditions during the design of the project and preparation on the site.

To this end occupational risks are to be taken into account at the following stages of the construction process:

- design and site organisation;
- execution of the work;
- future work on site; and
- the maintenance and upkeep of the building.

Thus from the very beginning of the project there has to be an overall approach to the well-being of the work-force. All firms, however large or small are obliged to comply with the safety rules.

On a practical level, these rules will apply whenever building or civil engineering works are to be, or are being, undertaken. The directive refers to 'temporary' sites but one might question whether construction sites are ever anything but temporary. Nevertheless for argument's sake even if a contractor were lucky enough to be engaged on a permanent work site then he would very probably be covered by the framework and other directives.

The Construction Sites Directive will also cover works which involve the presence on site of a number of contractors. Thus projects the size of house extensions might slip outside the scope of the directive. The number, though, is a question of fact. In most cases there will be more than one contractor on site or contracted to the project. Moreover, the construction industry is characterised by a predominance of small and medium sized enterprises, with work routinely being executed according to a clear division of labour between sub-contractors. Accordingly, the issue of whether the directive or national law will apply will rarely arise. One particular instance where it may do so is when two contractors belong to the same group. Under competition law exception is made for agreements between a parent and its subsidiary, but one could say that it would be unlikely that such a exception will be made in the context of the Construction Sites Directive. Here the spirit of the law comes into play. The object is to ensure co-ordination between enterprises so as to protect the well-being of workers. That necessitates co-ordination of management at the lowest level for that is often where the most important decisions are taken in health and safety terms.

The directive works on the basis of sharing responsibility amongst all participants. This results in a number of particular duties being placed on those persons whose decisions will affect the well-being of the workers. However, it must not be forgotten that such delegation does not discharge others from their own responsibilities.

Duties of the client

The client is defined as the person for whom the project is being carried out. His duty is to appoint the co-ordinators and to ensure that a safety and health plan is drawn up prior to commencement of the works although, as no doubt will usually be the case, he can delegate the task to the project supervisor. This is executed in part by displaying a notice at the construction site. Note that the prior notice acts in a way as a self-declaration of competence as well as to alert the competent authorities of the site so as to enable them to carry out checks and contribute to towards active prevention of accidents.

This does not necessarily mean that the client has overall responsibility for all health and safety matters, but it does require him to take the initiative to ensure that a framework in which health and safety matters can be accounted for and co-ordinated is established. Accordingly, the day-to-day co-ordination of health and safety matters is executed on behalf of the client. This continues for the life of the project, hence the duty to ensure health and safe working conditions are maintained.

Duties of the project supervisor

This will cover the architect, engineer, or surveyor and the role is defined as the person responsible for the design and/or execution and/or supervision of the execution of a project, acting on behalf of the client. It is his duty to appoint co-ordinators and see to the health and safety plan if required to do so by the client, and to take account of the general principles of prevention concerning safety and health referred to in the framework directive, in particular when architectural, technical and/or organisation aspects are being decided and when fixing the completion date. His duties do not end there but carry on, either by way of assumption of the role of project preparation co-ordinator or co-operation therewith.

Duties of the project preparation co-ordinator

This officer is defined as the person entrusted by the client and/or project supervisor, during the preparation of the project design, to account specifically for health and safety matters. He is appointed at the design stage and at the site organisation stage. Now this officer does not have to be a particular person. The appointee can be a separate person to the project supervisor, or the project supervisor can adopt the role, thus assuming duties which are additional to those relating to design.

Just as with the project supervisor, these particular health and safety duties become relevant at any time when architectural, technical and/or organisational aspects are being decided. The specific job is to co-ordinate implementation by the project supervisor of the general principles of prevention, namely avoiding risks, evaluating and combating unavoidable risks, and adapting the work to the individual. This is perhaps the most interesting task and it is possibly one which would not immediately spring to mind. Adapting the work to the individual can mean anything from not giving a sixteen year old who cannot drive sole responsibility for dumper trucks, or not expecting one man or woman to do the job of three. This principle is open to wide interpretation. It is there to prevent short cuts in labour costs by under-employing.

The co-ordinator is also responsible for keeping abreast of technical progress, replacing the dangerous with the safe or less dangerous and developing a coherent overall prevention policy covering production, organisation of work, working conditions and a dialogue between management and staff. This requires a positive approach to health and safety, not a 'wait and see' one. Likewise the co-ordinator must throughout give priority to collective protective measures, and ensure that all necessary information is available to those who need to know.

The safety plan

At the preparation stage the co-ordinator is particularly responsible for making sure that a health and safety plan is drawn up and prior notice is posted to the competent authorities. This safety plan contains an account of the potential risks to the work being performed on site from any other industrial activities being carried on in the immediate vicinity, for example if the construction site is located in a working industrial zone. It should also include specific preventive measures for certain categories of work, including work involving significant risks (e.g. falling from a height). This safety plan is the supervisor's proof that he is taking his health and safety responsibilities seriously. The safety plan should be supplemented by a file appropriate to the characteristics of the project containing the relevant safety and health information to be taken into account during any subsequent works. This file is intended to enable the general principles of prevention to be assimilated into the architectural decisions concerning the use of the building structure. That is to say, it is intended that the file will outlive the construction site for this information will determine the safety and health performance of the building or structure during its use, maintenance, alteration and demolition.

Duties of the project execution co-ordinator

This participant is defined as the person entrusted by the client and/or project supervisor with health and safety matters during execution of the project. This person can and probably will be the same as the project pre-paration co-ordinator. By definition the activities are confined to the third stage of a construction project. The specific duties are fairly self-explanatory. They include the duty to co-ordinate implementation by contractors and self-employed persons of the general principles of prevention and safety concerning deadlines, organisation and co-ordination, good housekeeping, traffic and on-site storage, materials handling operations on site, the environment surrounding the construction site, the safety and health plan and the project health and safety file.

Duties of employers

Employers face the full blast of health and safety law, and it is in the harmonised measures that one will find those duties. This is because they are geared towards preserving the well-being of employees. The number and range of duties is wide and getting wider. Basically, in every instance where employees are acting for or on behalf of an employer, then that will put the employer under a duty to look after the best interests of his staff. This is not a one-way street. There are reciprocal duties on workers to 'toe the line' and make the employer's job easier, but subject to this the ultimate responsibility is that of the employer.

The employer bears duties which are either of a general or specific nature. Some are very wide in their scope. Generally (derived from the framework directive) his duties are to:

- ensure the safety and health or workers in every aspect related to their work;
- adapt the work to the individual;
- properly organise the working time of the individual (see the Working Time Directive); and
- develop an overall safety and health policy.

Furthermore, he has to evaluate risks, combating them at source and updating preventive measures in the light of new circumstances and technical progress. In this regard he has to keep appropriate records on risks and accidents. At appropriate times he needs to inform employees and/or their representatives of the risks and the measures taken, consulting with them in a balanced way on all questions relating to safety and health at work, and providing adequate safety and health training. He can, in this regard, (and usually does) designate employees to carry out these activities related to the prevention of risks at the workplace.

The more specific duties arising out of the Construction Sites Directive include the duty to take into account directions from the project co-ordinator and to observe the minimum safety and health requirements for construction sites. These minimum requirements are extremely detailed and specific. For instance the installation of on-site work places needs to take account of:

- stability and solidity;
- emergency routes and exits;
- fire detection and fire fighting;
- ventilation and lighting;
- loading bays and ramps, and
- first aid.

The installation of on-site work stations (the distinction between work places and work stations being that work places are larger than work stations) needs to take account of stability and solidity, temperature, windows and skylights, escalators and travelators, room dimensions and air works, and space in the rooms.

Duties of self-employed persons

Finally, at least on the employment side, there are the small sub-contractors, or more generally, the self-employed persons. Their primary duty is not to disrupt the general health and safety plan set in place before they arrive. This requires them to co-operate with other persons working on site in implementing the relevant safety, health and occupational hygiene requirements and to co-ordinate action in protection and the prevention of risks. They must also take into account directions from the project co-ordinator and observe the minimum health and safety requirements for construction sites.

Rights and duties of workers

Turning to workers, whose benefit is the prime purpose of this legislation, not only do they have the privilege of protection but they also have rights and some duties. Generally, workers, whether public or private have the following rights (derived from the framework directive):

- to be informed and to make proposals concerning safety and health;
- to participate in a balanced way in accordance with national laws and/or practices;
- to appeal to the competent authority; and
- to cease work in the case of serious danger.

More specifically, workers are entitled (derived from the Construction Sites Directive) to information of all measures taken concerning their health and safety, to be consulted concerning specific health and safety measures, and to the proper co-ordination between workers in carrying out activities on site. No doubt in some countries where there is employee representation on works councils or management boards, taking account of health and safety proposals will be or already is easily accommodated. Under the directive there is no structure or forum specified by which such dialogue should take place. Neither are there restrictions on when or where proposals can be made.

On the other hand, there are also duties which impact on the worker. He must take care as far as is possible of his own safety and health and that of other persons affected by his acts or omissions at work, in accordance with the training and instructions received. He must also make correct use of machinery and personal protective equipment, obey the employer's instructions concerning safety and health, and point out potential dangers.

Conclusion

This book has endeavoured to give shape and definition to the European construction industry by reference to the principles of free movement, competition and the internal market. What end does this internal market have, and where do we go from here?

The author's personal view, after reflecting on the issue over a number of years, is that the internal market is not designed to enable every family-run construction firm or sole practising architect to achieve domination of the European market. The primary source of business will continue to be first and foremost in 'your own backyard'. Cross-border opportunities will be discovered only by being open and receptive to them. They will be few and far between initially, and over the long term they will become localised or focused on an particular region. After all, business either comes on recommendation or from a high market profile.

If the opportunities are as modest as these, then is it worth the sacrifice of new, common or harmonised laws on health and safety, technical specifications, environmental and consumer protection, and other laws which place restrictions on commercial activity? For instance, does it make sense for a house builder in Cork, Republic of Ireland to be following the same site safety procedures as his counterpart in Thessaloniki, Greece, when the two are very, very unlikely to compete directly with each other? Not a great deal. But people on the fringes of a region, whether it be Europe as a whole or a small country, have much less of an inclusive sense of regionalism than their counterparts who are more centrally located. The justification the centralists put forward for *common* safety rules is their need where cross-border activity and interaction will be most common.

The future of the European construction industry is inextricably linked to the shape, direction and events of the European Union. In this regard, there is at present and for the foreseeable future no more significant issue than economic and monetary union.

EMU will characterise Europe in ways in which the common market and then the internal market could never emulate. EMU does not simply deliver free movement of goods, workers, services, and capital. It is something much more than an area without internal frontiers. A single currency will enable businesses throughout Europe to talk the same commercial language. Price comparisons will become all too clear. The haze of exchange rates which blur on-the-spot judgements of price will be gone, although obviously transportation will still be a significant constituent of cost price. Yet the convergence of economic policies, and the eventual restraints that will be placed on fiscal policy, could have a considerable effect on the financial markets, government spending, and eventually industrial sectors such as construction.

A litmus test for EMU is whether it will bring about noticeable and rewarding integration of the national construction markets. Given that development projects are often funded from investment institutions then the large commercial and industrial regions in UK, France, Germany should continue to attract investment. So the market place itself is unlikely to shift as the sole result of EMU; it is only a question of whether the market will routinely be made up of traders who originate from several or more states. If it does then the local labour force, service suppliers, sub-contractors, and producers will all feel the pinch if (for instance) a developer in the UK chooses a main contractor from France who will bring with it its own labour, machinery and connections to suppliers and producers. In relation to a single construction project, the local industry will be the spectator, unless of course it is busy with another job in France, or Germany, etc.

The amount of cross-border activity to date makes this scenario a very realisable one. And certainly the legal, if not the economic, infrastructure is gradually being put in place: mutual recognition of diplomas, the right of establishment, the freedom to use one's own labour, the elimination of border restrictions on goods, and a more competitive and open procurement regime will all enable ever greater freedom of movement within a single market.

Table of Cases

Index